THE CONDUCT OF THE SERVICE
by the Rev. Dr. Arthur Carl Piepkorn

and

THE CONDUCT OF THE SERVICES
by Charles McClean

and

THE GENERAL RUBRICS
from *The Lutheran Liturgy*

Emmanuel Press ✠ Fort Wayne, IN

THE CONDUCT OF THE SERVICE
by the Rev. Dr. Arthur Carl Piepkorn
Originally printed 1965
Concordia Seminary Print Shop, St. Louis, Missouri
Public Domain

THE CONDUCT OF THE SERVICES
by Charles McClean
Originally printed 1972
Clayton Publishing House
P.O. Box 9258, St. Louis, Missouri 63117
Reprinted by permission from the author

THE GENERAL RUBRICS found in *The Lutheran Liturgy*
Originally printed by Concordia Publishing House
Public Domain

Emmanuel Press © 2023
Fort Wayne, Indiana
Originally printed 2006 by Redeemer Press

Cover Photo: Walther Chalice. Photo by Concordia Publishing House from the collection of Trinity Lutheran Church, St. Louis, Missouri. Used by permission. This ornate chalice is one of two that were brought by the Saxon immigrants to the United States from Germany in the 1830s for their new church.

All rights reserved. No part of this book may be reproduced, stored in a retrieval system, or transmitted, in any form or by any means, electronic, mechanical, photocopying, recording, or otherwise, for financial profit without the prior written permission of Emmanuel Press.

ISBN 978-1-934328-24-8

Preface

It has been nearly three years since our last reprint of Piepkorn and McClean. That second run sold out as quickly as the first and we realized immediately that we simply had to get more serious. But we were in the throes of other projects and parish work, and along the way Rev. Frese followed Piepkorn into the US Army chaplaincy and moved overseas. Yet by the grace of God, late as it is, this work is finally done.

Once again, we have not changed or "corrected" either Piepkorn or McClean. A revision of these works, like unto McClean's relationship to Piepkorn, would be quite useful. But part of understanding the liturgy is understanding its development. Careful readers of the Orders for Holy Communion in the Missouri Synod's 1981 *Lutheran Worship* and the 2006 *Lutheran Service Book* will see Piepkorn's influence. Those who can read between the lines and see the slow awakening we have undergone will also understand better why implementing higher ceremony and deliberate reverence, or even weekly Eucharist, can be a painful process. Reading Piepkorn and McClean teaches patience even as it teaches rites, rubrics, and ceremony. For every journey is informed by how it began. Our journey is not yet ended. Our learning is not yet complete. These books still have something to teach us, and part of that lesson is that we are on a journey and can never sit back and accept the status quo. Thus I find everything I wrote in the 2003 Preface to still be true.

What we have done with this edition is to try and make a better book. We have completely reformatted the text and placed it into a more convenient size and layout. We have cleaned up the diagrams and added some pictures.

Mr. Steve Blakey, the owner of BB Design and long-time elder at Redeemer, donated a great deal of time and expertise this round. Volunteer proof-readers, Michael Grooms, Sam Powell, Charles Lehmann, and Deacon David Muehlenbruch also helped, as did Heidi Mueller and Adriane Dorr. Once again Fr. Charles McClean has generously granted us permission to reprint his work, but retains the copyright.

It is our prayer that the knowledge and piety contained in these pages would be used by God for the edification of His people.

The Feast of St. Lucy, Virgin, Martyr
Anno ✠ Domini 2006

David H. Petersen
Pastor of Redeemer Lutheran Church
Fort Wayne, Indiana

Preface to the 2003 Edition

Legend has it that the Rev´d Dr. Arthur Carl Piepkorn found "how-to" books slightly distasteful. He was, above all, a theologian. He preferred to talk about what the Liturgy was confessing and the witness of heaven as opposed to describing the terrestrial reality of how the Celebrant held his hands. Yet to this day students and pastors are looking for these mundane descriptions. Within the Anglican Communion one can find such descriptions in Lamburn´s *Ritual Notes* and within the Roman Communion, a Pre-Vatican II description of Ceremony is still available in Fortescue´s monumental work, *The Ceremonies of the Roman Rite*. But to where do the Lutheran heirs of the Common Service and Luther´s Latin Mass go? A specifically Lutheran treatment and description is still hard to find.

Most of Piepkorn´s students had little experience with the ceremony, reverence, and decor that flowed from him so naturally. They recognized in his liturgical actions something of the Church that they wanted to imitate. Fortunately for us they continued to press him, until finally he relented and produced *The Conduct of the Service*, revised in 1965. It was printed by the Concordia Seminary print shop in St. Louis and sold in the seminary bookstore. He wrote it for his students, at their insistence. He never promoted it. And thus, it never enjoyed widespread dissemination and was quickly lost to the Church. Over the years it has been much sought after and much photocopied, but the copies that still exist are mostly torn and dog-eared.

When he finally acquiesced to their demands, his training and preference for systematics showed itself. He came at the description of ceremonies in a unique and systematic way. He went after the rules. The rules he used are the rubrics prescribed in *The Lutheran Hymnal* of 1941 and in the companion volume for that Hymnal, *The Lutheran Liturgy*. We have reproduced the latter in an appendix for easy reference. Incidentally, those rubrics have never been replaced by the LCMS. Unless they are explicitly contradicted, replaced, or restated in new Rites provided by the Commission on Worship, they are STILL the guide for the conduct of the Services in our churches. Where they have been updated and revised, Piepkorn´s descriptions and explanations tend to make even more sense. Thus, this is the best work up to our day on the practical execution of liturgy in the LCMS.

With that in mind we are making this volume available to the Church again in this durable format with additional features that were not in the original. We have not changed a single word, mind you, but we did expand the paragraph numbers, add page numbers, a table of contents, and an index. We have done this in order to make it a more useful reference tool, and, though Piepkorn may have cringed at the thought, a handier "how-to' book. Like his students then, we still desire to learn from him and his piety.

The other part of this volume is the Rev´d Father Charles McClean´s update and revision of Piepkorn´s work entitled *The Conduct of the Services* (1972). McClean´s reworking of Piepkorn is useful in several respects. Piepkorn only explained the Church´s main Service, that of Holy

Communion (TLH page 15). McClean expands that by adding commentary, explanation, and description for the Orders of Matins and Vespers. He also added explanations and descriptions for variables within the main Service, including varying configurations of assistants and servers and how they might be utilized in the Chancel, as well as how to make use of a free-standing altar. What students and pastors have loved most about McClean's revision over the years, and which is included here as well, are the helpful diagrams and illustrations.

Neither did we change a word of McClean's work. We did, however, expand his table of contents. We also eliminated two appendices from the original. They explained the conduct of the services in *Worship Supplement* 1969 and those services have mostly fallen out of use.

It is our prayer that these words would again serve the Church and help unclutter her Services from things that hinder and distract God's people from His gifts.

The Feast of the Resurrection
Anno ✠ Domini 2003

DAVID H. PETERSEN
Pastor of Redeemer Lutheran Church
Fort Wayne, Indiana

MICHAEL N. FRESE
Pastor of Emmanuel Lutheran Church
Adell, Wisconsin

THE CONDUCT OF THE SERVICE

by the Rev. Dr. Arthur Carl Piepkorn

CSPS 1965 (Revised Edition)

Contents

Notes on Reverence iii
General Rubrics of the Lutheran Liturgy 1
General Rubrics of the Lutheran Hymnal 5
The Order of Holy Communion 8
    The Confessional Service 8
    Hymn of Invocation and Baptism 8
    The Preparatory Service 9
        The Introit and Gloria Patri 11
        The Kyrie and Gloria in Excelsis 12
        The Salutation and Collect 12
        The Lection 14
        The Creed 19
        The Hymn and the Sermon 19
    The Service of the Sacrament 21
        The Offertory 21
        The Preparation of the Altar and accompanying ceremonies .22
        The General Prayer 24
        The Proper Preface 26
        The Sanctus 26
        The Lord's Prayer 26
        The Words of Institution and ceremonies 26
        The Pax 28
        The Agnus Dei and Distribution 28
        The Nunc-Dimittis, Thanksgiving, Post-Communion Collect, and Benediction 33
    Care of Altar and remaining consecrated elements 34

The Eucharistic Prayer of *Culto Cristiano* 37

Index 38

A Word of Explanation

The use of the Church-bodies composing the Evangelical Lutheran Synodical Conference of North America is contained in four books — The Lutheran Hymnal, The Lutheran Liturgy, The Lutheran Lectionary, and The Music for the Liturgy.

A use consists of two parts: the text of the services, called the rite; and the directions for conducting the services, called the rubrics.

One reason for the great diversity in the conduct of religious services in our churches is inadequate attention to the directions, or rubrics. Another is the difficulty which many pastors and parishes confess that they have in understanding and applying the rubrics.

To help such people is the purpose of this pamphlet.

One cardinal principle runs through this work: The rubrics are to be taken as they read not as the author of this guide thinks they ought to read! Accordingly, this is not a directory for a "liturgical" service, or for an "unliturgical" service.

Where the rubrics of our use contradict one another, this pamphlet suggests a solution to the dilemma.

Where the rubrics are inconsistent, this pamphlet tries to harmonize them.

Where the rubrics permit various possibilities, this pamphlet indicates which possible choice has the best historical warrant.

Where the rubrics say that something may or shall be done, but does not indicate how it is to be done, this pamphlet proposes a mode of procedure that accords with the best liturgical tradition of the Church of the Augsburg Confession.

But this pamphlet takes the rubrics as they read! Only as our pastors and parishes do likewise can our church achieve the degree of uniformity in our services that practical experience indicates is so desirable.

A. C. P.

Notes on Reverence

I

There is really only one basic rule of good form: "Be courteous!" And similarly there is really only one basic rule of altar decorum: "Be reverent!" Every other rule is simply a practical amplification of this basic charge.

To be reverent we must first of all be humble. We are ministers — ministers of Christ, serving Christ in the room and in the name of fellow-sinners. We minister not because of any virtue in ourselves. Our sufficiency is of God. We minister as temples of the Holy Ghost, as being bound in sacramental union to the Lord of the Church, as kings and priests living in mystic communion with the Most Holy Trinity, as those whom Christ has chosen that we might be with Him and that He might send us forth to preach (St. Mark 3, 13). We minister under the aspect of eternity and in the Presence of the Divine Majesty. Wherever we stand, we are on holy ground. In such a ministry there is no room for pride, only for all-pervading humility.

To be reverent we must be prepared. We must know what we are doing, and why we are doing it. The physical preparations, as far as may be, should be taken care of well in advance. There should be no last-minute running to and fro, no hasty final preparation, no distressed paging about. A meditation, brief if need be, but as long as the time permits, ought never to be overlooked; spiritual preparation is more essential to reverence than the proper ordering of the physical adjuncts.

To be reverent we must be calm. The unforeseen, the accidental, the disturbing must not be permitted to distract us. We are God's ambassadors and God's servants. We are speaking for and to God. Our entire lives ought to be, and our public ministry must be *en Christo* - in Christ! So must the calm peace of the changeless Christ in our souls be reflected in our outward demeanor.

II

The discussion of practical details which follows is intended to be neither "liturgical" nor "unliturgical." If certain individual suggestions seem to reflect a "liturgical" bias, it is because we are not persuaded that every parish and every parson must scale its or his ceremonial down to the lowest level in use among us. Those less "liturgically" inclined may depart from the norm suggested as widely as their vagrant fancy and their Christian liberty dictate, and they will unquestionably do so. These things are not matters of faith, and their doing or omission is neither mortal nor venial sin.

In general, services should be conducted, rites performed, and the Holy Sacraments administered in the place set aside for that purpose, the church. We need not ascribe intrinsic sanctity to a place or a building or an object to realize that devotion and reverence inevitably reflect surroundings and associations.

It is not a question of validity or efficacy. It is simply that it is usually easier to be reverent in church, and so the church should be the scene of our ministration except where inescapable exigencies direct that another place be employed.

Our service allows a wide range of individual liberty and gives full scope to parochial peculiarities. But the very rubrics which provide this beautiful freedom become gins of irreverence and confusion for the feet of the unwary and the uninstructed. Each Church might well have its Orders of Service, as used, mimeographed or printed and placed in the hands of the worshipers before The Service or rite begins.

III

It is proper to light the altar candles for all services. The Lutheran use is to have two single beeswax candles, set near the extremities of the altar, either on the gradine or as close as possible to the back of the mensa, if there be no gradine. Six candles is a Counter-Reformatory Roman use. Candelabra as substitutes for the two single candles are a Protestant sentimentality. The Epistle candle is lighted first; the Gospel candle last; they are extinguished in reverse order. Lighting with a match held in the hand is not reverent:—extinguishing with puffs of breath from bloating cheeks is even less so. Use a lighter and snuffer. The lights may be lit by the officiant if there be no one to assist him, or by a choirboy, or by a server appointed for the purpose. In any case the individual performing this task should be decently vested. New candles should be started before the service, or they may cause embarrassing difficulties. Candles, altar linens, frontals, frontlets, superfrontals, dossals, riddels, and carpets should be changed out of service time. Cut flowers (or potted plants) should not be placed on the altar, widespread practice not withstanding. Flowers are best placed in pottery jugs on the floor of the sanctuary or on stands rather than upon the altar. This should be done at least fifteen minutes before the service begins. The same applies to setting markers; placing books on the credence, lectern, and pulpit, and changing hymn-board numbers.

A credence table or bracket, preferably on the Epistle side of the sanctuary wall, is a convenience of such importance that it is almost a necessity. Upon it are disposed the extra books, memoranda, host-box, flagon, cruets, lavabo, and the other things which, when placed upon the altar, only cumber and clutter the Holy Table. The credence table or bracket may be covered unobtrusively by a white linen cloth.

Reverence dictates a complete set of Communion linens: A corporal, a burse to carry it from the sacristy to the altar and back; a pall to prevent foreign substances from falling into the uncovered chalice; a veil, unless the early medieval type of folded pall be in use; purificators; a towel. A houseling-cloth (a cloth preferably of white linen of suitable length held at each end by a server directly in front of the communicants to prevent the sacred species from falling to the ground through inadvertence) is not without good Lutheran warrant, and its use certainly makes for reverence.

It appears to be most seemly that on ordinary occasions the celebrant prepare the sacred vessels himself and that he carry them to and from the altar. In any case the candles should be lit before the sacred vessels are carried in and extinguished only after they have been carried away.

Arriving at the altar, the celebrant opens the burse, takes out the corporal, lays the burse at the rear of the altar left of the center, or leans it against the gradine or reredos to the left of the center, unfolds the corporal with a minimum of motion (to avoid confusion the corporal should always be folded into nine divisions thus: front, back, right, left); the chalice veil is adjusted to form a trapezoid when viewed from the front. If a hymn be sung meanwhile, the celebrant may return to his seat by the shortest route until it is concluded.

The clergy seat should not face toward the people. Few of our churches are so constructed that the clergy seat could not be placed on the Epistle (or Gospel) side with the occupant facing liturgical north (or south). Once having left the sacristy, the officiant should not return to it except for urgent reason. His proper place is at the altar, but if the choral rendering of any part of the service consumes much time, he is at liberty to read the section privately and to take his place in the clergy seat, to which he should go by the shortest route.

During the singing of the hymn the officiant should sing with the congregation, unless he be otherwise occupied with the conduct of the service. The time should not be employed looking at the lessons or other propers. Neither should the officiant beat time with his book, nor should he look about him, nor should he bellow at the top of his voice. If he knows the hymn well enough to dispense with a book, his hands should be extended upon his knees, palm down, right thumb crossed over the left thumb, or with one hand in the sleeve of the other arm. Under no circumstances should he cross his feet or legs.

Since the altar is a symbol of the constant presence of God and since it serves as the focus of devotion in the church (except during the reading of the Gospel when the focus of attention shifts to the book), it is appropriate to salute the altar with a profound bow when first entering and last leaving the sanctuary and to bow moderately whenever crossing, approaching, or leaving the midst.

In going to and from the altar, or when otherwise walking about, the officiant's hands should be folded reverently. It is possible that in ancient times it was custom to clasp the fingers, but by the time of the Reformation it was certainly a common custom to hold the hands palm to palm, fingers extended, generally with the thumb of the right hand over that of the left. In either case the hands should be held at the height of the breast, not hanging down below the midriff, "in the manner," as one baseball-minded clergyman put it, "of Willy Mays catching a fly." The hands should not be encumbered with books, nor should they be permitted to hang limp at the sides. When a book must be carried closed, it is held at the height of the breast a few inches in front of the person, upright.

In order to avoid the necessity of handling two books at the altar, the officiant could either type out the proper lessons or provide himself with an agenda or service book which contains the propers printed out in full.

In walking the head is always held erect, the eyes cast down. The gait should neither be too slow nor too fast. The steps should be short, but not mincing. The approach to the altar should always be made squarely, not at a diagonal. Turns should be made at right angles, but not with obtrusive precision. There should be no sidling or pivoting. When standing still, care should be observed to avoid the appearance of unsteadiness. Do not sway back and forth. Do not lean against the altar, especially when facing the congregation.

It is a confessional custom to bow the head at the Holy Name of Jesus, toward the Crucifix if at the Altar, toward the book if the Holy Gospel is being read, and straight ahead at other times. It is likewise proper to bow the head at the opening words of the Gloria Patri whenever it occurs, and at the Sanctus in the Preface and Te Deum.

The Sign of the Holy Cross is a confessional gesture. It is made with the hand disposed as for a blessing from the head ("My Lord Jesus Christ came down from heaven") to the breast ("and was incarnate for me") to the right side ("and was crucified for me") to the left side ("and entered into my heart"). When made over the people the same relative positions are observed, i.e., from the viewpoint of the officiant the last stroke is made from left to right. When made over the people the Holy Sign should be made at the same height and cover the same area as when made on the person. At the Holy Gospel the crosses are made with the right thumb in an area about an inch in diameter. At all times when the Holy Cross is signed, the left hand is held flat against the breast, unless otherwise engaged. This method of making the sign of the Holy Cross is older than the method in common use in the Roman Catholic Church where the right hand crosses from the left shoulder to the right.

An assistant, not necessarily another clergyman, can be of great help, for example, by transferring books, and holding and bringing objects as needed. He should be vested properly. The number of such assistants need not be restricted to one.

If a fellow-clergyman of the same communion be present, it is only common courtesy to offer him a part in the service. Such parts would be the preaching of the Sermon, the reading of the liturgical lessons, and the invitation to the Benedicamus ("Bless we the Lord") at the end of the Communion office. If he be a dignitary, he may be invited to pronounce the benediction. Unless there be a valid reason for refusing, it is highly discourteous to fail to act upon such an invitation.

Visiting clergy will be careful to observe the customs of the parish. Especially during the present period of transition back to older forms and usages, it is most advisable to inquire carefully on this point.

When a ministration takes place outside of church, the effort should be made to reproduce the conditions of church as far as possible, and as much of the ceremonial as conditions permit or warrant should be retained.

GENERAL RUBRICS OF THE LUTHERAN LITURGY
(The Lutheran Liturgy, pp. 417-419, 425-427)

Nota bene: The text of the rubrics as found in the designated sources has been underlined. The rubrics which apply to Matins and Vespers have been deleted from this chapter only because they do not apply to the immediate subject.

1. When the Officiant stands before the altar, he faces the altar for all sacrificial acts and the Congregation for all sacramental acts.
2. The sacrificial acts of the Morning Service and of the Order of the Holy Communion are the Trinitarian Invocation, the Confession, the Introit, the Hymns and Canticles, the Gradual, the Creed, the Prayers, the Offertory, the Preface, the Sanctus, and the Words of Institution. This listing is obviously intended to include the Kyrie, the Gloria in Excelsis, and the Collect.
3. The sacramental acts of the Morning Service and of the Order of the Holy Communion are the Invitation to Confession, the Declaration of Grace or the Absolution, the Salutation, the Lessons, the Sermon, the Votum, the Salutation, the Benedicamus and the Benediction.
4. The word" shall" in the rubrics makes that part of the Service obligatory, while the word "may" leaves it optional.
5. When turning at the altar, the Officiant shall ordinarily turn by his right side to face the Congregation and by his left side to face the altar.
6. Whenever the Holy Communion is celebrated in a Church Service, the Order of the Holy Communion shall be used in its entirety. At conference services, weddings, small Communion services in church, and evening Communion services, and on similar occasions, there is thus no authority for beginning the service with the Preface, combining parts of Vespers (or Matins) with parts of the Order for the Holy Communion, or omitting any part of the service that the rubrics make obligatory ("shall").
7. The Propria, or Propers (as distinguished from the fixed portions of the Service, called the Ordinary), that is, the Introit, the Collect, the Epistle, the Gradual, and the Gospel for the Day, shall be used throughout the week following, except on those Days for which other appointments are made. This rubric refers to the Propers for any given Sunday. If a Sunday is displaced by a festival which has no octave, the Propers of the festival are used on the Sunday itself, but the Propers of the Sunday are used during the week following except on those days for which other appointments are made.
8. The music of the Service is not a part of the Liturgy and may be altered as circumstances permit or require. Music may be omitted altogether and the entire service may be said. The normal service of the Christian community has, however, from earliest antiquity been choral. To vary the musical settings seasonally is desirable.
9. Liturgical chant, more so than any other type of church music, is not a musical interpretation of the text; it is only the bearer of the text and should be sung in a simple, straightforward manner. To chant is to speak on established pitches of musical sounds according to pre-

scribed formulae retaining natural rhythm and stress of speech (*choraliter legere*). The Officiant must not sing his part of the Service as if it were a recitative or a solo in an oratorio or opera. To a lesser extent, the same thing is true of Hymn tunes. This is in keeping with the spirit of the objective character of liturgical worship, which disdains sentimentalization and tawdriness, musical and otherwise.

10. <u>The Officiant shall chant those portions of the Service to which the Choir or the Congregation responds with chanting.</u> This rubric is obligatory, common practice to the contrary notwithstanding. If the Choir or Congregation responds with chant, the Officiant is required to chant the corresponding parts of the service assigned to him. He speaks these parts of the service only if the Congregation responds in a speaking voice.

11. <u>The primary function of the Choir is to lead the Congregation in the singing of the Liturgy and the Hymns, and to sing the Propers when they are beyond the capacity of the Congregation.</u> The singing of optional anthems and other compositions apart from the Ordinary, the Propers and Hymns is at best a secondary function of the Choir and should not be allowed to become its primary function or reason for existing.

12. <u>In view of the fact that the music presented by the Choir and organist is part of the Service of Worship, it is imperative that this music be in keeping with the spirit of the liturgical character of the Service.</u> This rubric does not contradict paragraph 8 above. *The Lutheran Liturgy* does not prescribe the music to be used nor does it even prescribe that any music be used. But if in a given service music is used it becomes part of the service of God's holy community on that occasion and must be in keeping with the liturgical spirit and character of the service.

13. <u>From time to time the Choir may sing parts of the Ordinary in more elaborate choral setting.</u> The ideal of maximum congregational participation in the service implies that the privilege accorded by this rubric will be used sparingly.

14. <u>Notices to the Congregation, except in connection with requests for Intercession, ought not to be read during the Services.</u> Such notices are best published in a parish bulletin or posted on a bulletin board in the narthex of the Church. If a notice must be brought to the Congregation's attention, it should be read after the service is over and after the worshippers have had an opportunity to offer their final private prayers.

15. <u>The liturgical colors are white, red, green, violet, and black.</u>

15.1 <u>White is used from and with Vespers of Eve of Nativity</u> (that is, Vespers on December 24) <u>through the Epiphany Octave</u> (that is, through the evening service on January 13); <u>on Maundy Thursday, when Communion is celebrated; from and with the Vespers of Easter through to</u> (but not at) <u>the Vespers of the Eve of Whitsunday; on the Feast of the Holy Trinity</u> (beginning with Vespers on the Saturday before) <u>and its Octave; all the other Festivals of Christ; i.e., Presentation, Annunciation, Visitation, and Transfiguration; on the Day of St. Michael and All Angels; on the Day of the Conversion of St. Paul; the Day of the Nativity of St. John the Baptist; All Saints' Day; the Dedication of a Church and its Anniversary; on days of general and special thanksgiving; and on the festivals of saints not martyrs.</u>

15.2 <u>Red is used from and with the Vespers on the Eve of Whitsunday through to</u> (but not at) <u>the</u>

- Vespers on the Eve of Holy Trinity, the Festival of the Reformation and its Octave, and on days commemorating the death of martyrs (except when Holy Innocents falls during the week).
- 15.3 Green is used from and with Matins on January 14 to (but not at) Vespers of the Eve of Septuagesima, and from Matins on the Monday before the Second Sunday after Trinity through the post-Trinity season to (but not at) the Vespers on the Eve of the First Sunday in Advent.
- 15.4 Violet is used from and with the Vespers on the Eve of (the first Sunday in) Advent to (but not at) the Vespers on the Eve of the Nativity; from and with Vespers on the Saturday before Septuagesima and throughout Pre-Lent and Lent, to (but not at) Vespers on the Eve of Easter; and for the Day of Humiliation. It is also desirable to use Violet from Matins on the Monday after Rogation Sunday until, (but not at), Vespers on the Wednesday before the Ascension Day; and on Holy Innocents' Day when it falls during the week.
- 15.5 Black is used on Good Friday only. The Solemnization of Holy Matrimony and the Order for the Burial of the Dead shall not affect the proper color for the Season in use when these Services are held.
- 16. The Fair Linen a cloth covering the altar, extending one third or two thirds or all the way to the floor at the narrow ends, shall always be upon the altar.
- 17. The Corporal, a square of very fine linen, is laid upon the center of the Fair Linen cloth. Upon it the sacramental vessels are placed. The practice of placing some of the sacramental vessels (usually the chalice and cruets) on the Gospel side of the altar ("wine" side) and some (usually the paten, pyx and ciborium) on the Epistle side of the altar ("bread" side) is thus contrary to the rubrics.
- 18. The Pall, a small square of stiff material covered or lined with linen, is used to cover the chalice. It should be removed at the Consecration. A corporal folded into thirds and then folded into thirds again, so that it is a square nine layers of cloth thick, each side of the square one-third the length of a side of the unfolded corporal, meets the requirement of the rubric. It is from this folded corporal that the modern chalice pall developed. It is doubtful if the modern chalice pall is any more convenient than a folded corporal. It is certainly more troublesome to wash.
- 19. The Purificators, squares of heavy linen, are used to cleanse the rim of the chalice during the Administration. They are also used to dry the tips of the celebrant's fingers at the Lavabo.
- 20. The Veil, made of silk or of the finest linen, is used to cover the sacramental vessels upon the altar or credence table. It is removed before the Preface and should be folded carefully and laid upon the altar and again placed over the sacramental vessels after the Administration at the Nunc Dimittis. The most common use is to make the veil of brocaded silk and to have it match the burse in color and material.
- 21. When not in use on the altar the sacramental linens should be properly folded and kept in the Burse, a square envelope made of strong cardboard, covered with silk or heavy linen. The most common use is to cover the burse with silk brocade. Where the resources of the parish permit, it should be in the color of the service in which it is used. This rubric obviously does not apply to the parish's whole supply of sacramental linens. It is intended to provide that a set of sacramental linens (the corporal, the pall or a corporal used as a pall, and two purificators) be kept ready in a burse at all times, and that they be carried to and from the altar in the burse.

22. It is a laudable custom based upon a Scriptural injunction (I Cor. 11:3-15), for women to wear an appropriate head covering in Church, especially at the time of divine service. "Appropriate head covering" includes a hat, a veil, a handkerchief, or a head-band. This custom is not only an ecclesiastical one, but also one that is dictated by good social usage.
23. On and after Easter Day, 1955, in any case of a contradiction between these General Rubrics as they are here printed and other rubrics published elsewhere in the official service books of the Evangelical Lutheran Synodical Conference of North America, these General Rubrics shall govern.

General Rubrics of The Lutheran Hymnal
The Lutheran Hymnal, Page 4

24. <u>Good usage permits the speaking of the Preparatory Service.</u> Congregations should avail themselves of this option. *The Lutheran Liturgy* (p. 419) asserts: <u>Since the Preparation is not a part of the Service proper, it is preferable that the Officiant and the Congregation speak the entire Preparatory Service.</u> It is desirable to distinguish the Preparatory Service from the Service not only by the position of the Minister (see note to par. 40), but also by the manner in which the officiant and congregation render this part of the service. If, however, the Congregation chants its responses, the Minister will chant the versicles and prayers of the Preparatory Service, in compliance with the General Rubrics (par. 10 above). *Concentus* (chanting by the Congregation) always implies *accentus* (chanting by the Minister); neither is proper without the other. *The Music for the Liturgy* declares: "The music for the chanting of the Confession of Sins is given for the convenience of those who desire to chant those parts; but this practice is not to be considered as being recommended by our Committee" (page 6).

25. <u>The Sign of the Cross may be made at the Trinitarian Invocation and at the words of the Nicene Creed "and the life of the world to come."</u> Make the Sign of the Holy Cross in this way: Hold the palm of the right hand flat, thumb and fingers together; touch with the tips of your fingers successively the forehead, the breast, the right shoulder and the left shoulder. The reference to the Trinitarian Invocation is general and applies whenever the words "In the Name of the Father and of the Son and of the Holy Ghost" are said. At the Trinitarian Invocation and at the closing words of the Creed, the Minister makes the sign of the Cross *on himself* just as the other worshippers do.

26. '<u>V stands for Versicle, said by the Minister; R designates the Response by the Congregation.</u> If the Minister speaks the Versicle, the congregation speaks the Response. The Congregation chants the Response only when the Minister has chanted the Versicle. See par. 10 above.

27. '<u>Instead of the Introit, a Psalm may be used. The Introit consists of Antiphon, Psalm and Gloria Patri.</u> No matter how the Introit is rendered, whether by the choir or by the Minister and the Congregation, the minimum requirement is the following: Antiphon; Psalm-verse; Gloria Patri (unless omitted, as on a Day of Humiliation and Prayer); Antiphon repeated. Never omit the repetition of the Antiphon at the very end of the Introit. On occasions of special solemnity, you may repeat the Antiphon after the Psalm-verse as well as after the Gloria Patri, thus: Antiphon, Psalm-verse, Antiphon repeated, Gloria Patri, Antiphon repeated. Our present Introits are simply remnants of Psalms sung by the choir and clergy on their way to the altar. If you substitute a Psalm for the Introit, it should always be the Psalm of which the Introit is

Conduct of the Service

an abbreviation. Usually the Psalm can be identified by referring to the Psalm-verse, which is normally the first verse of the Psalm. Thus the proper Introit Psalm for the Fourth Sunday in Advent (Rorate) would be Psalm 19 (*Coeli enarrant*) and the proper Introit Psalm for Christmas Day would be Psalm 98 (*Cantate Domino*).

Sometimes the Antiphon itself is the first verse(s) of the Psalm: a case in point is the Twelfth Sunday after Trinity, where the Antiphon of the Introit consists of verses 1 and 2a of Psalm 70 (*Deus in adjutorium*) and the Psalm-verse is verse 2b, so that Psalm 70 would be the proper Psalm to substitute for the Introit on that day. When you substitute a Psalm for the Introit, always retain the Antiphon; sing the Antiphon at least before the first verse of the Psalm and after the Gloria Patri (or last verse). On occasions of solemnity and in order to lengthen a short Psalm adequately, you may sing the Antiphon after *each* verse as well as after the Gloria Patri. If you substitute a long Psalm for the Introit, you need sing only as many verses as the circumstances call for; the Psalm may end at any point that the sense of the text permits, whereupon the Gloria Patri follows and the Antiphon is repeated. The only occasion on which *The Lutheran Liturgy* prescribes omission of the Gloria Patri is a Day of Humiliation and Prayer (*The Lutheran Liturgy*, page 184). Anciently the Gloria Patri was omitted from the Introit from the first Sunday in Passiontide (Judica) until, but not at, the first celebration of Holy Communion in memory of our Lord's resurrection. So in Paul Bunjes, *The Service Propers Noted*, Accompaniment Edition, Part I, Concordia Publishing House, Saint Louis, 1960, page 71ff. This practice is thus approved by the Commission on Worship, Liturgies and Hymnology.

28. <u>Other Collects may be used with the Collect for the Day; the Congregation shall chant or say "Amen" after each Collect.</u> Avail yourself of the privilege of saying other Collects with the Collect for the Day only at Matins and Vespers; at the Morning Service and the Holy Communion, restrict yourself to the Collect for the Day unless two holy days (such as St. Mary Magdalene's Day and the Ninth Sunday after Trinity) are being commemorated on the same day. The Congregation says "Amen" if the Minister has said the Collect; the Congregation chants "Amen" if the Minister has chanted the Collect. If a number of Collects are said under a single termination, they are regarded as a single collect (see par. 54).

29. <u>In the service other Scripture lessons may be read before the Epistle. The Epistle and the Gospel shall always be read.</u> This rubric authorizes you to restore an Old Testament lesson before the Epistle. Use column 4 (headed "Old Testament") in the lectionary on pages 159-160 of *The Lutheran Hymnal*. (Do not use a Psalm for this purpose.) Announce it in this way: "The Old Testament Lesson is written in the _____ Chapter of _____, beginning at the _____ Verse." If you chant the lesson, it is not necessary to indicate the end; if you read it, say at the end: "Here endeth the Lesson." Read the Old Testament Lesson from the place where you read the Epistle. The Epistle and the Gospel that "shall always be read" are the Epistle and the Gospel appointed for that occasion in *The Lutheran Liturgy* or *The Lutheran Hymnal* and printed out in *The Lutheran Lectionary*. You have no authority to omit the Epistle or Gospel because it is the text of the sermon. You likewise have no

authority to substitute an Epistle or Gospel either of your own choice or from another series of lessons (such as the Eisenach or Synodical Conference series).

30. Choir selections may be sung immediately after the Gradual. So used, they take the place of the ancient Sequence Hymn (*pro sequentia*).
31. On Trinity Sunday, at Matins, the Athanasian Creed may be used instead of the Psalmody. *The Lutheran Liturgy* authorizes you to use the Athanasian Creed in place of part of the Psalmody. When you use the Athanasian Creed, render it like a Psalm or Canticle; use Gloria Patri at the end and, if you wish, use an appropriate Antiphon at the beginning and the end. The Athanasian Creed should never be substituted for the Nicene (or the Apostles') Creed.
32. Silent prayer should be offered upon entering the church and after the Benediction. Kneelers help!
33. All necessary announcements which are not part of the special intercessions and Thanksgivings (see par. 14) should be made after the close of the Service.
34. Matins and Vespers end with the Benedicamus if the Minister is not conducting the service. If the Minister is the Officiant, he shall pronounce the Benediction, and the Benedicamus may be omitted. "The Minister" here means an ordained clergyman. The Benedicamus is an ancient and integral part of Matins and Vespers; even if an ordained clergyman officiates, do not avail yourself of the authority here given to omit the Benedicamus.
35. Congregations are urged to let the basic structure of the Service remain intact. The wide choice permitted in the Rubrics makes it possible to have the Service as simple or as elaborate as the circumstances of each Congregation may indicate.
36. The Hymnal is intended for use not only in the church service and in the school, but it may serve profitable also for family and private devotions. The Prayers and the tables for Bible-reading will be an aid for these uses.

The Order of Holy Communion
(*The Lutheran Hymnal*, pp. 5-31;
The Lutheran Liturgy, pp. 1-26, 419-422;
The Music for the Liturgy, pp. 11-34;
The Order of Holy Communion, pp. 3-24).

The Confessional Service

37. <u>If the Confessional Service immediately precedes the Communion Service, the latter shall begin with the Introit.</u> (*The Lutheran Liturgy*, page 420). The force of this rubric is in accordance with the best Lutheran tradition of the 16th century; when you have separated the Confession of Sins and Holy Absolution from the service proper by conducting a confessional service at another time before the service begins, then the Communion Service begins with the Introit. This rubric (*The Lutheran Liturgy*, p. 420) supersedes the second of the General Rubrics of *The Lutheran Hymnal*, page 4, which provided that the Trinitarian Invocation should precede the Introit in the case envisioned. Congregations should avail themselves of the rubric as found in *The Lutheran Liturgy*.

38. <u>When the Service begins with the Introit, the Officiant shall proceed to the altar at once.</u> This rubric (*The Lutheran Liturgy*, p. 419) clearly indicates that the Opening Hymn, which is obligatory when the service begins with the Preparatory Service, is to be omitted when the Service begins with the Introit.

Hymn of Invocation and Baptisms

39. <u>A Hymn of Invocation of the Holy Ghost or another Hymn shall be sung</u>. The Commission on Worship, Liturgies and Hymnology now authorizes omission of the Opening Hymn. At Confirmations, Ordinations, Installations and similar occasions, "Come, Holy Ghost, Creator Blest" (No. 233) is traditional. The Rubric does not prescribe the posture of the Minister and the Congregation; they are presumably seated, but they may stand, particularly for the last stanza of the Hymn if it is a doxology to the Triune God (that is, a rhymed version of the Gloria Patri). The Minister may proceed to the chancel during the singing of this Hymn, or, if he wishes to participate in the entire service with the Congregation, he may take his place in a clergy stall prior to the Hymn. In either case he may offer silent prayer as he kneels in his stall or at his chair, or as he kneels or stands at the entrance to the chancel. Normally there should be no procession of the choir into the church before the service and out of the church after the service. Processions should be reserved for special occasions (for example, Christmas, Palm Sunday, Maundy Thursday, Good Friday, Easter, April 25, whether or not Saint Mark's Day is being observed, the Monday, Tuesday and Wednesday after Rogate, the Ascension Day, Whitsunday, the Anniversary of the Dedication of the church, the patronal festival or feast of title of

the parish, a day of general or special thanksgiving, or a day of humiliation and prayer), when the procession helps to highlight the extraordinary character of the observance.

39.5 Note the General Rubric of *The Lutheran Liturgy* (p. 419): <u>Unless otherwise ordered in a Congregation, public Baptism may be administered after the Opening Hymn, in which case the Opening Hymn will be a baptismal Hymn.</u>

The Preparatory Service

40. <u>For the Invocation and the Preparatory Service, the Officiant may stand at the foot of the altar steps, advancing to the altar at the Introit.</u> If the altar is not raised one or more steps above the chancel floor, he may stand at a point about four feet in front of the altar. He has left his Hymnal at his seat or stall. *The Lutheran Liturgy* is open on the missal cushion or stand. In proceeding to the altar "at the Introit," the celebrant will normally proceed to the altar before he (or the choir) begins the Introit.

41. <u>The Congregation shall rise, if it is not already standing; and the Minister, facing the altar, shall say or chant: "In the name etc."</u> The Minister holds his hands before and close to his breast, palm to palm or folded, the right thumb over the left. If he reverences toward the altar, he inclines his head only; he does not bow from the hips nor does he arch his back. As he says the Invocation he and the members of the Congregation may make the Sign of the Holy Cross upon themselves (par. 4). While he makes the Sign of the Holy Cross, the Officiant holds his left hand flat to his body just below the breast. The Invocation is better spoken than sung (par. 3).

42. <u>The Congregation shall say or chant: "Amen."</u> The Congregation says the Amen if the Minister has said the Invocation; only if he has chanted the Invocation will the Congregation chant the Amen. Saying this part of the service is preferable (par. 3).

43. <u>Then shall be said or chanted The Confession of Sins.</u>

44. <u>The Minister, facing the people, shall say: "Beloved in the Lord! Let us draw near, etc."</u> The Minister, his hands joined, turns where he stands, keeping his right shoulder toward the Congregation as he does so, faces the Congregation, and says the invitation to the Confession of Sins. He may incline his head when he pronounces the Holy Name of JESUS.

45. <u>All may kneel.</u> This is a laudable custom. *The Lutheran Liturgy* (p. 419) declares: <u>The Congregation may kneel until the Declaration of Grace has been spoken.</u> After saying or chanting the invitation to the Confession of Sins, the Minister turns toward the altar again, his hands joined, his right shoulder toward the Congregation as he turns. He may kneel upon the lowest altar step, if there is one. If he does not kneel, he remains standing erect. Likewise, if the Congregation does not kneel, it remains standing.

46. <u>The Minister, facing the altar, shall say: "Our help, etc."</u> It is better to say the versicles and prayers which follow rather than to chant them. In the prayers, the Minister may incline his head when he pronounces the Holy Name of JESUS.

47. <u>Then the Minister, facing the altar, shall say with the Congregation: "O almighty God etc."</u> The Minister may incline His head when he pronounces the Holy Name

of JESUS. In saying the Confession of Sins, he should not pause between the words "death" and "of." The proper places to pause are after "mercy" and after "Christ."

48. <u>Then the Minister, facing the people, shall pronounce the Absolution.</u> The Minister turns to face the people by his right. As far as "unto all of you," he keeps his hands joined in front of his breast. Then he places his left hand flat against his body just below his breast and raises his right hand, fingers together and palm toward the congregation, to the level of his shoulder and continues. At the words "and of the Son" he makes the Sign of the Holy Cross over the people thus: He turns his right hand so that the open palm faces the side of the church; keeping the thumb and fingers together, he raises his right hand to a point in front of his face, then moves it vertically downward to the level of his waist, raises it again vertically to a point before his breast, moves it horizontally to a point in front of his left shoulder, moves it back horizontally to a point in front of his right shoulder, then moves it back before his breast. He holds it in this position until he has finished saying "Holy Ghost." As the Congregation responds, Amen, he rejoins his hands before his breast and turns by his left to the Altar, whereupon he proceeds to the altar and begins the Introit. The penitents may make the Sign of the Holy Cross at the words "and of the Son."

    If the Service be the Morning Service without Communion, at par. 47 the Minister shall face the altar and say "Almighty God, our Maker, etc." He may incline his head when he pronounces the Holy Name of JESUS. Then the congregation shall say with the Minister, facing the altar, "O Most merciful God, Who hast, etc." The Minister may incline his head as he pronounces the Holy Name of JESUS. Then the Minister, his hands joined, rises (if he has been kneeling), turns where he stands by his right toward the Congregation, and says (or chants) the Words of Assurance, "Almighty God our Heavenly Father, etc.," as far "He that believeth and is baptized shall be saved." Then, as the rubrics of *The Lutheran Liturgy* direct, he shall turn by his left to the altar and say (or chant): "Grant this, Lord, unto us all." The Congregation says (or chants) its Amen. The "sacrificial" character of the closing words is accented by the Minister's change of position, and the Congregation is given time for participation in the thought of the petition.

49. <u>Then all shall stand to the close of the Collect.</u> The Congregation, if it has been kneeling, rises. It makes for more attentive worship to stand for this part of the Service rather than to sit; it is also the older custom to stand. The permissive rubric of the Hymnal and the Liturgy has been superseded by a prescriptive rubric (*The Order of Holy Communion*, 1959, p. 3).

The Service of the Word

The Introit and Gloria Patri

50. <u>Then shall be said or chanted The Introit.</u> Whether you chant or say the Introit depends on whether the Service is a choral or spoken one. If the Service is fully choral, sing the Introit. If it is a spoken service, say the Introit. <u>The Introit for the Day with the Gloria Patri should be sung by the Choir. If no Choir is available, the Introit may be said or chanted by the Officiant. If the Antiphon and the Psalm are said by the Minister, facing the altar, the Gloria Patri may be said or chanted by the Congregation.</u> See par. 27 above. General Rubrics of *The Lutheran Liturgy* (pp. 419-420) supersede the directions of some of the other rubrics. The Introit is always the Introit for the Day of service, not one which the Minister has chosen from another set of propers or composed himself. The Introits have their proper music. If the setting is simple enough, the Congregation may sing the Introit or, if the Choir sings the Introit, the Congregation may unite in the Gloria Patri.

    If a more elaborate musical setting is used, the Choir may properly sing the Introit. The Gloria Patri is not an independent element of the Service; it is part of the Psalm of the Introit and we include it on the principle that an Old Testament Psalm becomes a New Testament hymn by adding the Gloria Patri. If the Minister says the Antiphon and Psalm of the Introit, the Congregation will properly say (not chant) the Gloria Patri. If the Choir and/or Congregation sing the Antiphon and Psalm to an Anglican chant or a plain-chant Psalm-tone, the Gloria Patri is sung to the same chant. *The Lutheran Liturgy* (p.420) asserts: <u>The Introit for the Day, including the Gloria Patri, should either be sung or spoken throughout.</u> The Gloria Patri should not be sung if the Antiphon and Psalm-Verse are read in a speaking voice. <u>The Antiphon, which announces the keynote of the Introit, shall be repeated after the Gloria Patri</u> (*The Lutheran Liturgy*, p.420). There is no exception to this rule.

    Prior to reading the Introit, or while the Choir and/or Congregation are singing the Introit, the Minister, his hands joined, goes to the altar and stands before it at the place where *The Lutheran Liturgy*, opened to the proper place, rests on its cushion or desk. Normally, this place will be either (1) the "Epistle" corner of the altar (at the officiant's right hand as he faces the altar), or (2) the center of the altar. Our use prescribes neither; the former represents the older and better tradition, the latter is probably more common. If the book is at the Epistle corner, the officiant goes to the center of the altar, then turns right until he comes to the book. The officiant faces the altar for the Introit, regardless of its content. If he reverences toward the Crucifix at "Glory be to the Father and to the Son and to the Holy Ghost" he merely inclines his head.

The Kyrie and Gloria in Excelsis

51. <u>Then shall be said or chanted by the Minister, facing the altar, and the Congregation The Kyrie.</u> If the whole service is choral, chant the Kyrie. If the service is not wholly choral, say the Kyrie. If the book is at the Epistle corner of the altar, the Minister turns to the left and goes back to the center of the altar and faces it throughout the Kyrie, his hands joined. *The Lutheran Liturgy* (p. 420) directs: <u>The Kyrie shall be said or sung by the Congregation.</u> This implies that the celebrant will not intone the Kyrie. *The Lutheran Liturgy* provides further: <u>A ninefold, but not a fourfold or sixfold (the Officiant speaking the first line; the Officiant speaking each line) Kyrie may be substituted for the threefold Kyrie. In place of the English text, the Greek, "Kyrie Eleison, Christe Eleison, Kyrie Eleison," may be used in either a threefold or a ninefold form.</u> There is no authority for substituting Hymn No. 6 for the Kyrie.

52. <u>Then shall be said or chanted The Gloria in Excelsis. If the Minister chants his part of the service, he, facing the altar, shall intone the opening sentence; if not, the people shall chant the entire Gloria in Excelsis.</u> The Minister intones this prayer by chanting: "Glory be to God on high." The second sentence of the rubric clearly applies only to choral services, since the first sentence authorizes saying the Gloria in Excelsis. If the service is not choral, the Minister and the Congregation will speak the entire prayer in unison. While the symbol R indicates that everything after the opening words is the Congregation's response, there appears to be no good reason why the Minister may not join the Congregation in saying this part of the prayer. The Minister remains at the center of the altar, facing it, throughout the Gloria in Excelsis, his hands joined. If he reverences at the words "worship," "give thanks," "Jesus," and "receive our prayer," he inclines only his head. *The Lutheran Liturgy* (p. 420) directs: <u>The Gloria in Excelsis shall be used on all Feast and Festival Days</u> (even when the Holy Communion is not celebrated), <u>at other times a versified form of the Gloria in Excelsis (Hymns 237, 238 in The Lutheran Hymnal) or another hymn of praise may be used.</u> (The Minister and Congregation remain standing during the singing of such substitutes.) The Gloria in Excelsis shall also be used at all services of worship in which the administration of Holy Communion takes place, except that in this case it may be omitted during the Seasons of Advent, Pre-Lent and Lent. At celebrations of Holy Communion, there is no authority for substituting either a metrical version of the Gloria in Excelsis or another hymn of praise for the Gloria in Excelsis. Although normally omitted during Advent, Pre-Lent and Lent, Gloria in Excelsis is to be used on Festivals (St. Andrew's Day, St. Thomas' Day, Conversion of St. Paul, Presentation, St. Matthias' Day, the Annunciation) and on Maundy Thursday.

The Salutation and Collect

53. <u>Then shall be said or chanted The Salutation. The Minister, facing the people, shall say or chant: "The Lord be with you."</u> The Minister, his hands still joined, turns to face the Congregation, keeping his right shoulder toward the Congregation as he

does so. If the service is fully choral, he chants the Salutation and the Congregation chants the response. If the service is not choral, both he and the Congregation speak their parts. The Minister does not incline his head at "The Lord," but, if he wishes, he may acknowledge the congregation's response by inclining his head slightly toward the Congregation *after* "And with thy spirit." If he wishes, as he says, "The Lord be with you," he may, in accordance with old tradition, separate his hands to the width of his body and rejoin them. He may repeat the action as he says, "Let us pray." He remains facing the congregation as he says "Let us pray." After "Let us pray," if the book is at the center of the altar, the Minister turns back to it, keeping his right shoulder toward the congregation. If the book is at the Epistle side of the altar, the Minister turns half way toward the altar, keeping his right shoulder toward the congregation, then walks to the place where the book is and turns to it.

54. <u>Then shall the Minister, facing the Altar, say or chant The Collect for the Day.</u> If the service is fully choral, he chants the Collect; if not, he speaks it. Do not substitute another Collect of your own choice or composition for the Collect for the Day printed out in *The Lutheran Hymnal*. On the rare occasions when two holy days are being kept on the same day, the first Collect is the one pertaining to the day that is receiving primary emphasis, the second Collect is the one pertaining to the day that you are "commemorating." *The Lutheran Liturgy* (p. 418) directs: <u>Whenever the Collect for the Day is said, the full termination as appointed shall be used. When the Petition is addressed to God the Father, the full termination is: through Jesus Christ, Thy Son, our Lord, who liveth and reigneth with Thee and the Holy Ghost, ever one God, world without end. When the Petition is addressed to God the Son, the termination is: who livest and reignest with the Father and the Holy Ghost, ever one God world without end. When the Petition is addressed to God the Holy Ghost, the termination is: Who livest and reignest with the Father and the Son, ever one God, world without end. When mention is made of Our Lord in the body of the Petition, the termination</u> (whether or not it is so printed out in the Service Book) <u>is: through the same Jesus Christ, Thy Son, our Lord, who liveth and reigneth with Thee and the Holy Ghost, ever one God, world without end. When mention is made of our Lord at the end of the Petition, the termination</u> (whether or not it is so printed out in the Service Book) <u>is: who liveth and reigneth with Thee and the Holy Ghost, ever one God, world without end. When mention is made of the Holy Ghost in the body of the Collect, the termination</u> (whether or not it is so printed out in the Service Book) <u>is: who liveth and reigneth with Thee and the same Holy Ghost, ever one God, world without end. When the Petition is addressed to the Holy Trinity, the termination is: who livest and reignest, ever one God, world without end.</u> If the Minister wishes, he may separate his hands the width of his body as he begins the Collect (or each Collect) and join them again at the beginning of the termination. If he reverences at the Holy Name of Jesus, he inclines only his head. The Congregation's "Amen" at the end of the Collect or each Collect is sung if the Minister has chanted the Collect, spoken if he has spoken the Collect. <u>Then</u>, the Amen having been said or sung, <u>shall the Congregation be seated.</u>

The Lection

55. <u>Before the Epistle for the Day an appointed Lesson from the Old Testament</u> (cf. pp.438, 439) <u>may be read, but the Epistle for the Day and the Gospel for the Day shall always be read</u> (*The Lutheran Liturgy*, p. 420). Historically, none of the Lessons at the Service were read from the lectern, which was reserved for use at choir offices, such as Matins and Vespers, if there was a lectern at all. To underline the difference between the Service and the choir offices, the lessons at the Service should be read from the altar, not from the lectern, even if one is available. Actually, the lectern is an ornament that a Lutheran church can well dispense with; most chancels would be improved by the omission (or removal) of the lectern. The Congregation is seated for the Old Testament Lesson. If the Epistle and the Holy Gospel are chanted in the Service, the Old Testament lesson should also be chanted. If the celebrant reads an Old Testament lesson, he takes the book containing the Old Testament lessons from the back of the Altar (where it has been placed before the service) and turns by his right after the Congregation has responded "Amen" to the Collect(s) for the Day. (In general, the mensa of the altar should be kept clear of all articles that are not essential to the conduct of the service.)

    If the celebrant has the assistance of a server, the server should go to the credence-table, where the book containing the Old Testament lessons will have been placed before the Service began, and bring the book to the celebrant.

    The Old Testament lesson may be read by a layman, suitably vested, that is, at least in surplice. If a person other than the celebrant reads the Old Testament lesson, he will go to the credence-table, take the book containing the Old Testament lesson, proceed to a point in the chancel on the chancel level in front of the Epistle corner of the altar; <u>after</u> the Congregation's "Amen" to the Collects for the Day, he will turn by his left, face the congregation and announce the Old Testament lesson. (There should be no moving about in the chancel while a prayer is being said or the Congregation is responding with its "Amen." After having read the lesson he will return to the credence-table and deposit the book on it.

56. <u>Then shall the Minister read the Epistle.</u>

    It may be read by a layman suitably vested, that is, at least in a surplice. Both the reader of the Old Testament lesson and the reader of the Epistle may wear an amice, an appareled, and girdled alb, and a tunicle. If another clergyman besides the celebrant is participating in the Service, he may properly be invited to read the Epistle.

    The Epistle will be announced with the words prescribed by The Service Book: "The Epistle for _____ is written in the _____ chapter of _____ beginning at the_____verse." You have no authority to vary this formula, even if the lesson read as the Epistle is taken from the Old Testament. Likewise, you have no authority to substitute another Epistle for the one prescribed.

    It may be noted that it was anciently customary to begin the reading of the Epistle with the salutation: "Brethren." The chanting of the Epistle has the authority of long precedent in the Church of the Augsburg Confession, and for generations after the Reformation the chanting of the Epistle and the Holy Gospel was one of the characteristic differences between the Lutheran and the Calvinistic communions.

57. <u>The Epistle ended, the minister shall say: "Here endeth the Epistle."</u> This conclusion, and no other, is used no matter who reads the Epistle.

58. <u>The Gradual for the Day or the Sentence for the Season should be sung by the Choir. If a choir is not available, the Officiant may say the Gradual or the Sentence for the Season; or the Congregation may simply sing the Hallelujah after the Epistle has been read. Hallelujah is not sung during Pre-Lent and Lent.</u> This rubric does not preclude the Gradual being chanted by a solo voice, or by the celebrant; the Gradual may also be sung by the Congregation to a simple musical setting. In any case, since the Gradual is Psalmody, it is desirable that it be sung rather than spoken.

    <u>If the Gradual be read by the Minister, the Hallelujah may be said or chanted by the Congregation</u> during those parts of the Church Year during which Alleluia is properly sung, that is, in general from Easter Day through the week of the last Sunday after the Epiphany. The Congregation may sing either the single Alleluia or the triple Alleluia. It is not necessary for the Congregation to respond to the Gradual, either with the Alleluia or with one of the Sentences. The Alleluia by the Congregation is best omitted.

    Sentences are provided for all of the Seasons of the Church Year except for the three Sundays of Pre-Lent. They represent a kind of abbreviated seasonal Gradual. Even when no choir is available, it is preferable to use the Gradual rather than the seasonal Sentence. Traditionally a sequence hymn was sung after the Gradual psalmody. Technically a Sequence Hymn is one that has been written specifically for this point in the service. For a list of Sequence Hymns for various occasions, see the article, "Sequences," by F. E. Warren and James Mearns in John Julian (editor), *A Dictionary of Hymnology*, revised edition (London: John Murray, 1915), pp. 1041-1053. The Sequence Hymn is always seasonal; conceivably another, equally seasonal, hymn, even though it were not written as a Sequence Hymn, might be substituted. There is some virtue in reserving Sequence Hymns for special occasions.

    If a Sentence or a Sequence Hymn is not used, the congregation will in any case make no response to the Gradual as sung by the choir or chanted by the celebrant during Pre-Lent and Lent, as well as on other occasions when Alleluia is not properly used.

    If the celebrant speaks or chants the Gradual, he will do so facing the altar at the Epistle corner and reading from the Service Book lying upon its cushion or stand. It is customary for him to place his hand at the edges of the book. If the Gradual is rendered by the choir or by someone other than the celebrant, he faces the altar, reads the Gradual to himself from the book lying on its cushion or stand, with his hands at the outside edges of the book.

    It should be observed that the Graduals are incorrectly printed in our *Hymnal* and *Liturgy*. In our rite, the term "Gradual" is a generic one to designate the Psalmody between the Epistle and the Gospel. In general, this Psalmody consists of two parts; originally the first part was sung between the Old Testament lesson and the Epistle, the second part between the Epistle and the Gospel. When the number of lessons was conventionally reduced to two, the two separate settings were combined into one. Through most of the Church Year, the Gradual consists of (1) the Gradual in the strict sense of the term (usually two Psalm verses), and (2) the Alleluia Verse. The double Alleluia does not belong to the verse after which it is printed in our *Hymnal* and *Liturgy*, but to the verse which follows. Account of this should be taken in the musical settings that are used. To differentiate the two parts, it is appropriate to use two different settings, even if they be simply Psalm-tones. In this case the first ends with the last word prior to the double Alleluia and the second begins with the double Alleluia. When the Gradual is merely read, account may be taken of the historic origin of the two parts of the Gradual by pausing before the double Alleluia and reading the remainder of the Gradual in such a way that the double Alleluia is clearly tied up with the Alleluia Verse. In Eastertide the Gradual in the strict sense is replaced by another Alleluia Verse. During the period when the Alleluia is not used in the Service, the Alleluia Verse is replaced by what is called the Tract; examples of this will be found in the Propers for the Sundays and various ferias (non-festival weekdays) of Pre-Lent and Lent. The phenomenon also appears, even though the term is not used, in the Propers for the Day of Humiliation and Prayer. In the Propers for the Presentation of our Lord and the Purification of the Blessed Virgin Mary, provision is made for an Alleluia Verse if the festival is kept before Septuagesima Sunday and for a Tract if the festival falls after Septuagesima Sunday. This was clearly the intention in connection with the Propers of the Annunciation as well, although apparently through an editorial error, the necessary rubric has been omitted. (During Lent the first six lines of the Gradual for the Annunciation as printed in the *Hymnal* are used; during Eastertide the first two and the last four lines of the Gradual as printed in the *Hymnal* are employed.)

59. Special choir music may be sung in place of, or preferably in addition to, the Gradual, between the Epistle and the Gospel. When this is done, it is important that the textual content of the choral selection harmonize with the theme of the Liturgy and of the Service for the day, where the latter can be determined. This rubric should not be interpreted as urging the inclusion of special choir music. It merely intends to say that if the choir sings an anthem of a seasonal character, it is appropriate to have it at this point in the Service.

60. *The Lutheran Liturgy* (pp. 420-421) provides: A hymn of Invocation to the Holy Ghost may be sung to replace the Gradual. The classic Gradual Hymn of the Lutheran Church is "We Now Implore God the Holy Ghost" (The Lutheran Hymnal, Hymn 231). The reason for this rubric is obscure. Historically, there is no evidence that a Hymn of Invocation of the Holy Ghost was ever actually in wide use as a substitute for the Gradual. Similarly, there is no evidence that *Nun bitten wir den Heiligen Geist* was ever actually in wide use as a "Gradual Hymn" in the Lutheran Church. Pastors and Congregations are well advised not to avail themselves of the provisions of this rubric.

61. On Trinity Sunday, the Athanasian Creed may be used after the Gradual in lieu of a Sequence (*The Lutheran Liturgy*, p. 421). If a Pastor or Congregation decides to use the Athanasian Creed at this point in the service on Trinity Sunday, there is no authority for omitting the Nicene Creed after the Holy Gospel.

62. <u>The Minister shall announce the Gospel for the Day:</u> "The Holy Gospel is written in the _____ Chapter of St. _____ beginning at the _____ Verse." <u>When the Minister announces the Gospel for the Day, the Congregation shall rise, (unless it has stood during the reading of the Epistle) and then chant, Glory be to Thee, O Lord.</u> (*The Lutheran Liturgy*, p. 420.) <u>The Minister shall then read the Gospel for the Day. The Gospel ended, the Minister shall say: Here endeth the Gospel.</u> Normally the congregation will have seated itself during the reading of the Epistle. While the rubric does not require the Congregation to stand until after the Gospel has been announced, both custom and convenience make it desirable for the Congregation to rise before the announcement of the Holy Gospel.

If the celebrant be the only clergyman participating in the Service, and if he has the assistance of a server, the latter should, as soon as the celebrant has finished reading the Gradual, either aloud to the Congregation or to himself, carry the Service-Book together with its cushion or its stand to the Gospel corner of the altar. Meanwhile the celebrant proceeds to the Gospel corner, pausing at the center of the altar to say the traditional prayers: "Cleanse my heart and my lips, Almighty God, Who didst cleanse the lips of the prophet Isaiah with a live coal, and do Thou, of Thy great mercy, vouchsafe so to purify me that I may worthily declare Thy Holy Gospel; through Christ, our Lord. Amen. Command, O Lord, Thy blessing to descend upon me. The Lord be in my heart and in my lips, that I may worthily and competently proclaim His Gospel, in the Name of the Father and of the Son (✠) and of the Holy Ghost. Amen." At the words "and of the Son," he makes the sign of the Holy Cross upon himself.

If he does not have the assistance of a server, he carries the book, together with its cushion or stand, to the Gospel corner of the altar.

If there be another ordained clergyman participating in the Service, it is most appropriate that he be invited to read the Gospel. In this case the reader of the Gospel takes the book containing the Gospel from the credence-table, where it has been deposited before the Service began, goes to the middle of the Altar, places the book containing the Gospel upon it, goes down to the footpace of the altar before the middle, kneels down, and says the prayer beginning "Cleanse my heart and my lips." In the meantime the celebrant goes to the midst of the altar, faces the clergyman who is to read the Gospel, and the latter says to the former: "Command, sir, a blessing." The celebrant responds with: "The Lord be in thy heart and upon thy lips that thou mayest worthily and competently proclaim His Gospel, in the Name of the Father and of the Son (✠) and of the Holy Ghost. Amen." At the words "and of the Son" the celebrant makes the sign of the Holy Cross over the reader of the Gospel. The celebrant then proceeds to the Gospel corner of the altar, the reader of the Gospel rises from his knees, takes the book containing the Gospel from the altar, and proceeds to a point in the chancel on the level of the chancel floor before the Gospel corner of the altar. (The lectern is not used for the reading of the Gospel). He turns to face the congregation by his left. Traditionally, the reading of the Gospel was the function of the deacon; traditionally the deacon turned toward the liturgical north to read the Gospel. Where no local objection exists, one of the deacons of the congregation may perform this function, suitably vested, that is, in a surplice at least. Traditionally, the reader of the Gospel wore an appareled amice and alb, a cincture, a stole over his left shoulder with the ends looped together at his right side at waist height, and a dalmatic.

Historically, instead of holding the book himself, the clergyman reading the Gospel on occasion had the book held before him by a server or by the reader of the Epistle. The person who held the book faced the reader of the Gospel, held the outside bottom edges of the book in his cupped hands at waist height and allowed the back of the book to rest against his chest. The reader of the Gospel according to ancient custom made the sign of the Holy Cross upon the beginning of the Gospel with his right thumb as he began to announce the Holy Gospel. As he continued with the announcement of the Gospel he made the sign of the Holy Cross in the same way, successively upon his forehead, upon his lips, and upon his breast.

These ceremonies are the survival of the primitive Church's "Little Entrance," ceremonially the climax of the first part of the Service. It will also be remembered that Blessed Martin Luther in his Form of the Mass and Communion for the Church at Wittenberg approved the retention of incense and of the traditional Gospel procession at this point. (Weimar Ausgabe, XII, 205-220.) In our own generation it is highly desirable that we do everything that we can in the course of our worship to encourage reverence for the written Word of God.

The chanting, rather than the mere speaking, of the Holy Gospel has the endorsement of centuries of precedent in the Church of the Augsburg Confession. The chant-pattern at the singing of the Gospel is traditionally at least slightly more elaborate than the chant-pattern for the singing of the other lessons.

If the celebrant reads the Gospel, he takes the Service Book in his hands and turns by his left to the congregation. This variation in the usual rubric recognizes the ghost of the deacon, who traditionally read the Gospel, still lingering about the altar.

No authority is given to vary the formula for announcing the Gospel nor to substitute another text from the Sacred Scriptures for the prescribed Gospel for the Day, even though the sermon may be on the Holy Gospel. After the celebrant says, "Here endeth the Gospel," the congregation sings, "Praise be to Thee, O Christ!"

Ancient custom, which survived after the Reformation in many parts of the Church of the Augsburg Confession, directed that while the congregation sang the response, the reader of the Gospel raised the book to his lips, kissed the beginning of the Gospel that he has read, and said in a low tone of voice: "By the Gospel words today may our sins be done away."

If the celebrant has read the Gospel, he turns by his right, replaces the book on its cushion or stand, moves the cushion or stand with both hands to within about a foot of the center of the altar, turns by his right and goes with joined hands to the midst of the altar.

If another person has read the Gospel, he (or the individual who held the book for him) carries the book containing the Gospel back to the credence-table and deposits it there.

The Creed

63. <u>Then shall be said or chanted the Creed.</u> *The Lutheran Liturgy* (p. 421) directs: <u>The Nicene Creed shall be chanted or said by the Congregation on all Feasts and Festivals and whenever there is a Communion; at other times the Apostles' Creed may be used in its stead, or a versified form of these Creeds may be sung. Cf. Hymns 251, 252, 253, in The Lutheran Hymnal.</u> Thus no authority is given for substituting another Creed for the Nicene Creed at any Feast or Festival or at any celebration of Holy Communion. The Nicene Creed is to be preferred to the Apostles' Creed even on non-festival occasions and when the Holy Communion is not being celebrated. The use of a metrical version of one of the Creeds, though allowed, is undesirable. It is better to chant the Creed than merely to recite it. During the saying of the Creed, the celebrant stands before the altar, facing it. If he has stood at some other point in the chancel for the Gospel, he invariably returns to the midst of the altar before beginning the Creed.

    The celebrant begins the Creed by saying: "I believe in one God." At this point the congregation joins in with "The Father Almighty, etc." As the celebrant says: "I believe," he may raise and extend his hands; as he says, "In one," he may join his hands; and as he says, "God," he may bow his head. He may also bow his head at the Holy Name of Jesus and, if he wishes, at the words "worshiped and glorified." He may bow from the waist at the words, "And was incarnate" and remain bowed through the words, "Was crucified also for us"; he raises himself erect again before the words, "Under Pontius Pilate." (The explanation given for this was that the soldiers of the Roman procurator knelt and bowed before Our Lord in mockery during His Passion.) In some parts of the Church of the Augsburg Confession the celebrant placed the extremities of his fingers on either side of the Corporal and knelt on his right knee from the words, "And was incarnate" through the words, "and was made man." *Culto Cristiano* (1964), authorized for Spanish-speaking parishes of The Lutheran Church—Missouri Synod, permits substitution of "Catholic" for "Christian."

    At the words, "The life of the world to come," the General Rubrics of the *Hymnal* authorize the sign of the Holy Cross, which the celebrant makes on himself just as the worshipers do.

The Hymn and the Sermon

64. <u>Then may a hymn be sung.</u> Originally the sixteenth century rites of the Church of the Augsburg Confession made no provision for a hymn at this point in addition to the Creed, either in prose or metrical form. The rubric of the *Hymnal* and *Liturgy*, which prescribes such a hymn at this point, has been superseded by a permissive rubric (*The Order of Holy Communion*, 1959, p. 12). The preacher need not enter the pulpit until the end of the hymn.

65. <u>Then shall follow the Sermon.</u> The traditional text for the sermon at the Service is the Gospel for the Day. The sermon should be strong with the power of the Gospel to move men, to give them the power to believe and to do those things which the total liturgical action of worship has been setting before them.

If the celebrant is also the preacher, he may find it convenient to remove his chasuble and maniple before beginning the sermon, although it is not necessary for him to do so. If someone other than the celebrant is the preacher, he wears into the pulpit the vestments appropriate to the ministry that he has exercised in the Service, except that he may for the sake of convenience and comfort lay aside his tunicle or dalmatic, if he wears either. If the preacher takes no other part in the service beyond delivering the sermon, he may be vested in a surplice, or he may content himself with wearing a plain black preacher's gown.

It is an ancient custom in the church to begin the sermon with the words: "In the Name of the Father and of the Son and of the Holy Ghost. Amen." While saying these words, the preacher should make the sign of the Holy Cross upon himself. If he has used this invocation, he ought not to follow it with another after reading his text, such as: "In the Name of Jesus."

66. <u>The Sermon ended, the Congregation shall rise, and the Minister shall say: "The peace of God, which passeth all understanding, keep your hearts and minds through Christ Jesus."</u> There is no authority given to vary this formulation. Although the General Rubrics of *The Lutheran Liturgy* (p. 421) authorizes the preacher to raise his hand in blessing and make the sign of the Holy Cross when saying the Votum at the close of the Sermon, it is better not to avail oneself of this privilege. The preacher may end his sermon with the Trinitarian Invocation, or he may close his sermon with an ascription of praise to the Holy Trinity.

The Service of the Sacrament

The Offertory

67. <u>Then shall the Offertory here following or the Proper Offertory be said or chanted, at the close of which the Congregation shall be seated</u> (*The Order of Holy Communion*, 1959, p. 12).

    The Minister goes from the pulpit to the center of the altar and then the Offertory is begun. The change of position and a deliberate pace will help to establish the Offertory as an expression of the sacrificial aspect of The Service rather than merely a response to the sermon.

    Anciently, the Offertory chant was one of the Propers of the Service. See, for instance, the Roman Missal. An effort to provide proper Offertories for the Lutheran rite has been made in Albert Olai Christensen and Harold Edward Schuneman, *Proper of the Service for the Church Year* (New York: The H. W. Gray Co., c. 1947). The original function of the Offertory was to cover the Offertory procession.

The Offering

68. <u>Then shall the Offerings be gathered and brought to the Altar</u> (*The Order for Holy Communion*, 1959, p. 13). The bringing of an offering is a prescribed part of the Service. The mode of gathering the offerings is not prescribed.

    There is no reason why, at least from time to time, the offerings should not be brought forward in an Offertory procession. If this is done, it is usual for the server to stand at the entrance to the chancel with a large basin or Offertory plate, into which the faithful place their offerings. If the offering is received by members of the congregation appointed for this Service, they may bring the offering plates or offering bags forward to the entrance of the chancel, where a server may receive them in a large offering basin and take them to the celebrant. The celebrant in turn holds them not higher than the level of his breast and places them upon the altar to the Epistle side of the corporal. The offerings may be removed to the credence table after the General Prayer.

    The reception of the offerings should not be made the occasion of a special prayer, the singing of a hymn stanza (such as the Long Meter Doxology), or some other ceremonial action. The General Prayer that follows contains a suitable formula of offering which does not require supplementing by the celebrant.

    Historically the Offertory is one of the climaxes of the service. In the primitive church the faithful brought offerings of bread and wine, as well as of other kinds of food, for the relief of the poor, for the support of the clergy and as symbols of their life of total worship, their self-dedication to the God of the creation, their redemption and their re-creation. From these offerings the loaves and wine needed for the celebration of the Sacrament of the Altar were taken. Later on, the offerings in kind were commuted into offerings of money for the convenience of both the worshipers and the administrators of the Church's financial affairs. The Offertory is still a reminder that, in Bl. Martin Luther's words, "we are the sacrifice in the Holy Eucharist."

Time for individual involvement in the self-offering expressed in The Offertory should be supplied as an understanding of its significance is shared by the worshipers.

The Preparation of the Altar and accompanying ceremonies
68.5 The General Rubrics of *The Lutheran Liturgy* authorize the celebrant to <u>make ready the Communion Vessels immediately after the Offertory.</u>

It was a not uncommon practice in the early years of the Church of the Augsburg Confession to prepare the elements for the celebration of the Holy Communion during the singing of the last part of the Creed. It would be equally appropriate to do so during the singing of the hymn before the sermon.

The celebrant may make ready the elements as described below, immediately after the singing of the Offertory, before the offerings are brought forward. The directions which follow assume that the celebrant is assisted by a server. If the celebrant is not assisted by a server, he may arrange to have all the necessary articles placed at the rear of the altar on the Epistle side before the service begins. He would proceed as described below with the changes necessitated by the absence of a server.

It is appropriate that at this point in the Service the celebrant wash his hands, for practical as well as for ceremonial reasons. Traditionally he does so in this way: With joined hands he moves toward the Epistle corner of the altar. If he wishes he may say in a low voice the Psalm *Lavabo* (Psalm 26). The server, who has gone to the credence-table, approaches him with the small basin for the washing of the celebrant's fingers in his left hand and with a napkin over his left arm. In his right hand he has the water cruet, unstoppered, while the celebrant continues to say the Psalm, he holds the extremities of his thumbs and forefingers over the basin while the server pours water on them. After he has washed his fingers, the celebrant takes the napkin from the server's arm and, facing the altar, wipes his fingers dry. He then replaces the napkin on the server's arm, turns once more to the altar and completes the Psalm. At the words: "Glory be to the Father... Holy Ghost, "he bows toward the crucifix and returns to an erect position at the words: "As it was in the beginning etc."

The washing of the celebrant's hands while he says the Psalm *Lavabo* is a ceremony that goes back at least to the fourth century, since it is described in the Catechetical Lectures of St. Cyril of Jerusalem. The server takes the water cruet, basin and napkin back to the credence-table and the celebrant returns to the midst of the altar.

It is presumed that chalice and paten have been brought to the altar, either at the beginning of the service, or at the Offertory, and are standing, veiled, in the center of the altar upon the outspread corporal. The burse in which the corporals and purificators are carried to the altar is on the rear of the altar to the left of the center. The server goes to the credence-table, takes the vessel containing the hosts to be consecrated in his right hand and goes with it to the Epistle corner of the altar; he remains standing on the chancel floor level. Meanwhile, the celebrant takes hold of the back part of the veil which covers the chalice and removes it with both hands. He folds it on the altar at the right of the corporal, then he places it close to the rear of the altar near the corporal. With his right hand he takes the chalice by the knop and moves it off the corporal towards the Epistle side. With his right hand he removes the pall (or folded corporal) from the chalice and places it upon the right side of the outspread corporal. Then he takes the paten, holding it in such a way that the thumb, forefinger, and middle finger of each hand surround the circumference, the ring and little fingers drawn together under the paten. Holding it in this way he goes to the Epistle side of the altar. The server uncovers the vessel containing the hosts and holds it out to the celebrant. Holding the paten in his left hand, the celebrant takes as many hosts as he deems sufficient for the celebration in question and places them on the paten. If he uses a large host to communicate himself, he will place the large host on top of the small hosts.

The celebrant does not consecrate more hosts or more wine than he actually expects to require at any given celebration. He should know quite accurately from the announcements of his intending communicants for how many to prepare; whether or not (and if so, how many) additional hosts should be provided beyond the number of communicants who have announced their intention of receiving is something that he must learn by experience. The peril of sacrilege, and even of scandal, is always present when the celebrant consecrates elements in excess of the actual need.

After the celebrant has placed the necessary number of hosts upon the paten he turns by his left and goes back to the middle of the altar, where he places the paten upon the forepart of the corporal.

If the number of communicants is so large that the hosts required cannot conveniently be placed upon the paten, a ciborium or a second chalice, the former with its own cover and the latter covered with a pall or a paten, should be used. The ciborium is placed on the altar before the Service or after the Offertory; and after the celebrant has spread the corporal, he places the ciborium behind the chalice. When he prepares the elements for the Holy Communion, he proceeds with the ciborium as he would have done with the paten.

As soon as the celebrant has taken the necessary number of hosts from the hostbox, the server replaces the box upon the credence-table. Then he removes the stoppage from the cruet and taking the wine cruet he returns to the Epistle corner, holding the chalice by the knop in his left hand. The server presents the wine cruet to the celebrant in such a way that the latter may take convenient hold of it by the handle or by the upper part of the cruet. The celebrant takes the wine cruet with his right hand, pours the requisite amount of wine into the chalice, and returns the cruet to the server.

In the preparation of the so-called "mixed chalice" the server takes the wine cruet in his right hand and the water cruet in his left hand. He gives the wine cruet to the celebrant and then transfers the water cruet to his right hand and receives the wine cruet with his left hand. The celebrant then takes the water cruet and pours a very small quantity of water into the chalice. The quantity of water must never be so great as to dilute the wine in the chalice appreciably. One ancient prescription decreed that the quantity of water should not exceed one part of water in six parts of wine. It must be conceded that the "mixed chalice" was relatively rare in the Church of the Augsburg Confession after the Reformation. At the same time, the custom is very ancient. Whatever the occasion may have been for the institution of the Holy Communion in the Cenacle, the Jewish ritual which our Lord followed calls for a mixed chalice. The primitive church retained the custom. There is no valid theological reason against its revival and if we wish to reduplicate the action of our Lord at the first celebration of Holy Communion as far as possible, we can properly include this feature as well. It should be noted that it is not forbidden by the Lutheran Symbols, and that the reasons assigned for its discontinuance are not persuasive in the light of our present knowledge. On the other hand, a mixed chalice is not essential to a valid celebration of the Holy Eucharist, obviously. Accordingly, if a pastor does not desire to employ this ancient ritual feature, it will be necessary for the server to bring him only the wine cruet.

After having placed the requisite amount of wine in the chalice, the celebrant carries the chalice in both hands, the foot in his left hand, the knop in his right, to the center of the altar, where he places it on the corporal behind the paten. He covers the chalice with the pall.

If the number of communicants be so large that the wine required cannot safely be contained in the chalice, an additional wine cruet can be prepared in advance of the Service and placed upon the credence-table. After the server has replaced the cruet from which the celebrant filled the chalice, he takes the supplementary cruet(s) to the Epistle corner of the altar, where he remains standing on the chancel floor level. The celebrant, after having covered the chalice with a pall, returns to the Epistle corner and receives the supplementary cruet(s) from the server. He takes them to the center of the altar and places them on the corporal behind the chalice.

The General Prayer

69. <u>Then shall follow the General Prayer.</u> The General Rubrics of *The Lutheran Liturgy* prescribe that <u>before the General Prayer at the Altar the officiant may announce special Petitions, Intercessions or Thanksgivings which have been requested. He may also make mention of the birth, contemplated marriage death etc. of members of the Congregation.</u> When special prayers are included in the General Prayer, it is desirable that an appropriate announcement thereof be made before the General Prayer. It is appropriate that in announcing the special petition, intercession, or thanksgiving which has been requested, the celebrant name the full name ("William Smith," "Mary Anderson," "Jane, the wife of Harold Peters,", etc.) of the persons concerned. In the prayer itself, however, he will be careful to mention only the Christian names

("William," "Mary," "Jane," etc.) of those prayed for, that is, the names given them in Holy Baptism, by which they are known in the Book of Life.

In selecting the intercessions to be used in connection with the General Prayer, the celebrant should be careful to choose prayers that are addressed to the Father, lest the structure of the General Prayer be violated by the interpolation of a prayer addressed to the Son or to the Holy Ghost.

69.5 The General Rubrics prescribe that <u>one of the General Prayers appointed for the Services shall always be used.</u> There is no rubrical place for the seasonal General Prayers in the Service. These prayers may be used in conjunction with sermons preached apart from the service, at special devotions, and in similar circumstances. The "General Prayers appointed for the Services" are those contained in *The Lutheran Liturgy* on pages 251-277 and in *The Lutheran Hymnal* on pages 13-14, 23-24, and 110-112. It should be noted that the 69.7 General Rubrics provide that <u>the Litany may be used instead of the General Prayer, except when there is a Communion;</u> that is, the Litany cannot replace the General Prayer at a celebration of the Sacrament of the Altar.

The rubrics do not prescribe the posture of the congregation during the General Prayer. It is desirable that the congregation stand or kneel for the General Prayer, although as far as the rubric goes, the congregation may remain seated for it. It should be noted that the Our Father is not said after the General Prayer.

Although the way in which the Amen at the end of the General Prayer is printed indicates that the celebrant will say the Amen, it is appropriate for the congregation to join with the celebrant in the Amen.

70. <u>Then may a hymn be sung.</u> It is better not to avail oneself of this authorization. The continuity of the Service from the offertory through to the completion of the Communion is stressed by proceeding at once to the Salutation. *The Order of Holy Communion*, 1959, p.12, makes no provision for a hymn at this point.

71. <u>The hymn ended, the congregation shall rise and stand to the end of the Agnus Dei. The celebrant turns by his right to the people and says: "The Lord be with you."</u> The ceremonial is the same as at the salutation before the Collects for the Day (see par. 53 above). After the response of the congregation, "And with thy spirit," the celebrant raises and extends his hands to the width of his breast, with palms facing each other, and says: "Lift up your hearts." After the response of the congregation, "We lift them up unto the Lord," he rejoins his hands before his breast and says: "Let us give thanks unto the Lord our God." The congregation responds: "It is meet and right so to do." The celebrant then turns to the altar, and, with his hands raised and extended as at the Collect, he proceeds with the Preface.

It should be noted that in some editions of *The Lutheran Hymnal* and *The Lutheran Liturgy* the Preface ends with the words: "Through Jesus Christ, our Lord" through an editorial mistake. The words should be struck at this point in those copies of these books in which they appear, and inserted at the beginning of the Prefaces for Advent, The Ascension, and Whitsunday.

The Proper Preface

72. <u>Here shall follow the Proper Preface.</u> Although the rubric does not so specify, the Preface of Christmas should be used through January 5, the Preface of the Epiphany through January 13, the Preface for Easter through the Wednesday after Rogate Sunday, the Preface for the Ascension Day through the Friday after Exaudi, and the Preface for Whitsunday from the Saturday before Whitsunday on throughout Whitsun-week. The Preface of the Holy Trinity may be used on any Sunday for which no other Preface is appointed, according to the General Rubrics of *The Lutheran Liturgy*; that is, on the Sundays of the post-Epiphany Season, the Sundays of Pre-Lent and on the Sundays of the season after Trinity.

The Sanctus

73. <u>Then shall be said or chanted the Sanctus.</u> The celebrant continues to face the altar. At the words: "Holy, Holy, Holy," he may join his hands and through the first "Hosanna in the Highest," he may bow moderately from the waist. Thereafter he resumes his erect position. This bow expresses the awe of the worshipers as they join in the hymn of the seraphim around the throne of grace. At the words, "Blessed is He," he may make the Sign of the Holy Cross upon himself.

73a. *Culto Cristiano* (1964), authorized for use in Spanish-speaking parishes of The Lutheran Church-Missouri Synod, on p. 37 permits the use of a Eucharistic Prayer (reproduced in English translation at the end of this manual), followed by the Our Father, in place of the Our Father and the Words of Institution.

The Lord's Prayer

74. <u>Then shall be said or chanted the Lord's Prayer.</u> *The Music for the Liturgy*, which is as authoritative as any of the other liturgical books of our rite, prescribes that the Our Father be introduced with the words: "Let us pray." At these words, the celebrant, still facing the altar, separates and then joins his hands again. The officiant, his hands extended, chants the Our Father through the petition: "But deliver us from evil." The so-called "Doxology"—which is not originally a part of the Our Father, as the ancient manuscripts, as well as the critical texts of the Greek New Testament, show—is sung by the congregation as a response to the Our Father. During the congregational response: "For Thine is the Kingdom" he joins his hands.

The Words of Institution and ceremonies

75. <u>Then shall the minister say or chant the words of Institution.</u> The celebrant continues to stand at the midst of the altar, facing it, as he says the Words of Institution. Before him on the altar is the outspread corporal, upon which there are the chalice and paten. If the number of communicants requires the use of cruets and a ciborium pyx, these also are upon the corporal. The Words of Institution are not only a rehearsal of the institution of the Holy Eucharist for the benefit of the congregation, but are also a consecration of the elements (Formula of Concord, Solid Declaration,

VII, paragraph 75-82; note the words "over the bread and chalice"). If a ciborium or pyx and cruets are used, the celebrant uncovers them at this point. At the words: "Took bread," he takes a host from the paten (the large host, if one is being used) raises it slightly and replaces it upon the paten. Thereupon he touches the ciborium or other vessel in which hosts to be consecrated are contained, thus indicating that he is including them in his intention.

The custom has become general in Lutheran churches for the celebrant to make the Sign of the Holy Cross over the hosts at the words: "This is My Body." In view of the connection between "giving thanks" and "blessing," both of which reproduce the Latin benedicere, it would be more appropriate to make the Sign of the Holy Cross over the hosts on the paten and over the other vessels containing hosts to be consecrated at the words: "When He had given thanks." In either case the Sign of the Holy Cross is made with the entire right hand, the fingers outstretched, the thumb held close to the index finger. The Holy Sign is made in a plane parallel to the mensa of the altar, not at right angles to it.

At the words, "He brake it," the celebrant may make a slight rent in the bottom of the large host or of one of the other hosts on the paten. At the words, "Take, eat," the celebrant takes the large host between thumb and forefinger of both hands, leans forward and rests his elbows on the altar, preferably outside the corporal, and says with particular distinctness, attention, and reverence, "This is My Body, which is given for you," over the host which he holds and over all the others which are to be consecrated.

After the words: "This do in remembrance of Me," it was anciently customary for the celebrant to elevate the large host. This he did by bowing profoundly from the waist and, keeping his eyes fixed on the host, reverently elevated it as far as he conveniently could so that it could be seen by the people. He then lowered it slowly and with his right hand placed it on the corporal (or paten). Thereupon he again bowed profoundly from the waist.

The celebrant was careful from this point on to keep his thumbs and forefingers joined, except when it was necessary to separate them, lest a fragment of one of the hosts adhering to his thumb or finger fall to the ground. With the same reverent concern he would later lightly rub his thumbs and forefingers together over the chalice to remove any fragments of the hosts which may be adhering to them. The use of the houseling-cloth (from the middle-English word Housel-Host) developed from the same concern.

The celebrant now uncovers the chalice. To obviate the danger of spilling, he holds the foot of the chalice with his left hand while he removes the pall with his right and places the pall on the chalice veil. At the words: "He took the cup" the celebrant takes the chalice in both hands and raises it three or four inches above the corporal and then replaces it. Thereupon he touches each vessel containing wine to be consecrated to indicate that he is including it in his intention. As in the case of the bread, it is more appropriate to make the Sign of the Holy Cross over the vessels containing the wine to be consecrated at the words: "And when He had given thanks."

At the words: "Drink ye all of it," the celebrant takes the chalice with his right hand, the thumb and forefinger together above the knop and other fingers below, and supporting the foot with his left hand, the thumb and forefinger above and the other fingers below, he inclines slightly, rests his elbows on the edge of the altar, lifts the chalice a little above the corporal, and holding it in such a way that it is perfectly upright, says with particular distinctness, reverence, and attention the words:

"This cup is the New Testament in My Blood, which is shed for you for the remission of sins." He then replaces the chalice on the corporal, saying: "This do, as oft as ye drink it, in remembrance of Me."

Anciently it was customary to elevate the chalice at this point in the same way in which the host had been elevated.

If the celebrant wears a maniple, he should be very careful that it does not come into contact with the hosts on the corporal or paten.

It was anciently customary to ring the bell in the church tower a total of seven strokes, the first at the beginning of the consecration, three strokes at the consecration of the hosts and three more at the consecration of the chalice. Later, with the multiplication of masses, hand bells were substituted. The widespread custom in the Church of the Augsburg Confession of ringing the church bell during the recitation of the Our Father is a survival of this ancient custom, transferred to another element in the Service after the custom of a celebration of Holy Communion every Sunday and major Holy Day unhappily fell into desuetude.

The Pax

The consecration completed, the celebrant places his left hand on the corporal and turns by his right to the congregation as far as he conveniently can. As he says the words of the Pax Domini: "The Peace of the Lord be with you alway!" he may make the Sign of the Holy Cross over the congregation three times or once, depending upon local custom. Where the congregation now says: "Amen," the ancient response was: "And with thy spirit." The latter response is now authorized in our rite also through inclusion in *The Order of Holy Communion*, 1959, p.21.

The Agnus Dei and Distribution

76. Then shall be said or chanted the Agnus Dei.

The significant words of the Agnus Dei should be a part of the worship of the entire congregation, people and ushers. There should, obviously, be no bustling about with kneeling cushions or rail gates. When necessary, these arrangements can be completed after the Agnus Dei.

During the singing of the Agnus Dei by the congregation, the celebrant may say the words of this prayer in a low voice. Traditionally, he strikes himself on the breast with the tips of the last three fingers of his right hand at the final word of each of the three petitions, his left hand resting meanwhile on the corporal.

Thereupon, in accordance with the best Lutheran precedent, the celebrant administers the Holy Communion to himself. In accordance with the Church's historic practice, he would do this even though there may be another clergyman present who might administer the Holy Communion to him. (If he celebrates twice on a given day, he normally receives the Holy Communion only at the first service of the day.)

By way of private preparation, the celebrant may say the following Prayer:

"O Lord Jesus Christ, Who saidest unto Thine Apostles, Peace I leave with you, My peace I give unto you, regard not my sins, but the faith of Thy Church, and grant unto her that Peace and Unity which is according to Thy will, Who livest and reignest God, world without end. Amen."

"O Lord Jesus Christ, Son of the Living God, Who according to the will of the Father, and by the cooperation of the Holy Ghost, hast by Thy death given life to the world; deliver me by this Thy Most Holy Body and Blood from all mine iniquities and from every evil, and make me ever to cleave unto Thy Commandments, and suffer me never to be separated from Thee, Who with the Father and the Holy Ghost livest and reignest one God, world without end. Amen."

"Let the partaking of Thy Body, O Lord Jesus Christ, which I, though unworthy, do presume to receive, according to Thy lovingkindness be profitable to me for the receiving of forgiveness of sins, life and salvation, Who with the Father and the Holy Ghost livest and reignest one God, world without end. Amen."

"I will receive the bread of Heaven and call upon the Name of the Lord."

"Lord, I am not worthy that Thou shouldst come under my roof; but speak the word only, and my soul shall be healed." (Anciently, this prayer, "Domine non sum dignus," was said three times, the celebrant striking his breast each time with the extremities of the last three fingers of his right hand.)

If the celebrant is using a large host, the accepted procedure is this: He should break it reverently twice across. (It will be remembered that a rent had been made in the Host at the Words of Institution.) Then taking the parts, one upon another, in his right hand, and holding the paten in his left hand under the host as he conveys it to his lips, he says in a low voice: "The Body of our Lord Jesus Christ, which was given for me, preserve my body and soul unto everlasting life. Amen." Then bending forward moderately, he reverently places the host upon his tongue. He replaces the paten on the corporal and rubs his thumb and forefingers over it to remove any fragments of the consecrated bread. Head erect, he joins both hands together before his face, and remains for a brief space in meditation on the Holy Eucharist.

Then he places the ends of the last three fingers of his left hand on the foot of the chalice and removes the pall with his right. He places both hands on the corporal, bows reverently from the waist, and says:

"What reward shall I give unto the Lord for all His benefits toward me? I will take the cup of salvation and call upon the Name of the Lord. I will call upon the Lord who is worthy to be praised; so shall I be saved from all mine enemies."

Then, still standing, the celebrant reverently raises the chalice as high as his breast and says:

"The Blood of our Lord Jesus Christ, which was shed for me, preserve my body and my soul unto everlasting life. Amen."

Thereupon he places the chalice up to his lips and receives the precious Blood. He replaces the chalice on the corporal and bows profoundly. Thereafter he remains for a short space meditating on the Gift which he has received.

76.5 The General Rubrics of *The Lutheran Liturgy* provide that <u>"if there be another minister to assist in the distribution, he may approach the altar during the singing of the Agnus Dei."</u> This rubric applies only where the clergyman who assists with the distribution takes no other part in the Service. Generally speaking, an ordained person present should be appropriately involved in other parts of the Service as well, wherever this is feasible. When a clergyman has assisted at other points in the Service, it is proper for him to accompany the celebrant to the altar at the offertory, standing at the celebrant's right and assisting the celebrant as the latter may require. For the Preface and Sanctus he may stand behind the celebrant. For the Our Father and the Words of Institution he may go the celebrant's left and turn the pages of the service book for him.

77. <u>During the Distribution the congregation may sing one or more hymns.</u> The singing of hymns during the Distribution of the Holy Communion is frequently distracting to the communicants. It would be better, in general, if the choir were to sing the proper Communion (a brief chant taken from the Psalter), or all or part of the Communion Psalm, or an appropriate anthem or motet, or if the organ were to be played during the Distribution (except, of course, during seasons when the organ is traditionally not played, such as Lent and Advent). The interpolation of long organ interludes between stanzas of hymns is particularly distracting.

78. <u>When the Minister giveth the bread, he shall say: "Take, eat; this is the true Body of our Lord and Savior Jesus Christ, given into death for your sins. May this strengthen and preserve you in the true faith unto life everlasting!" When he giveth the cup, he shall say: "Take, drink; this is the true blood of our Lord and Savior Jesus Christ, shed for the remission of your sins. May this strengthen and preserve you in the true faith unto life everlasting!" In dismissing the communicants, the minister may say: "Depart in peace."</u> If the *celebrant* is assisted by another person in the distribution of Holy Communion, the celebrant is properly the one who, as the responsible minister of the sacrament being celebrated, administers the Body of our Lord, while the assistant administers the Precious Blood, or, in the ancient phrase, "confirms with the chalice." (In the very earliest times, it appears that the deacons, who were full-time assistants to the bishop, distributed both the Body and the Blood of Our Lord. It was not long, however, before the celebrant assumed the responsibility of administering the Body of Our Lord and the assisting deacon administered the chalice.) This arrangement has undeniable pastoral advantages. In most cases the celebrant will be the pastor of the parish, that is, the individual who has *potestas iurisdictionis* in the parish. While it is happily very rare that a pastor must repel a person from the altar, this may happen on occasion. In such a case the embarrassment will be much greater if the assistant at the Holy Communion has already communicated the individual in question with Our Lord's Body.

It should be noted that the rubrics do not prescribe that the Words of Distribution be spoken over each communicant, or, for that matter, over each rail of communicants. The requirement of the rubric is adequately met if the minister who administers Our Lord's Body says the Words of Institution pertaining to the consecrated bread in a loud voice at the beginning of the Distribution and if the minister who distributes the Precious Blood of Our Lord does the same with the words pertaining to the chalice. Thereafter, following ancient precedent, the clergyman distributing the hosts need say to each communicant only "the Body of Christ" (or "The Body of Christ given for thee") and the clergyman who administers the chalice need say only "the Blood of Christ" (or "the Blood of Christ shed for thy sins."). It will greatly accelerate the distribution if the communicants are instructed to return to their respective pews immediately after receiving the Precious Blood, without waiting for the entire rail to be dismissed. As each communicant rises from his place at the rail, another can take his place and the clergymen distributing the Body and Blood of Our Lord will always know that the communicant kneeling before them has not as yet received the Holy Communion. If this procedure is followed, the number of communicants kneeling at one time is almost immaterial; it is possible, for instance, to dispense with gates, bars, and kneelers between the two rails and thereby to obviate the distraction which opening and closing the gates, putting bars and kneelers in place, and removing them again afterwards invariably involve. The time required to communicate a congregation in this way is only that required for the actual administration, plus the time needed to replenish supplies of hosts and wine in the paten (or ciborium) and chalice.

The clergyman who administers Our Lord's Body should, if he uses a paten, place upon the paten no more hosts than he will require to communicate one railful of communicants; the danger of dropping a host inadvertently is greatly increased if he has more than this number on the paten. It is perfectly appropriate to leave a small supply of hosts upon the outspread corporal.

It should not be necessary to indicate to the communicants when they are to kneel if the procedure set forth above is followed or if the communicants are instructed to kneel, as is proper, immediately upon arriving at their respective places before the rail. In many parishes it is customary for the communicant to bow moderately before kneeling to receive the host and to bow moderately again after having been dismissed or after having received the cup. This act of reverence is not a courtesy paid to the officiating clergymen and they should not acknowledge it by returning the bow!

While Lutheran clergymen will be careful to instruct their people that they are not to adore the bread and the wine as such, they will also be careful to instruct their communicants that "no one, unless he be an Arian heretic, can and will deny that Christ Himself, true God and man, Who is truly and essentially present in the Holy Communion in the right celebration thereof should be adored in spirit and in truth" (Formula of Concord, Solid Declaration, VI, paragraph 126).

The communicants should be instructed to hold their heads erect, to part their lips, and to place the tip of the tongue against the lower lip. In administering the hosts, the clergyman should hold the paten under the host until he has placed it between the lips of the communicant. Where the number of communicants is normally sufficiently great to fill several rails, it is desirable to use a ciborium or a second chalice for administering Our Lord's Body.

Similarly, the minister administering Our Lord's Precious Blood should be careful that the chalice is not too full, lest the danger of spilling be needlessly increased. He is well advised to hold the chalice by the knop in his left hand, with a folded purificator laid over the fingers of his left hand in such a way that approximately half of it is on either side of his left index finger. Any drops that may run down the outside of the chalice will be caught and absorbed by the purificator. With his right hand he should turn the chalice sufficiently as he passes from one communicant to another so that a fresh part of the chalice lip will be presented to each communicant. The communicants may be instructed to take hold of the foot of the chalice as they receive the Precious Blood.

After returning to the altar when he has finished administering the chalice to a railful of communicants, he should carefully wipe the outside of the chalice with a linen purificator. Paper tissues should not be used for this purpose. If the number of communicants is large, it will be necessary to have a fairly generous supply of purificators available on the altar. A single purificator should not be used too often. Used purificators should be folded neatly in such a way that the portions used for cleansing the rim of the chalice are each protected by a clean layer of cloth, both for the sake of appearance and to prevent the attraction of insects.

(Used purificators should be carefully rinsed in clear water several times before they are laundered, the water in which they are rinsed should be poured into the sacrarium; the same principle applies to other items of altar linen, such as corporals and palls.)

It has been stressed above that the celebrant should set aside no more hosts and wine than he actually expects to use in the course of any given celebration. If he has miscalculated,

78.5 however, the General Rubric of *The Lutheran Liturgy* prescribe that "if the consecrated bread and wine be spent before all have communed, the celebrant shall consecrate more, saying aloud so much of the Words of Institution as pertains to the elements to be consecrated." In this rubric, "aloud" does not requires a greater volume of voice than is necessary for those who are in the chancel to hear what the celebrant is saying. Under no circumstances should a clergyman administer hosts or wine that have not been previously consecrated. If the communicants are dismissed after each railfull has been communicated with the words: "Depart in peace," the minister may make the Sign of the Holy Cross over the communicants while repeating the words. In that case, he should not, if he holds the chalice, make the Sign of the Holy Cross with the chalice in his right hand, but he should transfer the chalice to his left hand and make the Sign of the Holy Cross over the communicants with his right.

78.7 The General Rubrics of *The Lutheran Liturgy* provide that "when all have received the Holy Sacrament, the celebrant shall cover what remains of the bread and wine with the veil."

The Nunc-Dimittis, Thanksgiving, Post-Communion Collect, and Benediction

79. The Distribution ended, all shall rise and say or chant the Nunc Dimittis.
80. Then shall be said or chanted the Thanksgiving. It should be noted that the celebrant faces the altar for the Versicle and Response as well as for the actual Prayer of Thanksgiving. When the celebrant says the closing Doxology of the Prayer ("through Jesus Christ, our Lord, etc."), he closes the book in such a way that the open edge is toward the center of the altar.

    (It will be noted that in the rite of the Church of the Augsburg Confession the Thanksgiving is a part of the "Common," not of the "Propers"; it is therefore not necessary, as it is in the rite of the Roman Catholic Church, to have the service book returned to the Epistle corner of the altar.)
81. Then may a Post-Communion hymn be sung. The service is needlessly lengthened by availing oneself of this option; it is better to omit this hymn.
82. Then may be said or chanted the Salutation and the Benedicamus. These are very ancient parts of the Eucharistic rite and should not be omitted. The celebrant, standing in the midst before the altar, turns by his right to the congregation and says: "The Lord be with you," to which the congregation responds: "And with thy spirit." The ceremonial is the same as that set forth in connection with the Salutation before the Collects for the Day. If the celebrant has been assisted by another clergyman who has read the Holy Gospel and has confirmed with the chalice at the distribution of the Holy Communion, it is fitting that the latter, standing in front of the celebrant on the level of the chancel floor, turn by his left to the congregation and chant: "Bless we the Lord," to which the congregation responds: "Thanks be to God."
83. Then shall the minister say or chant the Benediction. The minister places his left hand flat against his breast, raises his right hand, fingers together and palms toward the congregation, not higher than his head and pronounces the prescribed blessing. (The elevation of both hands for the blessing appears among Lutherans to be a late seventeenth century imitation of a Reformed practice. It has not been possible to trace the source of the relatively recent and localized custom of curling the fourth and fifth fingers into the palm.) He may incline his head slightly at each reference to "The Lord." At the words: "and give thee peace," he moves his right hand to a point in front of his face and makes the Sign of the Holy Cross over the congregation, being careful not to make the down-stroke of the Cross below the level of his waist and confining the cross-stroke to the width of his own shoulders. He rejoins his hands before him and faces by his left toward the altar while the congregation responds with: "Amen." (Neither this nor any other blessing should be introduced with "And now.") Thereafter all engage in silent prayer. In returning to the sacristy from the altar, the celebrant is the last to leave the chancel.

Care of Altar and remaining consecrated elements

84. The General Rubrics of *The Lutheran Liturgy* provides that <u>"when the Service has been completed, the celebrant or a deacon shall remove the sacramental vessels from the altar to the sacristy and dispose of that part of the bread and wine which remains as follows: He shall carefully remove the bread from the paten and ciborium to a fit receptacle, there to be kept against the next Communion. He shall pour what remains of the consecrated wine into the piscina or upon the ground at a proper and convenient place outside the Church."</u> As the responsible "steward of the Mysteries of God," the celebrant should carry out these prescriptions himself and should not delegate them to a deacon. That which has been formally consecrated and blessed for sacramental use should be treated with due respect. The rubric does not prescribe the nature of the "fit receptacle"; it is very clear however, that the consecrated hosts are not to be mixed with un-consecrated hosts but are to be carefully segregated; it is the celebrant's responsibility to insure that they are the first to be distributed at the next Communion (which need not necessarily be the next parochial Communion Service but might conceivably be a bedside celebration for a sick communicant). "Fit receptacle" could well be a special pyx or ciborium. The consecrated wine is to be poured into the sacrarium, or piscina.

There should be a sacrarium in the sacristy as well as in the chancel; in either case it is connected with a drainpipe to mother earth, under no circumstances to the common sewer. In the event that there is no sacrarium in the Church, "a proper and convenient place outside the Church" should be prepared.

This should be at the side of the building, appropriately protected from animals. The simplest arrangement is to dig a pit at least 12 inches by 12 inches and at least 18 to 24 inches deep. The bottom should be of gravel, the top surface of small crushed stone (in order to discourage the growth of grass and weeds). After what remains of the consecrated wine has been poured into the sacrarium or upon the ground at the proper and convenient place outside the Church referred to, a sufficient quantity of clear water should be poured in afterwards to rinse the consecrated wine down, lest it attract insects.

If the celebration of Holy Communion has taken place outside a parish church (for instance, in an inadequately equipped chapel or in a private house), the celebrant, following an ancient tradition in the Church of the Augsburg Confession, should reverently consume what remains of the consecrated Bread and Wine. If through a serious miscalculation the amount be very great, he may solicit the assistance of those who have received Holy Communion at the preceding celebration in consuming the remaining Bread and Wine.

After he has removed the hosts from the paten, he holds the paten over the chalice with his left hand and, with the thumb and forefinger of his right hand, he rubs the paten from top to bottom so that any fragments which have adhered to the paten fall into the chalice. He then pours the contents of the chalice into the sacrarium. Next, a server pours a small quantity of wine into the chalice and the celebrant moves the wine gently about in the chalice and pours it into the sacrarium. Thereupon the celebrant holds his thumbs and forefingers over the bowl of the chalice and the server pours a small quantity first of wine and then of water over the celebrant's thumbs and forefingers while the celebrant rubs his thumbs and forefingers together; then the celebrant pours the contents of the chalice into the sacrarium and carefully dries the chalice, inside and out, with a purificator. If a ciborium was used to communicate the people, the celebrant, immediately after cleansing the paten, will also cleanse the ciborium over the chalice in the same way in which he cleansed the paten. If need be, he may cleanse the ciborium in the same way in which he has been directed to cleanse the chalice.

It may be well in this connection to remember that a reverent attitude in the sacristy on the part of the clergy, the servers, the deacons, and the ushers cannot be too highly stressed and will inevitably be reflected in the attitude of the whole congregation toward the forms and the things of divine worship. Unnecessary conversation and noise (and, of course, smoking) should be conscientiously avoided after as well as before the service.

Thereupon the celebrant may say an appropriate short prayer with those who ministered with him in the Service. Then he proceeds to unvest (in the reverse order of vesting), washes his hands, and goes to make his personal thanksgiving for the Holy Communion.

The Eucharistic Prayer of *Culto Cristiano* (1964) Conformed to RSV Principles

It is truly meet, right and salutary, that we should at all times and in all places give thanks to thee, O Lord, holy Father, almighty, everlasting God:
(Here shall follow the proper Preface. If no proper Preface is appointed, the Minister shall continue:)
Through Jesus, Christ, our Lord. Therefore with angels and archangels and with all the company of heaven, we praise and magnify thy glorious name, ever adoring thee and saying: Holy, holy, holy is the Lord God of hosts! Heaven and earth are full of thy glory! Hosanna in the highest! Blessed is he who comes in the name of the Lord! Hosanna in the highest!

Holy art thou, O God, almighty and most merciful Lord. Holy art thou and great in the majesty of thy glory. Thou didst so love the world that thou gavest thine only Son, that whoever believes in him should not perish but have eternal life, and thou didst send him into the world to fulfill for us thy holy will and to accomplish our salvation.

He, Our Lord Jesus Christ, on the night when he was betrayed, took *(Here the Minister shall take the paten in his hand)* bread, and when he had given thanks, he broke it and gave it to the disciples, and said:

Take, eat; this is my body, which is given for you. Do this in remembrance of me.

In the same way also he took *(Here the Celebrant shall take the chalice in his hand)* the cup after supper, and when he had given thanks, he gave it to them, saying:

Drink of it, all of you, this is my blood of the new covenant, which is poured out for you for the forgiveness of sins. Do this, as often as you drink it, in remembrance of me.

Remembering therefore his salutary precept, his life-giving passion and death, his glorious resurrection and ascension, and the promise of his coming again, we give thanks to thee, O Lord God almighty, and we beseech thee mercifully to accept our praise and thanksgiving, and to bless us, thy children, so that all we who partake of Christ's holy body and of his precious blood may be filled with thy heavenly peace and joy; and also that we, in receiving the forgiveness of sins, together with the gifts of life and salvation, may be sanctified in body, soul and spirit and have our portion with all thy saints in light.

To thee, O God, Father, Son and holy Spirit, be all honor and glory in thy holy church for ever and ever. Amen.

Let us pray. Our Father. .
For Thine is the kingdom. .
The peace of the Lord be with you always.
And with your spirit.
O Lamb of God...

Index

The page number is always given and is always given first. Where there is a rubric number it is given after the colon.

Absolution/Preparatory Service	9:40; 10:48
At page 5 service (Words of Assurance)	10:48
Adoration at Communion	30-32:78
Alleluia Verse	15-16:58
Announceents in the Service	7:33
Announcing	
Old Testament	6:29
Epistle	14:56
Gospel	17-19:62
Antiphon with Introit	5-6:27
Athanasian Creed	7:31; 16-17:61
Baptism (Service of, Hymn)	9:39.5
Benedicamus	33:82
Benediction	33:83
Black, use of	3:15.5
Bowing (inclining the head)	19:53; 19:64
At the Name of Jesus	v; 9:44; 9-10:46-47
At Sanctus (at waist)	26:73
Breaking the Host	26-28:75; 28-30:76
Burse	3:21
Candles, candelabra, lighting candles	iii
Celebrant's reception	28-30:76
Ceremonies while preparing for the Eucharist	22-24:68.5
Chanting	1-2:9-10; 5:24; 11:50; 14:56; 17:62
Choir	2:11-12; 14:56
Sequence Hymn substitution	7:30; 16:59
Gradual	15-16:58
Clearing the Altar after Service	34-35:84
Collect of the Day	6:28; 13:54
Terminations	2:15
Colors, liturgical	iii
Communion linens, what consists of	28-30:76
Communion prayers	8:37
Confession and Absolution/Confessional Service	9:40; 9:43-47
Confession and Absolution/Preparatory Service	8:37
Confessional Service	8:37

Consecreation 26-28:75
Consecration of additional elements 32:78.5
Corporal 3:17
Credence tables iii
Creed, Nicene 5:25; 7:31; 16-17:61; 19:63
Dalmatic 17-18:62
Deacon, vestments 17-18:62
Distribution 28-33:76-79; 30-32:78
    Assistance 30:76.5
    Hymns during 30:77
    Veiling Vessels after 33:78.7
Doxological hymn stanzas 8:39; 33:80
Elevation 26-28:75
Epsitle 14:56
Epistle Corner of Altar (use) 11-12:50-51; 33:80; 22-24:68.5
Eucharistic Prayer 26:73a; 7:36
Fair linen 3:16
Flowers iii
Fraction 26-28:75; 28-30:76
General Prayer 24-25:69
Genuflect (during the Creed) 19:63
Gloria Patri 5-6:27
Gloria in Excelsis 12:52
Gospel, reading of 17-18:62
    Blessing an ordained reader 17-18:62
    Deacon, reading 17-18:62
    Incense 17-18:62
    Kissing 17-18:62
    Proccession 17-18:62
Gradual 15-16:58
Green, use of 3:15.3
Hallelujia Verse 15-16:58
Hand position . . . . .iv; 12-13:53
Hand covering 4:22
Hymn of Invocation (Opening Hymn) 8-9:39
Incense (at the Gospel) 17-18:62
Introit 5-6:27; 8:38; 11:50
Invocation 9:41
Kyrie (threefold, fourfold, and ninefold) 12:51
Lavabo Ceremony 22-24:68.5
Lavabo Towel/purificator 3:19; 22-24:68.5
Lay readers 14:55
Lectern 14:55

Lection 14:55-56
Lent
    Omission of greater Glroia 12:52
    Omission of Hallelujiahs 15-16:58
    Omission of music during Distribution 30:77
"Let us give thanks." 25:71
"Let us pray." 12-13:53; 26:74
"Lift up your hearts." 25:71
Litany 25:69.5
Liturgical colors 2-3:15
Lord's Prayer 26:74
Maniple 19-20:65; 26-28:75
Matins with Communion, forbidden 1:6
Maundy Thursday addition of greater Gloria 12:52
"May" versus "shall" rubrics 1:4
Nunc Dimittis 33:79
Offering 21:68
    Placing on Altar and then Credence 21:68
Old Testament 6-7:29; 14:55
Opeing Hymn (Hymn of Invocation) 8:39
Oremus 12:53; 26:74
Our Father 26:74
Pall 3:18; 22:68.5; 28:76; 30-33:78
Pax 26-28:75
Piscina 34:84
Post-Communion Collect 33:80
Post-Communion Hymn 33:81
Posture iv
Potted plants iii
Preface 25:71
Preface wording error in TLH 25:71
Preparation of the Altar during the Service 22:68.5
Preparatory Service 9:40; 9-10:43-47; 5:24
Preparation the Altar (for the Eucharist) 22-24:68.5
Procession 8:39
Proper Preface 26:72
    For Epiphany season and Pre-Lent use Trinity 26:72
Purificator 3:19; 30:78
Reading the rubrics i
Red, use of 2:15.2
Reliquae 34:84
Reverence ii
Sacramental acts 7:30

Sacramental Vessels on Altar, location 3:17
Sacramental Vessels, cleaning 34:84
Sacrarium 34:84
Sacrificaial acts 1:2
Salutation (posture and ceremonies) 12:53
   Before the Collect of the Day 12:53
   Before the Preface 25:71
   Post-Communion/Pre-Benediction 33:82
Saluting the Altar (bowing, reverenceing) iv
Sanctus 26:73
Self-communion 28-30:76
Sentence 15-16:58
Sequence Hymn 7:30; 15:58
"Shall" versus "may" rubrics 1:4
Sign of the Cross
   At the Benediction 33:83
   At the Creed 19:63
   At the Dismissal 32:78.5
   At the Gospel 18:63
   At Invocation and Creed .5:25; 9:41; 10:48
   At the Sanctus 26:73
   Form and purpose of 5:25
   On the forehead, lips, and breast at the Gospel 17:62
   On the Gospel 17:62
   Over others (at the Absolution) 10:48
   Over the Host and Chalice 26:75
Standing for doxological hymn stanzas 8:39
Thanksgiving 33:80
Tract 15-16:58
Tunicle 19:65; 14:56
Veil 3:20
Verba 26:75
Versicle/Response - Preparatory Service 5:26
Vespers with Communion, forbidden 1:6
Vesting of laymen/acolytes 14:56
Violet, use of 3:15.4
White, use of 2:15.1
Words of Institution 26:75

The Conduct of the Services

Edited by Charles McClean

Preface to the First Edition

Readers familiar with The Conduct of the Service by the Rev. Arthur Carl Piepkorn will immediately recognize how largely indebted this manual is to that work.

This manual was prepared in cooperation with the members of the worship division of the department of practical theology at Concordia Seminary, St. Louis: the Rev. George W. Hoyer, the Rev. Mark P. Bangert, the Rev. Robert R. Bergt, and the Rev. Dr. John S. Damm. The. Rev. David C. Yagow, registrar of Concordia Seminary and the Rev. Dr. Carl Bergen of St. Louis, assisted in the editorial process. The Rev. Earle Hewitt Maddux, of Catonsville, Maryland, and the Rev. Arthur L. Gillespie, of Maspeth, New York, also provided valuable help in the preparation of this manual.

The Rev. Michael Hiller, of Raynham, Massachusetts, prepared the diagrams and art work.

Charles McClean
Maundy Thursday 1972

Preface to this Reformatted Edition

The ceremony of the Divine Service plays an integral role in our perception of who God is, who we are, and how God comes to us. It is our hope that a reformatted edition of The Conduct of the Services will foster a renewed interest, among pastors and laity, in the rich piety that confessional Lutheranism has always practiced.

We have simply reproduced what the department of practical theology at Concordia Seminary, St. Louis published in 1972. Aside from deleting two appendices which explained the ceremony of the Divine Services found in the hymnal supplement of 1969, we have left all of the original work generally unchanged. We updated the Forward and slightly extended the Table of Contents to aid use of this Manual. The diagrams showing the censing of the altar were traced first instead of being scanned directly into the text for enhanced clarity.

I would like to thank the Reverend Father Charles McClean for granting permission for this reprint.

Michael N. Frese
25th Sunday after Trinity 2002

Contents

Preface .... *i*
Key to Diagrams .... *vi*
Forward 1

Introduction 2

Chapter One: General Considerations 5
General Deportments 5
Position of Hands 6
Bowing 6
Sign of the Cross 7
Reading 7
Music of the Service 8
Arrangement of the Altar and Chancel 9
Sacred Vessels 10
Sacramental Linens 11
Liturgical Colors 11
Vestments 12
Offertory Procession 13
Greeting of Peace 14
Point of Courtesy 15
Other Matters 15

Chapter Two:
General Notes on the Celebration of the Sacrament of the Altar 16

Chapter Three: The Propers 20

Chapter Four: The Rite of the Order of Holy Communion 22
The Opening Hymn 22
The Confession of Sins 22
The Introit 23
The Kyrie 24
The Gloria in Excelsis 25
The Salutation 26
The Collect for the Day 26
The Old Testament 26
The Epistle 27
The Gradual 28
The Holy Gospel 29
The Nicene Creed 30
The Hymn 30

The Sermon	30
The Offertory	31
The General Prayer	31
The Preface	32
The Sanctus	32
The Lord's Prayer	33
The Words of Institution	33
The Pax Domini	33
The Agnus Dei	33
The Distribution	33
The Nunc Dimittis	34
The Thanksgiving	34
The Salutation and Benedicamus	34
The Benediction	34

CHAPTER FIVE: THE CELEBRATION OF THE HOLY EUCHARIST 35
I. Preparation for the Celebration of the Holy Eucharist 35
II. The Celebration of the Holy Eucharist: Celebrant and Server 37

The Confession of Sins	37
The Introit	38
The Kyrie	38
The Gloria in Excelsis	38
The Salutation	39
The Collect for the Day	39
The Old Testament	39
The Epistle	39
The Gradual	39
The Holy Gospel	40
The Nicene Creed	41
The Hymn	42
The Sermon	42
The Offertory	42
The General Prayer	43
The Preface	44
The Sanctus	45
The Lord's Prayer	45
The Words of Institution	45
The Pax Domini	47
The Agnus Dei	47
The Distribution	48
The Nunc Dimittis	49
The Thanksgiving	49
The Salutation and Benedicamus	49

  The Benediction 49

 III. The Celebration of the Holy Eucharist: Celebrant, Deacon, Subdeacon, and Acolytes 50
  The Introit 50
  The Kyrie 50
  The Gloria in Excelsis 50
  The Salutation 51
  The Collect for the Day 51
  The Old Testament 50
  The Epistle 51
  The Gradual 51
  The Holy Gospel 52
  The Nicene Creed 52
  The Hymn 53
  The Sermon 53
  The Offertory 53
  The General Prayer 54
  The Preface 54
  The Sanctus 54
  The Lord's Prayer 54
  The Words of Institution 54
  The Pax Domini 55
  The Agnus Dei 55
  The Distribution 55
  The Nunc Dimittis 55
  The Thanksgiving 55
  The Salutation and Benedicamus 55
  The Benediction 56

CHAPTER SIX:
THE CELEBRATION OF THE HOLY EUCHARIST FACING THE PEOPLE 57
I. Introduction 57
II. The Arrangement of the Altar and Chancel 59
III. Preparation for the Celebration of the Holy Eucharist Facing the People 62
IV. A Simple Way of Celebrating the Holy Eucharist Facing the People 62
 Eucharist Facing the People 62
 The Confession of Sins 62
 The Introit 62
 The Kyrie 62
 The Gloria in Excelsis 62
 The Salutation 62
 The Collect for the Day 62
 The Old Testament 63

The Epistle	63
The Gradual	63
The Holy Gospel	63
The Nicene Creed	63
The Hymn	63
The Sermon	63
The Offertory	63
The General Prayer	65
The Preface	65
The Sanctus	65
The Lord's Prayer	65
The Words of Institution	65
The Pax Domini	66
The Agnus Dei	66
The Distribution	66
The Nunc Dimittis	67
The Thanksgiving	67
The Salutation and Benedicamus	67
The Benediction	67

V. *The Celebration of the Holy Eucharist Facing the People: Celebrant, Deacon, Subdeacon, and Acolytes* 67

The Confession of Sins	67
The Introit	67
The Kyrie	67
The Gloria in Excelsis	67
The Salutation	67
The Collect for the Day	68
The Old Testament	69
The Epistle	69
The Gradual	69
The Holy Gospel	70
The Nicene Creed	71
The Hymn	71
The Sermon	71
The Offertory	71
The General Prayer	72
The Preface	72
The Sanctus	72
The Lord's Prayer	72
The Words of Institution	72
The Pax Domini	73
The Agnus Dei	73

The Distribution	73
The Nunc Dimittis	73
The Thanksgiving	73
The Salutation and Benedicamus	73
The Benediction	74

CHAPTER SEVEN: MATINS AND VESPERS 75
I. *The Rite of the Order of Matins* 75
II. *The Rite of the Order of Vespers* 82
III. *The Ceremonial of Matins and Vespers* 85

CHAPTER EIGHT: PROCESSION 89

APPENDIX C: THE MANNER OF CENSING THE ALTAR 93

Key to the Diagrams

▢	Altar
C	Celebrant
D	Deacon
SD	Subdeacon
S	Server
Cr	Crucifer
Th	Thurifer
T	Taperer

Forward: How to Use this Manual

This manual has been prepared as a practical tool to aid the pastor in the conduct of the service. Pastors and congregations will remember the teaching of the Lutheran symbols:

> We believe, teach, and confess that no church should condemn another because it has fewer or more external ceremonies not commanded by God, as long as there is mutual agreement in doctrine and in all its articles as well as in the right use of the holy sacraments, according to the familiar axiom, "Disagreement in fasting does not destroy agreement in faith" (Formula of Concord, Ep., X 7).

Most pastors and congregations may find chapters one, two, three, four, parts one and two of chapter five (in churches where the altar has been placed away from the wall of the chancel, parts one through four of chapter six), and all of chapter seven useful in the regular conduct of the church's worship. The remaining sections of this manual will be useful to pastors and congregations who make larger use of the church's ceremonial tradition. In preparing this manual, the attempt has been made to provide directions for the most complete ceremonial tradition known in the church of the Augsburg Confession. But it is hoped that those who use this manual will feel free to omit this or that ceremonial feature, while retaining whatever they may find of value.

Much of the material in part two of chapter five applies very generally to any form of celebration of holy communion. In other sections of this manual which describe the eucharistic liturgy, it is assumed that the reader is familiar with part two of chapter five or, if he is not familiar with it, that he will consult it from time to time.

It will be noted that in part two of chapter five some paragraphs are double indented, and that certain directions in the remaining paragraphs of the text are in parentheses. It is possible to disregard these materials and still conduct the service in faithfulness to the authorized service books of the church. The indented directions and those in parentheses in some instances provide more detailed instructions on how some action may most conveniently be done; in other instances they describe the procedure commonly followed in the western church at the time of the Reformation.

The diagrams have been included as an aid in understanding the written directions. Local circumstances may require different arrangements and positioning of participants in the service.

Page references are to this manual unless otherwise indicated.

All references to the Hymnal Supplement are taken from The Commission on Worship's supplement to The Lutheran Hymnal of 1969 published by Concordia Publishing House.

✠ Soli Deo Gloria ✠

Introduction

The practice of ceremonial worship is closely related to the heart of the Christian faith. The Scriptures teach and the church confesses that Christ redeemed the whole man. Our bodies share in the redemption accomplished by the Son of God, who Himself took flesh and blood of His virgin mother. Christ chose earthly, tangible elements—water, bread, and wine—to impart to men the salvation He accomplished. It is impossible to use these material elements without some basic ceremonial action. This basic ceremonial might be called functional or utilitarian ceremonial. There is also interpretative ceremonial—actions and the use of objects to express the meaning of the actions Christ Himself instituted. For example, a crucifix is usually placed at the altar to remind the congregation that the Eucharist is the memorial of the sacrifice which was offered once for all on Golgotha. People usually kneel to receive Holy Communion to express adoration in the presence of the living Christ, who gives His body and blood with the blessed bread and wine.

Bodily, external action in worship is a sign of God's creation of the material and of His all-embracing redemptive work. It is a sign of the hope that in the resurrection—in a way we cannot imagine—"the creation itself will be set free from its bondage to decay and obtain the glorious liberty of the children of God" (Rom. 8:21).

While ceremonial worship is closely connected with the heart of the Christian faith, the precise form worship takes is not divinely ordained, apart from the actions and elements involved in Christ's institution. There is, therefore, no one "right" way of celebrating the Eucharist. We can speak of "right" and "wrong" only when faithfulness to Christ's institution is involved. Lutheran pastors will be guided in their conduct of worship by the doctrine of the Sacred Scriptures and the symbolical books to which they have been obligated at the time of their ordination.

Beyond this, what is said and done in church is, strictly speaking, a matter of Christian liberty.[1] But since liberty is not license, we will be guided in what we say and do by certain sound principles. We will be guided by the rites and rubrics of the church body to which we belong.[2]

---

1 "We believe, teach, and confess, that no church should condemn another because it has fewer or more external ceremonies not commanded by God, as long as there is mutual agreement in doctrine and in all its articles as well as in the right use of the holy sacraments, according to the familiar axiom, 'Disagreement in fasting does not destroy agreement in faith.'" Formula of Concord, Epitome X 7.

2 See Augsburg Confession XV 1, XXVIII 53-56; Apology of the Augsburg Confession XV 38, XXVIII 7; Formula of Concord, Epitome X 4; Formula of Concord, Solid Declaration X 9. Note Article III 5 and Article VI 4 of the "Constitution of The Lutheran Church—Missouri Synod." "The objects of Synod are ... 5. The endeavor to bring about the largest possible uniformity in church practice, church customs, and, in general, in congregational affairs" (Handbook of The Lutheran Church—Missouri Synod, 1969 Edition, p. 16). "Conditions for acquiring and holding membership in Synod are ... 4. Exclusive use of doctrinally pure agenda, hymnbooks, and catechism in church and school" (ibid., p. 17). Note also that the *General Rubrics of The Lutheran Hymnal* state: "Congregations are urged to let the basic structure of the Service remain intact. The wide choice permitted in the Rubrics makes it possible to have the Service as simple or as elaborate as the circumstances of each Congregation may indicate" (*The Lutheran Hymnal*, p. 4). The *General Rubrics* of *The Lutheran Liturgy* state: "The word 'shall' in the rubrics makes that part of the Service obligatory, while the word 'may,' leaves it optional" (*The Lutheran Liturgy*, p. 417). "On and after Easter Day 1955, in any case of a contradiction between these *General Rubrics* as they are here printed and other rubrics published elsewhere in the official service books of the Evangelical Lutheran Synodical Conference of North America, these *General Rubrics* shall govern" (*The Lutheran Liturgy*, p. 427).

These rites and rubrics constitute the use of our church. They exist for the sake of decency and order and reflect a long history of Christian experience. The following directions try to be faithful to the authorized service books of our synod—*The Lutheran Liturgy*, *The Lutheran Lectionary*, *The Lutheran Agenda*, *The Lutheran Hymnal*, *The Music for the Liturgy*. Reference is also made to the *Worship Supplement* and *The Holy Communion* prepared by the Inter-Lutheran Commission on Worship.

In addition to the rites and rubrics of our authorized service books, three principles have shaped the following directions: historic precedent, ecumenical consensus, and contemporary need.

In an age that seems to have little sense of historic continuity, the appeal to historic precedent may seem pointless. Besides, some of the ceremonial described in the following pages may not be immediately intelligible to every worshiper. Yet while the historic ceremonial is not always immediately intelligible, it can be made meaningful. But why, some will ask, should we burden ourselves with ceremonial that requires explanation, ceremonial from the dim past? The answer to that question can partially be suggested by referring to the words of St. Paul: "What! Did the Word of God originate with you, or are you the only ones it has reached?" (1 Cor. 14:36). The ceremonial of the liturgy, no less than the rite, reminds us of our continuity with that host of believers who have gathered to "do this" in remembrance of the Lord ever since the night when He was betrayed. Unthinking bondage to historic precedent is, of course, deadening. Besides, a reading of the numerous rites of Christendom would quickly show that one could find precedent for almost anything he would want to do. This, then, implies that in appealing to historic precedent, one must also consider historic consensus—insofar as that exists—and the intrinsic meaningfulness of a usage. Lutherans will in most cases give greatest weight to Lutheran precedent, in this way visibly asserting Lutheran confessional identity.

The appeal to ecumenical consensus springs from the conviction that we are, in spite of our divisions, one with all who have been baptized into our Lord's death and resurrection. While Lutheran pastors must not introduce or abolish ceremonies with the intention of suggesting that there is no essential difference between the Church of the Augsburg Confession and churches adhering to a different confessional position, it is also true that Lutheran liturgical usage has not been sectarian. The symbolical books themselves appeal to non-Lutheran usage in cases where such usage is not contrary to the Gospel and where it furthers the devotion and piety of the people (Apology of the Augsburg Confession XXIV 6, 93). Therefore, where there is a growing consensus among Christians regarding the fitness of a given procedure in worship, we may well follow it, provided we do not follow blindly.

The third principle for these guidelines for ceremonial is contemporary need. Historic precedent and ecumenical consensus can be approximately established without too much difficulty. We can, perhaps, begin by noting a strong contemporary reaction to a purely intellectualized approach to reality—an approach to reality reflected in a strongly intellectualized approach to worship. There is a grasping for more than the purely rational, an awareness that reality is something more than can be grasped by words addressed to the intellect. "The communications revolution has provided a type of perception radically different from that provided by the spoken or written word, one in which perception of reality is achieved by direct participation, by involvement."[3]

---

3   James F. White, "Worship in an Age of Immediacy," *The Christian Century*, LXXXV (Feb. 21, 1958), 227.

Historic Christian ceremonial probably helps in some measure to meet this situation. The appeal of ceremonial worship is not merely to the intellect via verbal communication, but its appeal is to the total person via all the senses. This does not mean that the received tradition, or the ceremonial described in the following pages, is a wholly adequate solution to our contemporary liturgical problems, but it does mean that in the received tradition there are resources for contemporary need, and that the tradition may be used as a point of departure and helpful pattern for future developments.[4]

The foregoing principles—historic precedent and ecumenical consensus—themselves relate to contemporary need. We have already spoken of the apparent lack of historic consciousness in our time. And yet a consciousness of being rooted in the long history of the people of God should be an integral part of a Christian's experience of the church. For this reason a historically rooted ceremonial is helpful. A historically rooted ceremonial speaks to more or less rootless contemporary man of his share in the ongoing life of the community of believers across the centuries. While not a phenomenon unique to our time, contemporary man seems to be afflicted by a sense of isolation from his fellow man. A ceremonial guided by ecumenical consensus speaks to him of oneness with the whole people of God. Therefore, what initially may appear to be the irrelevance of historic ceremonial to contemporary man is finally, in part, its actual relevance.

But we live in a time of rapid change. We cannot expect our worship to remain unaffected by the nature of the times in which we live. There will, therefore, be some tension between faithfulness to the authorized use of the church and responsible experimentation. Responsible experimentation takes place when a pastor carefully studies the problems involved, adequately prepares his people for the experiment, and provides opportunity for evaluation of what has been done.

The material in this manual may at times appear overly precise and, when attempted in practice, may seem unnatural and even stiff. On the one hand, increased familiarity will lead to greater ease and freedom of movement and gesture. On the other hand, individuals will learn from experience which actions and usages edify and make for vital and genuine worship, and which actions and usages have, perhaps, outlived their usefulness in a given community of worshiping Christians.

---

4 Eugene Brand, "Ceremonial Forms and Contemporary Life," *Response*, VIII (St. Michael and All Angels, 1966), 91–99.

Chapter One: General Considerations

There is really only one basic rule of good form: "Be courteous."

And similarly there is really only one basic rule for those who lead the church in worship: "Be reverent!" Every other rule is simply a practical application of that basic charge.

To be reverent we must first of all be humble. We are ministers—ministers of Christ, serving Christ in the name of fellow-sinners. We minister not because of any virtue in ourselves. "Our sufficiency is of God" (2 Cor. 3:6). We minister as temples of the Holy Spirit, bound in sacramental union to the Lord of the church, living in mystic communion with the most holy Trinity. We are those whom Christ has chosen to be with him, and he has sent us to preach (Mark 3:13). We minister under the aspect of eternity and in the presence of the divine Majesty. Wherever we stand, we are on holy ground. In such a ministry there is no room for pride, only for all-pervading humility.

To be reverent we must be prepared. We must know what we are doing, and why we are doing it. Physical preparations should be taken care of well in advance.[5] There should be no last-minute running around, no hasty final preparation, no distressed paging about. A meditation, brief if need be, but as long as time permits, should never be overlooked. Spiritual preparation is more essential to reverence than the proper ordering of the physical adjuncts of worship.

To be reverent we must be calm. The unforeseen, the accidental, the disturbing must not be permitted to distract us. We are God's ambassadors and God's servants. We are speaking for and to God. Our entire lives ought to be, and our public ministry must be, *en Christo*—in Christ. So must the calm peace of the changeless Christ in our souls be reflected in our outward demeanor.

General Deportment

Whenever the minister walks, he should hold his head erect, his eyes forward and cast down. Keeping his eyes cast down helps the minister to think about what he is doing and to avoid staring at the people. He should not walk too slowly nor too rapidly, and he should take rather short steps. He should approach the altar squarely, not at a diagonal. He turns at right angles, but not with obtrusive precision. He should not sway or pivot, and when standing still, he should be careful to avoid the appearance of unsteadiness. He should not lean against the altar, especially when facing the congregation.

---

5   The preparation of the church for worship should be completed at least fifteen minutes before the service begins. Such preparations include: placing books on the altar, credence, lectern and pulpit, changing hymn-board numbers, placing flowers in the chancel, changing the frontal and frontlet, placing the necessary vessels on the credence before a celebration of holy communion, lighting the candles. Candles should be lighted by a lay server decently vested, he should wear at least a cassock. The candle on the epistle side is lighted first; the candle on the gospel side is lighted last. They are extinguished in reverse order. New candles should be started some time before the service or they may cause embarrassing difficulties. It should be noted that the lighting and extinguishing of the candles is a purely utilitarian matter and that the pomp which attends this action in many places is wholly unnecessary.

During the singing of hymns the minister should sing with the congregation, unless he is otherwise occupied with the conduct of the service. The time should not be used to locate the lessons or other propers. The minister should not beat time with his book, look around him, nor bellow at the top of his voice. If he knows the hymn well enough to dispense with a book, his hands should be deliberately placed and still. Customarily, the minister places his hands on his knees, palms down. He should not cross his feet or legs.

Position of Hands

In going to and from the altar, or when otherwise walking around, the minister's hands should be folded reverently. It is possible that in ancient times it was customary to clasp the fingers, but by the time of the Reformation it was certainly a common custom to hold the hands palm to palm, fingers extended, generally with the thumb of the right hand over that of the left. In either case the hands should be held at the height of the chest.

The hands should not be encumbered with books, nor should they hang limp at the sides. When a book must be carried closed, it is held upright at the height of the chest, a few inches in front of the person.

Whenever the minister's right hand only is engaged in some action, e.g. turning the pages of the service book, his left hand is placed flat against his chest or flat on the altar.

The ancient posture of prayer was that of hands uplifted, eyes raised "to heaven." (Cf. 1 Kings 8:22, 1 Tim. 2:8)

> The hands are raised level with the head, the palms of the hands are half-way between facing forwards and facing together, the wrists slightly bent back, and, unless reading from the book is necessary, the eyes are raised "to heaven." ... In medieval times [this position] was modified first to the position of one crucified, and then reduced to a position easier to hold, where the hands are level with the shoulders.[6]

By convention this gesture is used only for the prayers that belong to the oldest strata of the eucharistic liturgy. When the eucharist is celebrated facing the people, this ancient position may be adopted. When the eucharist is celebrated in the customary eastward position, the late medieval practice of holding the hands as high as the shoulders, the palms of the hands facing each other, may well be adopted—or the older gesture may be retained.

Bowing

Since the altar is a symbol of the presence of God and since it serves as the focus of devotion in the church (except during the reading of the gospel when the focus of attention shifts to the book), it is appropriate to reverence the altar with a profound bow before it when first entering and last leaving the sanctuary. It is also appropriate to bow moderately when crossing, approaching, or leaving the midst of the altar.

A person carrying the holy sacrament does not bow.

---

6   Basil Minchin, *The Celebration of the Holy Eucharist Facing the People* (n.p., n.d.), p. 33.

It is a confessional custom to bow the head at the name of JESUS—toward the crucifix if at the altar, toward the book if the gospel is being read, straight ahead at other times. It is proper to bow the head at the words, "Glory be to the Father and to the Son and to the Holy Ghost." It is also proper to bow the head at the words, "Holy, holy, holy, Lord God of Sabaoth," in the *sanctus*, and at the words, "Holy, holy, holy, Lord God of Sabaoth! Heaven and earth are full of the majesty of thy glory," in the *te deum*.

The Sign of the Cross

When a person makes the sign of the cross on himself, he holds the palm of his right hand flat, thumb and fingers together, and with the tips of his fingers he touches in succession his forehead, chest, right shoulder and left shoulder. The left hand is held flat against the chest. (This method of making the sign of the cross is older than the method in common use in the Roman Catholic church, in which the right hand crosses from the left shoulder to the right.) The formula "My Lord Jesus Christ came down from heaven–and was incarnate for me–and was crucified for me—and entered into my heart"–may aid in interpreting this method of making the sign of the cross.

When the gospel is announced, the sign of the cross may be made with the tip of the right thumb on the forehead, lips, and heart. The silent prayer which accompanies this action reads as follows: "May thy gospel be in my mind, on my lips, and in my heart."

When making the sign of the cross over the people or over a person, the minister places his left hand—fingers together—flat against his chest, raises his right hand at a right angle to his face, moves his right hand vertically downward to the level of his waist, raises it again vertically to a point before his chest, moves it horizontally to a point in front of his left shoulder, moves it back horizontally to a point in front of his right shoulder, then moves it back to a point before his chest and joins both hands before him.

When the celebrant of the eucharist makes the sign of the cross over the bread and wine, he places his left hand flat on the altar. With fingers together he makes the sign of the cross—in a plane parallel to the mensa of the altar, not at right angles to it—over the element to be consecrated. Then he rejoins his hands before him.

Reading

The minister must be careful to read the service distinctly and fittingly.

He should read slowly enough to give devout attention to what he reads, but not too deliberately, lest he weary the hearers. He should avoid all theatrical and elocutionary emphasis, but should also avoid a monotonous utterance, such as will create the impression of boredom. His tone should be grave and full, not conversational; but he should use the best tones of his own natural voice, and not an affectedly deep or orotund resonance.[7]

The minister should read loudly enough to be heard by everyone in the church building, but he should not shout. The ancient private prayers prayed by the celebrant before reading the gospel and before receiving the holy communion are said in a tone loud enough to be heard only by the celebrant himself. (The text of these prayers will be found on **p. 31 in this manual.)

---

7 (Cambridge, Massachusetts: 1951), p. xxvi. Before the service the minister should try out the church's loudspeaker system if there is one.

When a layman reads a lesson in church, the pastor may first discuss the meaning of the lesson with him. Good reading presupposes understanding what is read. Then the reader may silently read the lesson to himself. Then he may read it aloud until the pastor is satisfied that the lesson will be understood by the congregation. The reader should read the lesson at least once prior to the service in the church building, so that he may have some idea of the volume needed if the lesson is to be heard. Whoever reads a lesson should keep his eyes **on the book** as a sign that he is reading the words of another.

The Music of the Service

The service of the Christian community—as of the people of God under the old covenant—has historically been a **choral** service. The **spoken** eucharist is a medieval development: the multiplication of masses made a choral eucharist on every occasion impossible. In the Lutheran church the celebration of the sacrament of the altar has also been a choral service. The common practice of the minister speaking his part of the service is an innovation which can be traced to Reformed influence. It is desirable that our churches return to the ancient Christian and historically Lutheran custom of a fully choral service. Of course, when the minister **cannot** sing the liturgy in an acceptable way, it is obviously preferable that he speak it. And even where the choral service is the norm, there may be occasions when the service must be spoken, e.g. at daily matins and vespers during the week, or at a weekday eucharist attended by few communicants.

When the liturgy of the holy communion is sung, the service may be called "choral eucharist." When the eucharistic liturgy is sung, and a deacon and subdeacon assist the celebrant, the service may be called "solemn choral eucharist."

When the eucharist is sung, it is traditional to sing the following parts of the service: introit, kyrie, gloria in excelsis, salutation, collect, Old Testament lesson, epistle, gradual, gospel, creed, hymn, offertory, preface, sanctus, our father, words of institution, pax domini, agnus dei, nunc dimittis, thanksgiving, salutation, benedicamus, benediction. When the lessons are sung, the conclusion of the lessons—"Here endeth the epistle," "Here endeth the gospel"—may be omitted. If the conclusion is not omitted, it is spoken, not sung.

The *General Rubrics* of *The Lutheran Liturgy* state that "The music of the Service is not a part of the Liturgy and may be altered as circumstances permit or require" (*The Lutheran Liturgy*, p. 418). This means that music may be omitted altogether and the entire service may be said. But it must be remembered that the service of the church has from earliest antiquity been choral. To vary the musical settings seasonally is desirable.

The *General Rubrics* also state that "The officiant shall chant those portions of the Service to which the Choir or the Congregation responds with chanting" (*The Lutheran Liturgy*, p. 419). This rubric is obligatory, common practice to the contrary notwithstanding. If the choir or congregation responds with chant, the officiant is required to chant the corresponding parts of the service assigned to him. He speaks these parts of the service only if the congregation responds in a speaking voice. *Concentus* (chanting by the congregation) always implies *accentus* (chanting by the minister): neither is proper without the other.

"Liturgical chant, more so than any other type of church music, is not a musical interpretation of the text; it is only the bearer of the text and should be sung in a simple, straightforward manner" (*The Lutheran Liturgy*, p. 418). To chant is to speak on established pitches of musical sounds according to prescribed formulae retaining natural rhythm and stress of speech (*choraliter legere*). The minister must not sing his part of the service as if it were a recitative or a solo in an oratorio or opera. "To a lesser extent, the same thing is true of Hymn tunes. This is in keeping with the spirit of liturgical worship, which disdains sentimentalization and tawdriness, musical and otherwise" (*The Lutheran Liturgy*, p. 419).

"The primary function of the Choir is to lead the Congregation in the singing of the Liturgy and the Hymns, and to sing the Propers when they are beyond the capacity of the Congregation" (*The Lutheran Liturgy*, p. 419). The singing of optional anthems and other compositions apart from the Ordinary, the Propers and Hymns is at best a secondary function of the Choir and should not be allowed to become its primary function or reason for existing. "In view of the fact that the music presented by the Choir and organist is part of the Service of Worship, it is imperative that this music be in keeping with the spirit of the liturgical character of the Service." "From time to time the Choir may sing parts of the Ordinary in more elaborate choral settings" (*The Lutheran Liturgy*, p. 419). The ideal of maximum congregational participation in the service implies that the privilege accorded by this rubric will be used sparingly.

The Arrangement of the Altar and Chancel

The altar is the one absolutely essential piece of furniture in the church building. If there is to be a meal, there must necessarily be a table on which to prepare it. The altar should indicate by its size and dignity and position its role as the table for the eucharistic meal and the symbol of the presence of the exalted Christ among his people.

The altar should be vested in a frontal of the color of the day or season; it may also be vested in a frontlet. In many places there is a tendency to dispense with the frontal, but this is contrary to the bulk of tradition. People normally clothe their tables at meal-time. Of the omission of the frontal Cyril Pocknee writes: "The altar symbolizes Christ in the midst of his church; and if his ministers are arrayed in costly vesture, why is the Table of the Lord to be treated in this"—that is, omitting the frontal—"manner?"[8] Vesting the altar in a frontal is not only a mark of reverence for the Lord whom the altar represents, but also serves to make the altar the focus of attention. The use of the frontal in the proper liturgical color also prevents the monotony of the altar appearing the same throughout the year. There may, of course, be circumstances in which one may feel free—or be compelled—to omit the frontal. This might happen when the altar is itself an extraordinary work of art or where its shape unfortunately makes impossible its vesting in the customary way.

---

8   Cyril E. Pocknee, *The Christian Altar* (London: A. R. Mowbray and Co., 1963), p. 14.

The altar must be vested in a fair linen cloth (*The Lutheran Liturgy*, p. 426). At the narrow ends of the altar the fair linen cloth should reach the floor.

A candle is placed at the back of the mensa at each end of the altar. If there is a gradine, the candles may be placed on the gradine. The candles are lighted at every service.

There should be a crucifix somewhere in the church in full view of the people.[9] The crucifix may be placed on the altar at the back of the mensa, or on the gradine, or it may be hung over the altar, or on the east wall of the church, or over the entrance to the chancel.

Flowers should not be placed on the mensa.[10]

If there is a gradine on the altar, the flowers may be placed on the gradine. A better custom is to place flowers in jars on the floor of the chancel. If the jars are low, they may be placed on low wooden stools so that the flowers may be seen.

There should be a credence table at the epistle side of the chancel. It should be vested in a clean linen cloth.

A lectern is not a necessity. The lessons may be read from the altar or at some convenient place within the chancel.

A crucifix may be hung near the pulpit as a reminder to pastor and people that Christ crucified is the heart of all that is preached from that place.

The Sacred Vessels

The sacred vessels are the chalice, paten, ciborium, pyx or bread-box, cruets and flagons. In places where the celebrant washes his hands at the offertory a lavabo bowl is also needed.

Reverence demands that we provide the best vessels we are able to afford for the distribution of the true body and blood of our Lord. The sacred vessels should be made of sterling silver. Silver vessels are customarily lined with gold. Vessels of good quality and honest workmanship should be obtained.

The chalice is used for the distribution of the consecrated wine. The foot of the chalice should be heavy enough that the chalice does not become top heavy when filled with wine.

The paten may be used for the distribution of the consecrated bread. Patens with a slight depression in the middle are probably preferable to perfectly smooth patens. When perfectly smooth patens are used the danger of dropping the hosts is greatly increased.

The ciborium may be used for the distribution of the consecrated bread, and is a fit receptacle for the consecrated hosts which remain after the celebration. The ciborium is really nothing more than a chalice with a cover.

The pyx or bread-box is customarily used to hold the bread before it is brought to the altar at the offertory. In parishes which have no ciborium, it may also be used for the distribution of the consecrated bread and as a fit receptacle for consecrated hosts which remain after the celebration.

---

9 Pictures of Lutheran churches show that since the sixteenth century the crucifix rather than the bare cross has been used in the overwhelming majority of Lutheran churches.

10 Flowers are obviously not of necessity. It is customary to dispense with flowers during Advent and Lent. Flowers may be used on the Third Sunday in Advent ("Gaudete Sunday") and on Laetare, the Fourth Sunday in Lent; these Sundays are in a sense regarded as anticipations of Christmas and Easter respectively. Flowers may be used on festivals during Advent and Lent, and at the holy communion on Maundy Thursday.

The cruets are customarily used to bring the wine (and water) to the altar at the offertory. The water cruet is also used for the washing of the celebrant's hands in parishes where that ceremony is customary. The cruets of wine and water are also used for the cleansing of the sacred vessels after the celebration. The cruets may be made of silver or glass. In parishes which have no flagon, a cruet may be used for the additional supply of consecrated wine when the chalice cannot safely hold all of the consecrated wine.

The Sacramental Linens

The sacramental linens are the corporal, pall, purificators, veil and burse.

"The Corporal, a square of very fine linen, is laid upon the center of the Fair Linen Cloth. Upon it the sacramental vessels are placed" (*The Lutheran Liturgy*, p. 426). The practice of placing some of the sacramental vessels (usually the chalice and cruets) on the gospel side of the altar ("wine" side) and some (usually the paten, pyx and ciborium) on the epistle side of the altar ("bread" side) is thus contrary to the rubrics.

"The pall, a small square of stiff material covered or lined with linen, is used to cover the chalice. It should be removed at the Consecration" (*The Lutheran Liturgy*, p. 426). A corporal folded into thirds and then folded into thirds again, so that it is a square nine layers of cloth thick, each side of the square one-third the length of a side of the unfolded corporal, meets the requirements of the rubric. It is from this folded corporal that the modern chalice pall developed. However, the folded corporal may prove inconvenient to handle.

"The Purificators, squares of heavy linen, are used to cleanse the rim of the chalice during the Administration" (*The Lutheran Liturgy*, p. 426).

"The Veil, made of silk or of the finest linen, is used to cover the sacramental vessels upon the altar or credence table. It is removed before the Preface and should be folded carefully and laid upon the altar and again placed over the sacramental vessels after the Administration at the Nunc Dimittis" (*The Lutheran Liturgy*, p. 426). The most common use is to make the veil of brocaded silk and to have it match the burse in color and material.

"When not in use on the altar, the sacramental linens should be properly folded and kept in the Burse, a square envelope made of strong cardboard, covered with silk or heavy linen" (*The Lutheran Liturgy*, p. 427). The most common use is to cover the burse with silk brocade. Where the resources of the parish permit, it should be in the color of the service in which it is used. This rubric does not apply to the parish's whole supply of sacramental linens. It is intended to provide that a set of sacramental linens (the corporal, the pall or folded corporal, and two purificators) be kept ready in a burse at all times, and that they be carried to and from the altar in the burse.

In parishes where the celebrant washes his hands at the offertory, a lavabo towel will also be necessary.

A houseling cloth (a cloth preferably of white linen of suitable length held at each end by a server directly in front of the communicants to prevent the consecrated bread and wine from falling to the ground through inadvertence) is not without good Lutheran warrant, and its use certainly makes for reverence.

The Liturgical Colors

The *General Rubrics* of *The Lutheran Liturgy* (pp. 425f) state:

The liturgical colors are white, red, green, violet and black...**White** is used from and with Vespers of [the] Eve of the Nativity [that is, Vespers on December 24] through the Epiphany Octave [that is, through the evening service on January 13]; on Maundy Thursday, when Communion is celebrated; from and with the Vespers of Easter through to [but not at] the Vespers of the Eve of Whitsunday; on the Feast of the Holy Trinity [beginning with Vespers on the Saturday before] and during its Octave; all the other Festivals of Christ, i.e. Presentation, Annunciation, Visitation, and Transfiguration; on the Day of St. Michael and All Angels; on the day of the Conversion of St. Paul; the day of the Nativity of St. John the Baptist; All Saints' Day; the Dedication of a Church and its Anniversary; on days of general or special thanksgiving; and on the festivals of saints not martyrs.

Red is used from and with Vespers on the Eve of Whitsunday through to [but not at] the Vespers on the Eve of Holy Trinity; the Festival of the Reformation and its Octave; and on days commemorating the death of martyrs [except when Holy Innocents falls during the week].

Green is used from and with Matins on January 14 to [but not] at Vespers of the Eve of Septuagesima, and from Matins on the Monday before the Second Sunday after Trinity through the post-Trinity season to [but not at] Vespers on the Eve of [the first Sunday in] Advent.

Violet is used from and with the Vespers on the Eve of [the first Sunday in] Advent to [but not at] the Vespers on the Eve of the Nativity, from and with Vespers on the Saturday before Septuagesima and throughout Pre-Lent and Lent, to [but not at] Vespers on the Eve of Easter; and for the Day of Humiliation. [It is also desirable to use] Violet...from Matins on the Monday after Rogation Sunday until, but not at, Vespers on the Wednesday before the Ascension Day, and on Holy Innocents' Day when it falls during the week.

Black [is used on] Good Friday only...The Solemnization of Holy Matrimony and the Order for the Burial of the Dead shall not affect the proper color for the Day or Season in use when these Services are held.

The *Lutheran Church Year Calendar, Lutheran Liturgy Edition*, published annually by the Ashby Company, Erie, Pennsylvania, accurately indicates the correct use of the liturgical colors.

The use of violet on Holy Innocents Day is not obligatory. Red may be used as on any feast of martyrs. The use of violet is connected with the custom of treating Holy Innocents' Day as a penitential feria; gloria in excelsis was not said and alleluia was omitted. Since our rite does not omit the alleluias and makes no provision for the omission of gloria in excelsis, it is probably desirable to use red vestments on this feast.

Vestments[11]

There is no consistent usage of vestments in the Lutheran churches. In fact, the use of vestments is not even prescribed by the rubrics of our authorized service books.

---

11 On the whole subject of vestments, see Arthur Carl Piepkorn, *The Survival of the Historic Vestments in the Lutheran Church After 1555*, 2nd Edition (St. Louis: Concordia Seminary, School for Graduate Studies, 1958).

However, on the basis of the history of the use of vestments in the church of the Augsburg Confession, it is possible to speak of approximately four types of vestment use.

First, there is the use of the black gown, with or without the bands or "Bäffchen."

Secondly, there is the use of the surplice. (The surplice in use at the close of the middle ages reached the ankles; its skirt was full as were its sleeves.)

Third, there is the use of the ankle-length surplice or alb, with a chasuble at celebrations of holy communion.

Fourth, there is the full historic use: At the holy eucharist, the celebrant wears the amice, alb, cincture, stole, maniple and chasuble.

At matins, vespers and the order of morning service (*The Lutheran Hymnal*, p. 5) the minister wears a surplice. At baptisms, confirmations, weddings, and ordinations he wears a stole over his surplice or alb; he may also wear a cope. A cope—but not a stole—may be worn over the surplice at matins and vespers. A cope may be worn over the surplice or alb on any occasion of great solemnity and in procession. If a minister only preaches at a service—and performs no other function—it is perfectly correct for him to wear a black gown.

Those assisting in a service vest according to the vestment use of the officiating minister.

If the minister wears a black gown, assisting clergymen wear black gowns.

If the minister wears a surplice, assisting clergymen and lay servers wear surplices.

If the full historic use is followed, assisting clergymen and lay servers are vested as follows. If two ministers assist the celebrant at the holy eucharist, the minister who reads the gospel and administers the chalice wears an amice, alb, cincture, stole (worn "deacon-wise," over the left shoulder, fastened under the right shoulder), maniple, and dalmatic. The minister who reads the epistle wears an amice, alb, cincture, maniple and tunicle. The dalmatic and tunicle may be omitted if they are not available. Other clergymen assisting in the distribution of holy communion may wear surplice and stole. The lay servers may wear an amice, alb, and cincture, or a surplice, or a rochet with or without sleeves. Ministers participating in the laying on of hands may—if the ordinator is wearing eucharistic vestments or surplice and stole (and cope)—wear surplice and stole. At all other services assisting clergymen and lay servers may wear a surplice, or an amice, alb, and cincture, or a rochet with or without sleeves.

Offertory Procession

In some places an offertory procession of the people has been restored. The people bring their offerings of money, bread, and wine to the front of the church. Where this ancient custom is restored, these directions may prove helpful: A server stands at the head of the main aisle of the church with a large alms bason. The people come forward by the main aisle, place their offerings in the alms bason and return to their seat by the side aisles. Last of all, one or more members of the congregation bring forward the bread and wine, and present the bread and wine to the celebrant, or to the subdeacon, or the server, depending on the type of service being held.

---

12 In many places the maniple is no longer used. The maniple apparently fell into disuse in the Lutheran church in the seventeenth century. Cf. Piepkorn, p. 119.

13 Our synod's *Worship Supplement* describes the offertory action in this way: "During the singing of the Offertory the Offerings shall be brought to the altar, together with the bread and wine to be used in the Sacrament. These are to be considered as tokens of the offering of self" (*Worship Supplement*, p. 51).

A simpler procedure is this: the bread, wine and money are brought forward by representatives of the people at the appropriate point in the service.

Where local customs permit, each communicant may, as he enters the church, place a host in the ciborium or bread box placed on a credence near the door of the church. This practice underscores the meaning of the offertory—that the elements of the eucharist are tokens of our life and work offered to Christ for this purpose. The practice also has the great practical advantage of eliminating the possibility of consecrating more hosts than needed for the communion on a given day. Where this practice is followed, it will be necessary to have two containers for the hosts—one containing the supply of hosts, the other into which the hosts will be placed by the communicants. For the sake of cleanliness a pair of tongs may be used for transferring the hosts from one container to the other.

It is possible to place an alms bason on a credence near the door of the church: when the people enter they will place their offering in the alms bason. At the offertory the alms bason is brought forward. This practice reduces the length of the service by eliminating the "collection." When the alms bason is placed on the credence near the door of the church together with the bread and wine, the meaning of the offering is again underscored. The gifts of money are an offering representing our very selves given up to our Lord.

The Greeting of Peace

In some places the greeting of peace has been restored. The *Worship Supplement* directs:

> If the ceremony of the Greeting of Peace is used, the celebrant shall begin the ceremony immediately after the Pax by extending both his hands to the right hand of his assistant, saying "Peace be with you." The assistant shall respond with the same words. The assistant shall then greet the others in the chancel and they may, if this is desired, extend the greeting to the congregation.

Anciently, the greeting of peace was given before the total eucharistic action of offertory–consecration–communion, rather than before a single element of the eucharistic action, i.e. the communion. "The Holy Eucharist I" of our synod's *Worship Supplement* prescribes that the greeting of peace be given immediately after the pax i.e. before the communion. This is also the current Roman Catholic usage. The more ancient use—giving the greeting of peace before the total eucharistic action of offertory-consecration-communion—is prescribed by "The Holy Eucharist II" and "The Holy Eucharist III" of the *Worship Supplement* (*Worship Supplement*, pp. 60, 64) and in "The Holy Communion" prepared by the Inter-Lutheran Commission on Worship. Exchanging the greeting of peace before the total eucharistic action seems to agree very well with the words of St. Matthew 5:23f. (These words are actually read before the greeting of peace in "The Holy Eucharist II", *Worship Supplement*, p. 60). When "The Order of the Holy Communion" (*The Lutheran Hymnal*, p. 15) is used, the greeting of peace may be exchanged after the pax domini or immediately before the offertory.

---

14 *Worship Supplement*, p. 52.

In exchanging the greeting of peace the rubric quoted above is helpful. "The Holy Eucharist III" speaks of extending one's hand(s) to his neighbor or placing hands on one another's shoulders. There is no need for rigid prescription in this matter. Spontaneity is desirable at this point in the liturgy. "It should be a moment of joyous informality." ("The Holy Communion," ILCW, p. xvi)

The simplest procedure for "passing" the greeting of peace throughout the congregation is this: At the appointed time, the worshipers simply start exchanging the greeting of peace with fellow worshipers around them. A more elaborate procedure is this. The celebrant greets his assistant, e.g. the deacon, at a solemn choral eucharist. The celebrant's assistant then greets the next assistant and so on. The last two persons receiving the greeting of peace in the chancel—probably two lay servers—go down to the nave. Beginning at the first pew on either side of the main aisle, each server greets the person nearest the main aisle on one side of the main aisle. That person then greets the person next to him and so on. After the servers have greeted the person nearest the main aisle in each pew on both sides of the aisle the servers return to the chancel.

Points of Courtesy

If a fellow-clergyman of the same communion is present it is only common courtesy to offer him a part in the service. Such parts would be preaching of the sermon, the reading of the liturgical lessons, and the benedicamus ("Bless we the Lord") at the end of the communion service. If he is a dignitary, he may be invited to pronounce the benediction. Unless there is a valid reason for refusing, it is courteous to accept such an invitation.

Visiting clergy will be careful to observe the customs of the parish. Especially during the present period of transition, it is advisable to inquire carefully about these matters.

Other Matters

"Silent prayer should be offered upon entering the church and after the Benediction" (*The Lutheran Hymnal*, p. 4). Kneelers help.

"All necessary announcements which are not part of the special intercessions and Thanksgivings should be made after the close of the service" (*The Lutheran Hymnal*, p. 4). "Notices to the Congregation, except in connection with requests for Intercession, ought not to be read during the Services" (*The Lutheran Liturgy*, p. 419). Such notices are best published in a parish bulletin or posted on a bulletin board in the narthex of the church. If a notice must be brought to the congregation's attention, it should be read after the service is over and after the worshipers have had an opportunity to offer their final private prayers.

It is a laudable custom, based upon a Scriptural injunction (1 Cor. 11:3–15) for women to wear an appropriate head covering in Church, especially at the time of divine service" (*The Lutheran Liturgy*, p. 427). "Appropriate head covering" includes a hat, a veil, a handkerchief, or a head-band. This custom is not only an ecclesiastical one, but also one that has been dictated by social usage.

"The Hymnal is intended for use not only in the church service and in the school, but it may serve profitably also for family and private devotions. The Prayers and the tables for Bible reading will be an aid for these uses" (*The Lutheran Hymnal*, p. 4).

---

15 One minister should preside throughout the entire celebration of the eucharist. The parts of the service that may be assigned to other ministers are the Old Testament lesson, the epistle, the gospel, the sermon, and the benedicamus. But sections of the service should not be distributed among several ministers, such as one minister leading the service of the word, and another leading the service of the sacrament.

Chapter Two: General Notes on the Celebration of the Sacrament of the Altar

The celebrant does not consecrate more hosts or more wine than he actually expects to require at any given celebration.[16] He should know quite accurately from the announcements of his intending communicants for how many to prepare; whether or not (and if so, how many) additional hosts should be provided beyond the number of communicants who have announced their intention of receiving the sacrament is something that he must learn by experience.

The celebrant may add a small quantity of water to the chalice after he has poured wine into the chalice. The quantity of water should never be great enough to dilute the wine in the chalice appreciably. One ancient prescription decreed that the quantity of water should not exceed one part of water in six parts of wine. It must be conceded that the "mixed chalice" was relatively rare in the church of the Augsburg Confession after the Reformation. At the same time the custom is very ancient. Whatever the occasion may have been for the institution of the holy communion in the cenacle, the Jewish ritual which our Lord followed calls for the mixed chalice. The primitive church retained the custom. There is no valid theological reason against its revival and if we wish to reduplicate the action of our Lord at the first celebration of holy communion as far as possible, we can properly include this feature as well. It is not forbidden by the Lutheran symbols. The reasons assigned for its discontinuance are not persuasive in the light of our present knowledge. On the other hand, a mixed chalice is obviously not essential to a valid celebration of the eucharist.

The words of institution are not only a rehearsal of the institution of the eucharist for the benefit of the congregation, but are also a consecration of the elements (Formula of Concord, Solid Declaration, VII, 75–82). The words of institution are, therefore, to be spoken over the bread and the wine and **under no circumstances are hosts or wine that have not been previously consecrated to be administered to communicants**. The *General Rubrics* of *The Lutheran Liturgy* (p. 421) reflect the doctrine of the church of the Augsburg Confession when the rubrics prescribe that "if the consecrated bread and wine be spent before all have communed, the celebrant shall consecrate more, saying aloud so much of the Words of Institution as pertains to the elements to be consecrated." In this rubric, the word "aloud" does not require a greater volume of voice than is necessary for those who are in the chancel to hear what the celebrant is saying.

If the celebrant is assisted by another person in the distribution, the ***celebrant***, as the responsible minister of the sacrament being celebrated, is the one who should administer the body of our Lord, while the assistant should administer the precious blood, or, as was anciently said, "confirm with the chalice."[17] This arrangement has undeniable pastoral advantages. In most cases the celebrant will

---

16 The rubrics of *The Lutheran Liturgy* prescribe: "In making ready the elements for the Holy Communion, so much of the bread and the wine shall be placed in the proper vessels as in the judgment of the Celebrant will be required for the Administration." (p. 421)

17 In the very earliest times, it appears that the deacons, who were full-time assistants to the bishop, distributed both the body and blood of our Lord. It was not long, however, before the celebrant assumed the responsibility of administering the host and the assisting deacon administered the chalice.

be the pastor of the parish, that is, the individual who has the potestas jurisdictionis in the parish (Apology of the Augsburg Confession XXVIII, 12–14). While it is happily very rare that a pastor must repel a person from the altar, this may happen on occasion. In such a case the embarrassment will be much greater if the assistant has already communicated the individual in question with our Lord's body.[18]

While Lutheran pastors will be careful to instruct their people not to adore the bread and wine as such, they will also be careful to instruct their communicants that "no one, unless he be an Arian heretic, can and will deny that Christ himself, true God and man, who is truly and essentially present in the holy communion in the right celebration thereof should be adored in spirit and truth" (Formula of Concord, Solid Declaration, VII, 126).

It will greatly accelerate the distribution if communicants are instructed to return to their respective pews after receiving the chalice, without waiting for the entire rail to be dismissed. It is courteous to wait until the next communicant has received the chalice. As each communicant leaves his place at the rail, another can take his place, and the clergymen distributing the sacrament will always know that the communicant kneeling before them has not as yet received the holy communion. If this procedure is followed, the number of communicants kneeling at one time is almost immaterial; it is possible, for instance, to dispense with gates, bars and kneelers between the two rails and thereby to eliminate the distraction which opening and closing the gates, putting bars and kneelers in place, and removing them again afterwards invariably involve. The time required to communicate a congregation in this way is only that required for the actual administration plus the time needed to replenish supplies of hosts and wine in the paten (or ciborium) and chalice.

The clergyman who administers the host should, if he uses a paten, put no more hosts on the paten than he will need to communicate one group of communicants at the rail. The danger of dropping a host inadvertently is greatly increased if he has more than this number on the paten. It is possible to leave a small supply of hosts on the outspread corporal.

It should not be necessary to indicate to the communicants when they are to kneel if the procedure described above is followed or if the communicants are instructed to kneel, as is proper, immediately upon arriving at their respective places before the rail. In many parishes it is customary for the communicant to bow moderately before kneeling to receive the host, and to bow moderately again after having been dismissed or after having received the cup. This act of reverence is not a courtesy paid to the officiating clergymen and they should not acknowledge it by returning the bow!

The communicants should be instructed to hold their heads erect, to part their lips, and to place the tip of the tongue against the lower lip. In administering the hosts, the clergyman should hold the paten under the host until he has placed it between the lips of the communicant. When there are enough communicants to fill several rails, it is desirable to use a ciborium or a second chalice to administer the hosts.

---

18   If an individual has been communicated with the body of the Lord under no circumstances should the chalice be withheld. That is, even though an individual should actually be repelled from the altar, if he has, through inadvertence or ignorance, been communicated with the host, he should also be given to drink of the chalice. Cf. C. F. W. Walther, *Amerikanisch-Lutherische Pastoral-theologie* (St. Louis: Concordia Publishing House 1885), p. 197.

The person administering the chalice should be careful that it is not too full. He should not needlessly increase the danger of spilling. The minister may hold the chalice by the knop in his left hand, with a folded purificator laid over his right hand. The right hand, with the purificator laid over it, is held against the bowl of the chalice. After each communicant receives the consecrated wine, the celebrant wipes the place on the chalice from which the communicant drank and turns the chalice. Communicants may be instructed to take hold of the foot of the chalice as they receive it. This procedure is almost a necessity when holy communion is distributed to communicants who are standing.

Paper tissues should not be used to cleanse the rim of the chalice. If the number of communicants is large, it will be necessary to have an ample supply of purificators available on the altar. A single purificator should not be used too frequently. Used purificators should be folded neatly in such a way that the portions used for cleansing the rim of the chalice are each protected by a clean layer of cloth, both for the sake of appearance and, if this is a problem, to prevent the attraction of insects. Used purificators should be rinsed in clear water several times before they are laundered. The same principle applies to other items of sacramental linen, such as corporals and palls. The water in which they are rinsed should be poured into the sacrarium or on the ground.

If the communicants are dismissed after each group at the altar rail has been communicated, the minister may make the sign of the cross as he says, "Depart in peace."

If holy communion is received in the standing position, the ministers may pass before the people with the bread and cup or the ministers may stand in one place—e.g. at the head of the main aisle or at the altar step—and let the people pass before them, the people first receiving the host from the celebrant, then receiving the cup from the assisting minister who stands at the celebrant's right. Where large numbers of communicants present themselves before the altar every Lord's Day, it may be useful to appoint a second assistant to stand at the celebrant's left with a second chalice. Each communicant would then receive the host from the celebrant and then step to the right or left to receive the cup from an assisting minister.

The *General Rubrics* of *The Lutheran Liturgy* (p. 421) say:

> when the Service has been completed, the celebrant or a deacon shall remove the sacramental vessels from the altar to the sacristy and dispose of that part of the bread and wine which remains as follows: He shall carefully remove the bread from the paten and ciborium to a fit receptacle, there to be kept against the next Communion. He shall pour what remains of the consecrated wine into the piscina or upon the ground at a proper and convenient place outside the church.

As the responsible "steward of the mysteries of God" the celebrant should carry out these prescriptions himself and should not delegate them to a deacon. The rubrics make clear that the consecrated hosts are not to be mixed with unconsecrated hosts, but are to be carefully segregated. The rubrics do not, however, prescribe the nature of the "fit receptacle." Tradition would suggest the use of a ciborium or pyx. It is the celebrant's responsibility to insure that these hosts are the first to be distributed at the next communion. The consecrated wine is to be poured into the sacrarium or piscina.[19] If a large quantity of consecrated wine remains in the cruets or flagons it may be kept in a decent vessel, e.g. a glass cruet, until the next communion. The consecrated elements should be kept under lock and key to avoid superstition and profanation. An aumbry in the sacristy of the church would provide a fit place for consecrated elements kept for the next communion. Consecrated elements so kept may well be used for the communion of the sick.

If the celebration of holy communion has taken place in an inadequately equipped chapel or in a private house, the celebrant, following an ancient tradition in the church of the Augsburg Confession, should reverently consume what remains of the consecrated bread and wine. If the amount is excessive he may ask for the assistance of those who received at the preceding celebration in consuming the remaining consecrated bread and wine.

After the consecrated hosts have been removed to a fit receptacle or consumed, and the consecrated wine has been poured into the piscina or upon the ground or has been consumed, the celebrant proceeds with the cleansing of the sacred vessels. Traditionally, this was done in the following way. After the celebrant has removed the hosts from the paten, he holds the paten over the chalice with his left hand and with the thumb and forefinger of his right hand he rubs the paten from top to bottom so that any fragments which have adhered to the paten fall into the chalice. He then pours the contents of the chalice into the sacrarium. Next, a server pours a small quantity of wine into the chalice, the celebrant moves the wine gently around in the chalice, and pours it into the sacrarium. Then the celebrant holds his thumbs and forefingers over the bowl of the chalice and the server pours a small quantity first of wine and then of water over the celebrant's thumbs and forefingers while the celebrant rubs his thumbs and forefingers together. Then the celebrant pours the contents of the chalice into the sacrarium and carefully dries the chalice, inside and out, with a purificator. If a ciborium was used to communicate the people, the celebrant, immediately after cleansing the paten, will also cleanse the ciborium over the chalice in the same way in which he cleansed the paten. If need be, he may cleanse the ciborium in the same way in which he has been directed to cleanse the chalice. If wine was consecrated in a cruet or flagon, the cruet or flagon should also be cleansed in the same way in which the celebrant cleansed the chalice. Wherever there is no piscina or sacrarium, the liquid contents will in all cases be consumed or poured on the ground.[20]

---

19 There should be a sacrarium in the sacristy as well as in the chancel. In either case it is connected with a drainpipe to the earth, under no circumstances to the common sewer. In the event there is no sacrarium in the church, "a proper and convenient place outside the Church" should be prepared. This should be at the side of the building, appropriately protected from animals. The simplest arrangement is to dig a pit at least 12 inches by 12 inches and at least 18 to 24 inches deep. The bottom should be of gravel, the top surface of small crushed stone (in order to discourage the growth of grass and weeds). After what remains of the consecrated wine has been poured into the sacrarium or on the ground, a sufficient quantity of clear water should be poured in afterwards to rinse the consecrated wine down so that insects are not attracted.

20 On the history of the disposition of the consecrated elements, the ceremonial cleansing of the vessels, and the like, see William Lockton, *The Treatment of the Remains at the Eucharist after Holy Communion and the Time of the Ablutions* (Cambridge: University Press, 1920). See also Edward Frederick Peters, *The Origin and Meaning of the Axiom: "Nothing Has the Character of a Sacrament Outside of the use,"* in Sixteenth-Century and Seventeenth-Century Lutheran Theology, Unpublished Doctor's Thesis, Concordia Seminary, St. Louis, pp. 188ff, 316ff, 328f, 418, 504ff, and his article on that subject in *Concordia Theological Monthly*, XLII, 10 (Nov. 1971), 643-52. Martin Luther held that the consecrated hosts and wine should be consumed. Cf. Walther, pp. 189f. See also Arthur Carl Piepkorn, "Digests of Recent American and European Lutheran Discussions of the Sacrament of the Altar," *Lutherans and Catholics in Dialogue III The Eucharist as Sacrifice*, published jointly by Representatives of the U.S.A. National Committee of the Lutheran World Federation and the Bishops' Committee for Ecumenical and Interreligious Affairs, pp. 125–147.

Chapter Three: The Propers

The Lutheran Liturgy directs:

"The Propria, or Propers (as distinguished from the fixed portions of the Service, called the Ordinary), that is, the Introit, the Collect, [the Old Testament Lesson] the Epistle, the Gradual, and the Gospel for the Day shall be used throughout the week following, except on those Days for which other appointments are made."[21]

This rubric refers to the propers of any given Sunday. If a Sunday is displaced by a festival which has no octave, the propers for the festival are used on the Sunday itself (the collect for the Sunday is said after the collect for the festival), but the propers of the Sunday are used during the week following except on those days for which other appointments are made.

Our rite has no directions indicating which Sundays are displaced by festivals and which Sundays take precedence over any festivals occurring on them. The table of precedence in the *Service Book and Hymnal* is here cited as a guide.

Precedence of Festivals and Days

I. The following days shall be observed invariably as appointed in the Calendar. A Day or Festival concurring with any of these here noted may be observed the first open day thereafter.

Greater Festivals and Days

The Sundays of Advent	Easter Day and the Day following[22]
The Nativity	The Sundays after Easter
The Circumcision	The Ascension and the Sunday following
The Epiphany	Pentecost and the Day following
Septuagesima	Trinity Sunday
Sexagesima	Reformation Day
Quinquagesima	All Saints' Day
Ash Wednesday	
The Sundays in Lent	
The Days of Holy Week	

II. When a Lesser Festival falls on a Sunday not noted in Rubric I, the Introit, Collect, Epistle, Gradual and Gospel for the Festival shall be used, and the Collect for the Sunday shall be said after the Collect for the Day.

---

21 *The Lutheran Liturgy*, p. 417.
22 Traditionally, every day in Easter week and Pentecost week was regarded as having the dignity of the Lord's Day and no feasts were observed on any day in either of these weeks. For example, if Saint Mark's Day fell within the week after Easter, it was transferred to the next open day, i.e. the Monday after Quasimodogeniti. This ancient custom has much to commend it since it emphasizes the supreme importance of Easter and Pentecost.

Example of Rubric I: Should Septuagesima Sunday fall on January 25, the Conversion of Saint Paul, the propers of Septuagesima Sunday would be used, and the Conversion of Saint Paul would be observed on Monday, January 26. Example of Rubric II: Should the ninth Sunday after Trinity fall on July 22, Saint Mary Magdalene's Day, the propers of Saint Mary Magdalene's Day would be used on Sunday, July 22, and the collect for the ninth Sunday after Trinity would be prayed after the collect for Saint Mary Magdalene's Day. During the week following, however, the propers of the ninth Sunday after Trinity would be used, except on July 25, Saint James the Elder's Day, when the propers for Saint James the Elder's Day would be used.

When a festival occurs during the week, the collect *of the Preceding Sunday* is **omitted** unless that Sunday is a feast with an "octave." (For example, if the fifth Sunday after Trinity falls on June 28, Saint Peter and Saint Paul the Apostles' Day would be celebrated on Monday, June 29. The propers for Saint Peter and Saint Paul the Apostles' Day would be used on Monday, June 29, and the collect for the fifth Sunday after Trinity would not be said.)

Our rite does not provide instructions for the observance of the "octave" of greater festivals, that is, the seven days following a festival. Our rite mentions the Epiphany octave, the octave of the Holy Trinity, and the octave of Reformation Day, although—apart from specifying the color use—it gives no instructions indicating how they are to be observed. Since our rite assigns octaves to Epiphany, Trinity Sunday, and Reformation Day, we may assume that festivals of greater dignity—Christmas, Easter, and Pentecost—also have octaves.

The following directions for the observance of octaves are based on tradition. During an octave, the propers of the festival are used, *except* on a Sunday or other festival occurring during the octave. On such a Sunday or other festival occurring during the octave, the propers are those of the Sunday or other festival, and the collect of the festival in the octave of which the Sunday or other festival occurs is said after the collect for the Sunday or other festival. (For example, on Saint Stephen's Day, the propers of Saint Stephen's Day are used, but the collect for Christmas Day is said after the collect for Saint Stephen's Day. Should there be any more days until the following Sunday after the conclusion of an octave, the propers of the preceding Sunday are resumed. For example, in 1971 the Epiphany of our Lord occurs on Wednesday, January 6. On January 6, 7, 8, 9, 11, 12 and 13 the propers of the Epiphany of our Lord are used. On Sunday, January 10, the propers of the first Sunday after the Epiphany are used, and the collect for the Epiphany of our Lord is said

after the collect for the first Sunday after the Epiphany. On January 14, 15 and 16, the propers of the first Sunday after the Epiphany are used.)

Our rite prescribes that "the Collect for Ash Wednesday is said in every Lenten Service after the Collect for the Day" (*The Lutheran Liturgy*, p. 418). This means that on every day of Lent from Ash Wednesday through Holy Saturday the collect for Ash Wednesday is said after the collect for the day. (For example, on the second Sunday in Lent, the collect for Ash Wednesday is said after the collect for the second Sunday in Lent. If Saint Matthias' Day occurs during Lent, the collect for Ash Wednesday is said after the collect for Saint Matthias' Day. On Tuesday in holy week, the collect for Ash Wednesday is said after the collect for Tuesday in holy week.)

In general, it is best to consult the *Lutheran Church Year Calendar*, *The Lutheran Liturgy* Edition, published annually by the Ashby Company, Erie, Pennsylvania. The proper observance of the church year is there carefully noted.

Further instructions on the use of the propers will be found in the following chapter.

Chapter Four:
The Rite of the Order of the Holy Communion[23]

The Lutheran Liturgy prescribes: "If the Confessional Service immediately precedes the Communion Service, the latter shall begin with the Introit" (p. 420). (See below under "The Confession of Sins"). Note that this rubric supersedes the second of the *General Rubrics* of *The Lutheran Hymnal* (p. 4), which provided that the Trinitarian invocation should precede the introit in the case envisioned. The rubric as found in *The Lutheran Liturgy* should be followed. For the rubric "When the Service begins with the Introit, the Officiant shall proceed to the altar at once" (*The Lutheran Liturgy*, p. 419) clearly indicates that the opening hymn, which is obligatory when the service begins with the preparatory rite, is to be omitted when the service begins with the Introit.

The Opening Hymn

The Commission on Worship now authorizes the omission of the opening hymn, even when the service begins with the preparatory service.

Normally there should be no procession of the choir into the church before the service and out of the church after the service. The choir may enter the church during the organ prelude, or, during Advent and Lent—when the organ is traditionally used only to support the singing of the choir and congregation—in silence. The choir likewise leaves the church during the organ postlude or, during Advent and Lent, in silence. Processions should be reserved for special occasions, when the procession helps to highlight the extraordinary character of the observance. (See Chapter Eight, Processions.)

Note the rubric of *The Lutheran Liturgy* (p. 419): "Unless otherwise ordered in a congregation, public Baptism may be administered after the Opening Hymn, in which case the Opening Hymn may well be a Baptismal Hymn."

The Confession of Sins

The text of the confession of sins should be spoken throughout. If, however, the congregation chants its responses, the minister will chant the versicles and prayers of the preparatory service, in compliance with the rubrics (*The Lutheran Liturgy*, p. 419). *The Music for the Liturgy* says: "The music for the chanting of the Confession of Sins is given for the convenience of those who desire to chant those parts; but this practice is not to be considered as being recommended by our Committee" (p. 6).

It is desirable to **separate** the confession of sins from the eucharist proper. There are genuine problems involved in pronouncing absolution over an entire congregation. Unbaptized persons may be present. But confession and holy absolution, because they are a return to baptism, are obviously

---

[23] *The Lutheran Liturgy* states: "Whenever the Holy Communion is celebrated in a Church Service, the Order of the Holy Communion shall be used in its entirety" (*The Lutheran Liturgy*, p. 417). At conference services, weddings, small communions in church, evening communion services, and on similar occasions, there is thus no authority for beginning the service with the preface, combining parts of vespers (or matins) with parts of the order for holy communion, or omitting any part of the service that the rubrics make obligatory ("shall").

meant only for those who have been baptized. There is also the possibility that persons may be present who, although they have been baptized, should not be absolved, for example, excommunicated persons. The ideal solution to such problems is a return to the regular use of private confession and absolution. (See the Augsburg Confession XI, XXV 13; Apology of the Augsburg Confession XI). A partial solution, where the number of worshippers is not large, is to pronounce individual absolution at the altar rail. If this practice is followed, the minister says the absolution through the words, "announce the grace of God unto all of you." At that point the minister pauses and the people come forward to the altar rail, just as they would for holy communion. The minister then walks along the rail. He places both hands on the head of each penitent and says: "In the stead and by the command of my Lord Jesus Christ, I forgive you all your sins in the name of the Father … Holy Ghost." At the words, "and of the Son," he makes the sign of the cross with his left hand still resting on the head of the penitent.

The desirability of separating the confession of sins from the service proper has been recognized in a number of ways in our authorized service books. "Since the Preparation is not a part of the Service proper, it is preferable that the Officiant and the Congregation speak the entire Preparatory Service" (*The Lutheran Liturgy*, p. 419). "Good usage permits speaking the Preparatory Service" (*The Lutheran Hymnal*, p. 4). "If the Confessional Service immediately precedes the Communion Service, the latter shall begin with the Introit" (*The Lutheran Liturgy*, p. 420). "For the Invocation and the Preparatory Service, the Officiant may stand at the foot of the altar, advancing to the altar at the Introit" (*The Lutheran Liturgy*, p. 419). The thrust of all of these rubrics is that it is desirable to distinguish the confession of sins as an action preparatory to the service of holy communion itself.

If the confession of sins is separated from the eucharistic liturgy, the minister can be certain that only those persons are present who actually want to receive absolution. If the confession of sins is separated from the service proper, the minister will come into the church in advance of the hour appointed for the celebration of the eucharist, conduct the confession of sins, and return to the sacristy. At the hour appointed for the service, the introit is sung, the minister comes into the church, and goes to the altar.

The Introit

The introit consists of antiphon, psalm-verse, gloria patri (unless omitted—see below), and antiphon repeated.[24] "The Antiphon, which announced the keynote of the Introit, shall be repeated after the Gloria Patri" (*The Lutheran Liturgy*, p. 420). There is no exception to this rule. On a day of humiliation and prayer (*The Lutheran Liturgy*, p. 184) the gloria patri is omitted. Anciently, the gloria patri was omitted from the introit from the first Sunday in Passiontide (i.e. Judica, the Fifth Sunday in Lent) until (but not at) the first celebration of the eucharist in memory of our

---

24   The gloria patri is not an independent element of the service; it is part of the psalm of the introit and is included on the principle that an Old Testament psalm becomes a New Testament hymn by adding the gloria patri. The gloria patri is not a ***primitive*** element in Christian worship. Even after it was introduced into the liturgy in general, it was never added to the eucharistic liturgy for passiontide, i.e. the fifth Sunday in Lent through holy Saturday, and was never added to matins and vespers of Maundy Thursday, Good Friday, and Holy Saturday. "This is not a deliberate omission of a feature considered to be too festal for such a day; it is simply that the solemnity of this day has resisted what was felt to be an innovation." (E. C. R. Lamburn, *Behind Rite and Ceremony* [London: W. Knott and Son Limited, 1961], 5)

Lord's resurrection. (See Paul Bunjes, *The Service Propers Noted, Accompaniment Edition*, Part I [St. Louis: Concordia Publishing House, 1960], 71ff. This practice is thus approved by the Commission on Worship.)[25]

The *General Rubrics* of *The Lutheran Hymnal* say: "Instead of the Introit, a psalm may be used" (p. 4). If a psalm is substituted for the introit, it should always be the psalm of which the introit is an abbreviation. Usually the psalm can be identified by referring to the psalm-verse, which is normally the first verse of the psalm. Thus the proper introit psalm for the fourth Sunday in Advent (Rorate) would be psalm 19 (Coeli enarrant) and the proper introit psalm for Christmas Day would be psalm 98 (Cantate Domino). (*The Lutheran Church Year Calendar*, *The Lutheran Liturgy* Edition, notes all of the proper introit psalms on the reverse side of the calendar sheet for each month.) Sometimes the antiphon itself is the first verse(s) of the psalm: a case in point is the twelfth Sunday after Trinity, where the antiphon of the introit consists of verses 1 and 2a of psalm 70 (Deus in adjutorium) and the psalm verse is verse 2b, so that psalm 70 would be the proper psalm to substitute for the introit on that day. In this case verses 1 and 2a would be repeated after the gloria patri: these verses are the antiphon. When a psalm is substituted for the introit, the antiphon should be sung at least before the first verse of the psalm and after the gloria patri (or when the gloria patri is omitted, as noted above, after the last verse of the psalm). On occasions of solemnity, and in order to lengthen a short psalm adequately, the antiphon may be sung after each verse of the psalm as well as after the gloria patri. If a long psalm is substituted for the introit, only as many verses as circumstances call for need be sung. The psalm may end at any point that the sense of the text permits, whereupon the gloria patri is sung and the antiphon is repeated.

"The Introit for the Day, including the Gloria Patri, should be either sung or spoken throughout" (*The Lutheran Liturgy*, p. 420). There is, therefore, no authority for the common practice of the minister reading the antiphon and psalm-verse and the people singing the gloria patri. If the minister reads the antiphon and psalm-verse, the people say the gloria patri and may join in reading the repetition of the antiphon. If the minister sings the antiphon and psalm-verse, the people sing the gloria patri and may join in singing the repetition of the antiphon. "The Introit for the Day with the Gloria Patri should be sung by the Choir. If a Choir is not available, the Introit may be said or chanted by the Officiant; in this case the Gloria Patri may be said or chanted by the Congregation." (*The Lutheran Liturgy*, pp. 419f.)

The Kyrie

The Lutheran Liturgy (p. 420) directs: "The Kyrie shall be said or sung by the Congregation." This implies that the celebrant will not intone the kyrie, i.e. that he will not intone the first line of the kyrie, "Lord, have mercy upon us," the people then responding by singing the entire kyrie, "Lord, have mercy upon us; Christ, have mercy upon us; Lord, have mercy upon us." *The Lutheran Liturgy* provides further: "A nine-fold, but not a four-fold or six-fold (the Officiant speaking the first line; the Officiant speaking each line) Kyrie may be substituted for the threefold Kyrie. In place of the English text, the Greek Kyrie eleison, Christe eleison, Kyrie eleison, may be used in either a threefold or ninefold form."[26]

---

25 Our present introits are simply remnants of psalms sung by the choir and clergy on their way to the altar.
26 In the ninefold form, the kyrie reads: "Kyrie eleison, Kyrie eleison, Kyrie eleison. Christe eleison, Christi eleison, Christe eleison. Kyrie eleison, Kyrie eleison, Kyrie eleison"—or the English equivalent.

The Gloria in Excelsis
The Lutheran Liturgy (p. 420) directs:

"The Gloria in Excelsis shall be used on all Feast and Festival Days (even when the Holy Communion is not celebrated); at other times a versified form of the Gloria in Excelsis (Hymns 237, 238 in *The Lutheran Hymnal*) or another hymn of praise may be used. The Gloria in Excelsis shall also be used in all services of worship in which the Administration of Holy Communion takes place, except that in that case it may be omitted during the Seasons of Advent, Pre-Lent and Lent."

At celebrations of the holy communion there is no authority for substituting either a metrical version of the gloria in excelsis or another hymn of praise for the gloria in excelsis. Although the gloria in excelsis should be omitted during Advent, Pre-Lent, and Lent, it is used on festivals occurring during those seasons (Saint Andrew's Day, Saint Thomas' Day, the Conversion of Saint Paul, the Presentation of our Lord, Saint Matthias' Day, and the Annunciation of the Blessed Virgin Mary) and on Maundy Thursday.[27]

The Salutation
If the service is fully choral, the celebrant chants the salutation and the congregation chants the response.

The Collect for the Day
If the service is fully choral, the celebrant chants the collect; if not, he speaks it. The collect for the day printed out in *The Lutheran Liturgy* and *The Lutheran Hymnal* must be said; it is not permissible to substitute another or a collect of one's own composition for the appointed collect for the day.[28] The rubrics for the termination of the collects are found in *The Lutheran Liturgy*, p. 418. The termination of each collect is accurately printed out in full in *The Lutheran Liturgy*.

The congregation's "Amen" at the end of the collect is sung if the celebrant has chanted the collect; it is spoken if he has spoken the collect.

---

27 The Maundy Thursday eucharist commemorates the institution of the sacrament of the altar. There is a close connection between the eucharist and the incarnation, since it is the incarnate Christ who is present in the holy sacrament. With the consecrated bread we eat the "body...born of Mary" (Hymn 313, stanza 1). For these reasons the "hymn of the angels" (Luke 2:14) is sung at the Maundy Thursday eucharist.

28 When a eucharistic liturgy in contemporary English is used, e.g. "The Holy Eucharist I" of the *Worship Supplement*, some pastors may feel compelled to translate the collect for the day into contemporary English. (This is a most difficult task—if due attention is given both to the sense of the original Latin text and to the nature of the English language.) If the minister wishes to do this, he should consult the original Latin text of the collect. See, for example, Luther D. Reed, *The Lutheran Liturgy*, Revised edition (Philadelphia: Muhlenberg Press, 1959), 465–575).

The Old Testament Lesson

The Lutheran Liturgy directs: "Before the Epistle for the Day an appointed lesson from the Old Testament (cf. pp. 438, 439) may be read, but the Epistle for the Day and the Gospel for the Day shall always be read" (*The Lutheran Liturgy*, p. 420). The table of Old Testament Lessons also appears on pp. 159f of *The Lutheran Hymnal*. The "Report of the Commission on Worship" to the 1969 convention of The Lutheran Church-Missouri Synod states:

"The lectionaries of the *Service Book and Hymnal*—both in the RSV and in the AV—have been authorized by the commission for use as alternates to *The Lutheran Lectionary* (published by Concordia Publishing House) until such time as an I(inter) L(utheran) C(ommission on) W(orship) Lectionary becomes available."[29]

This statement of the Commission on Worship therefore authorizes the use not only of the Old Testament lesson but also of the epistle and gospel of the lectionary of the *Service Book and Hymnal*.

The Old Testament lesson is announced in this way: "The Old Testament lesson is written in the _____ chapter of _____ beginning at the _____ verse." The reading of the liturgical lessons at the eucharist is not the place for taking up isagogical questions. The person who reads the lessons should, therefore, carefully adhere to the title of the book of the Bible from which the lesson is taken, exactly as the title is given in the version of the Bible from which he is reading. It should also be noted that this is not the place to comment on the lesson. The place for commentary on the lesson is the sermon. If the minister feels that more explanation is needed than can be given in the sermon, he may enter the church before the service begins and briefly comment on the propers for the day, or he may print comments on the propers in the parish bulletin.

If the lesson is chanted, it is not necessary to indicate the end. If it is read, the lesson is concluded with the words: "Here endeth the lesson."

The person who reads the Old Testament lesson—and any lesson in the church service—should not attempt to establish eye contact with the congregation. He should rather keep his eyes on the book as a visible sign that he is ***reading*** the words of another.

The Epistle

The epistle is announced with the prescribed formula of our authorized service books: "The Epistle for _____ is written in the _____ chapter of _____ beginning at the _____ verse." The epistle is concluded with the words: "Here endeth the epistle."

The chanting of the lessons of the service has the authority of long precedent in the church of the Augsburg Confession, and for generations after the Reformation the chanting of the epistle and gospel was one of the characteristic differences between the Lutheran and the Reformed communions.[30]

It may be noted that it was anciently customary to begin the reading of the epistle with the salutation, "Brethren."

---

29 *The Edifying Word, Convention Workbook (Reports and Overtures) 48th Regular Convention, The Lutheran Church—Missouri Synod*, Denver, Colorado, July 11–18, p. 71.
30 See the excellent discussion of the rationale for chanting the lessons in Peter Brunner, *Worship in the Name of Jesus*, translated by Martin H. Bertram (St. Louis: Concordia Publishing House, 1968), 270.

The Gradual[31]

"The Gradual for the Day or the Sentence for the Season should be sung by the Choir. If a choir is not available, the Officiant may say the Gradual or the Sentence for the Season; or the Congregation may simply sing the Hallelujah after the Epistle has been read. Hallelujah is not sung during Pre-Lent and Lent" (*The Lutheran Liturgy*, p. 420). This rubric does not preclude the chanting of the gradual by a solo voice or by the celebrant; the gradual may also be sung by the congregation to a simple musical setting. In any case, since the gradual is psalmody, it is desirable that it be sung rather than spoken.

"If the Gradual be read by the Minister, the Hallelujah may be said or chanted by the Congregation" during those parts of the church year during which alleluia is properly sung, that is, from Easter Day through the week of the last Sunday after the Epiphany (*The Lutheran Liturgy*, p. 14). The congregation may sing either the single alleluia or the triple alleluia. It is not necessary for the congregation to respond to the gradual, either with the alleluia or with one of the sentences. The alleluia by the congregation should probably be omitted.

Sentences are provided for all of the seasons of the church year except for the three Sundays of Pre-Lent.

---

31 It should be noted that the graduals are incorrectly printed in our Hymnal and Liturgy. In our rite, the term "gradual" is a generic one to designate the psalmody between the epistle and gospel. In general, this psalmody consists of two parts; originally the first part was sung between the Old Testament lesson and the epistle, the second part between the epistle and gospel. When the number of lessons was conventionally reduced to two, the two separate settings were combined into one. Through most of the church year, the gradual consists of (1) **the gradual in the strict sense of the word** (usually two psalm verses) and (2) **the alleluia verse.**
1. Behold, O God, our Shield: and look upon Thy servants. V. O Lord God of hosts: hear our prayer.
2. Alleluia. Alleluia. V. The king shall joy in Thy strength, O Lord: and in Thy salvation, how greatly shall he rejoice! Alleluia. (Gradual for the fifth Sunday after Trinity)
Note that the double alleluia does not belong to the verse after which it is printed in our Hymnal and Liturgy, but to the verse which follows. Account of this should be taken in the musical settings that are used. To differentiate the two parts, it is appropriate to use two different settings, even if they are simply psalm tones. In this case the first ends with the last word prior to the double alleluia and the second begins with the double alleluia. When the gradual is merely read, account may be taken of the historic origin of the two parts of the gradual by pausing before the double alleluia and the remainder of the gradual in such a way that the double alleluia is clearly tied up with the alleluia verse. In Eastertide the gradual **in the strict sense** is replaced by another alleluia verse.
3. Alleluia. Alleluia. V. Then was the Lord Jesus known of the disciples in the breaking of bread. Alleluia.
4. Alleluia. V. I am the Good Shepherd: and know my sheep and am known of mine. Alleluia. (For Misericordias Domini)

During the period when the alleluia is not used in the service, the alleluia verse is replaced by what is called the tract; examples of this will be found in the propers for the Sundays and various ferias (non-festival weekdays) for Pre-Lent and Lent.
1. Let the nations know that Thy name is Jehovah: Thou alone art the Most High over all the earth. V. O my God, make them like a wheel and like chaff before the wind.
2. Tract. Thou, O Lord, hast made the earth to tremble and hast broken it. V. Heal the breaches thereof, for it shaketh. V. That Thy beloved may be delivered, save with Thy right hand. (For Sexagesima)
The phenomenon also appears, even though the term is not used, in the propers for the day of humiliation and prayer. In the propers for the Presentation of our Lord and the Purification of the Blessed Virgin Mary, provision is made for an alleluia verse if the festival is kept before Septuagesima Sunday and for a tract if the festival is kept after Septuagesima Sunday. This clearly was the intention in connection with the propers of the Annunciation as well, although apparently through an editorial error, the necessary rubric has been omitted. (During Lent the first six lines of the gradual for the Annunciation as printed in the Hymnal are used; during Eastertide the first two and the last four lines of the gradual as printed in the Hymnal are employed.)

While there is no rubrical authority in our rite for doing so, the celebrant may, in view of the origin of the gradual and alleluia verse or tract, feel justified in splitting the gradual proper from the alleluia verse or tract, and thus read the gradual proper before the epistle, and the alleluia verse or tract before the gospel. This, of course, is done only if an Old Testament lesson is read before the epistle.

They represent a kind of abbreviated seasonal gradual. Even when no choir is available, it is preferable to use the gradual rather than the seasonal sentence.

Traditionally a sequence hymn was sung after the gradual psalmody.[32] The sequence hymn is always seasonal; conceivably another, equally seasonal, hymn, even though not written as a sequence hymn, might be substituted. "On Trinity Sunday, the Athanasian Creed may be used after the Gradual, in lieu of a Sequence" (*The Lutheran Liturgy*, p. 421). If the Athanasian Creed is used as a sequence in the service of Trinity Sunday, there is no authority for omitting the Nicene Creed after the gospel.

The Holy Gospel

If the celebrant reads the gospel, he may, before reading it, pause at the center of the altar and say silently the traditional prayers:

> Cleanse my heart and my lips, almighty God, who didst cleanse the lips of the prophet Isaiah with a live coal, and do thou, of thy great mercy, vouchsafe so to purify me that I may worthily declare thy holy gospel; through Jesus Christ, our Lord. Amen.
> Command, O Lord, thy blessing to descend upon me. The Lord be in my heart and on my lips, that I may worthily and competently proclaim his holy gospel, in the name of the Father and of the Son and of the Holy Ghost. Amen.

If there is another ordained clergyman participating in the service, it is appropriate to invite him to read the gospel. The ceremonial directions for this are given on pp. 52 and 68. The reader of the gospel first silently offers the prayer, "Cleanse my heart... through Jesus Christ our Lord. Amen." In a low voice he then asks the celebrant's blessing with the words: "Sir, give me your blessing," or "Pray, Father, a blessing" (The Latin text reads: "Jube, domine, benedicere"). The celebrant responds: "The Lord be in your heart and on your lips that you may worthily and competently proclaim his holy gospel, in the name of the Father and of the Son and of the Holy Ghost." At the words, "and of the Son," the celebrant makes the sign of the cross over the reader of the gospel.

---

32 Technically, a sequence hymn is one that has been written specifically for this point in the service. For a list of sequence hymns for various occasions see the article, "Sequences," by F. E. Warren and James Mearns in John Julian (editor), *A Dictionary of Hymnology*, revised edition (London: John Murray,1915), pp. 1041–1053. The ancient sequences for Easter (Victimae paschali) and Pentecost (Veni, Sancte Spiritus) are given together with their traditional plain-song melodies in *The Graduals for the Church Year*, edited by Erwin Kurth an Alter E. Buszin (St. Louis: Concordia Publishing House, 1944), pp. 32, 44–47. *The Lutheran Hymnal* contains a paraphrase of the Easter sequence; see Hymn 191. The *Worship Supplement* includes the Easter sequence, *Victimae Paschali*, WS 741. *The Lutheran Hymnal* also contains a translation of the Pentecost sequence; see Hymn 227. The use of the sequences is noted—insofar as possible—on the reverse side of the calendar sheet for each month of the *Lutheran Church Year Calendar, The Lutheran Liturgy Edition*. (continued on following page)

The gospel is announced according to the prescribed formula of our authorized service books: "The holy gospel is written in the _____ chapter of _____ beginning at the _____ verse." The gospel is concluded with the words: "Here endeth the gospel."

Ancient custom, which survived after the Reformation in many parts of the church of the Augsburg Confession, directed that while the congregation sang the response, "Praise be to thee, O Christ," the reader of the gospel raised the book to his lips, kissed the beginning of the gospel that he had read, and said in a low tone of voice: "By the gospel words today may our sins be done away." This is a mark of reverence for the written word of God.

The chanting, rather than the mere speaking, of the gospel has the endorsement of centuries of precedent in the Lutheran church. The chant-pattern at the singing of the gospel is traditionally at least slightly more elaborate than the chant-pattern for the singing of the other lessons.

The Nicene Creed

The *Worship Supplement,* El *Culto Christiano* (authorized for Spanish-speaking parishes of The Lutheran Church-Missouri Synod), and the text of the creed provided by the International Consultation on English Texts, use the word "catholic" instead of "Christian" in the creed. See *Prayers We Have in Common* (Philadelphia: Fortress Press, 1970), p. 11.

The Hymn[33]

Originally the sixteenth century rites of the church of the Augsburg Confession made no provision for a hymn at this point in addition to the creed. The rubric of the Hymnal and Liturgy, which prescribes such a hymn at this point, has been superseded by a permissive rubric (*The Order of Holy Communion*, 1959, p. 12). It must be remembered that in the present state of transition, the problem of what constitutes liturgical or rubrical authority is by no means wholly clear.

This hymn is the **Hauptlied** of the service and historically almost became an additional proper. The hymn of the week listed in *The Lutheran Annual* is intended to be the chief hymn for the service of a given Sunday or festival.

The Sermon

The traditional text for the sermon at the eucharist is the gospel for the day. The sermon should be strong with the power of the gospel to move men, to give them the power to believe and do those things which the total liturgical action of worship has been setting before them.

It is an ancient custom in the church to begin the sermon with the words: "In the name of the Father and of the Son and of the Holy Ghost. Amen." While saying these words, the preacher may make the sign of the cross on himself. If he has used this invocation, he should not follow it with another after reading his text, such as, "in the name of Jesus."

There is no authority to vary the text of the votum at the end of the sermon: "The peace of God, which passeth all understanding, keep your hearts and minds through Christ Jesus."

---

32 (cont.) *The Lutheran Liturgy* provides that "special choir music may be sung in place of, or preferably in addition to, the Gradual, between the Epistle and the Gospel. When this is done, it is important that the textual content of the choral selection harmonize with the theme of the Liturgy and of the Service for the day," where the latter can be determined. This rubric should not be interpreted as urging the inclusion of special choir music. It merely intends to say that if the choir sings an anthem of a seasonal character it is appropriate to have it at this point in the service.

The Lutheran Liturgy says: "A hymn of invocation of the Holy Ghost may be sung to replace the Gradual. The classic Gradual Hymn of the Lutheran Church is "We now implore God the Holy Ghost" (*The Lutheran Hymnal*, Hymn 231). The reason for this rubric is obscure. Historically, there is no evidence that a hymn of invocation of the Holy Spirit was ever actually in wide use as a substitute for the gradual. Similarly, there is no evidence that "Nun bitten wir den Heiligen Geist" was ever actually in wide use as a "gradual hymn" in the Lutheran church.

Although the *General Rubrics* of *The Lutheran Liturgy*, p. 421, authorize "the preacher" to "raise his hand in blessing and make the sign of the holy cross when saying the Votum at the close of the Sermon," it is better not to do this. The preacher may end his sermon with the Trinitarian invocation, or he may close his sermon with an ascription of praise to the Holy Trinity.

The Offertory[34]

The Order of Holy Communion, 1959, p. 12, states: "Then shall the Offertory here following or the Proper Offertory be said or chanted, at the close of which the Congregation shall be seated." Anciently, the Offertory was one of the propers of the service. An effort to provide proper offertories for the Lutheran rite has been made in Albert Olai Christensen and Harold Edward Schunemann, *Proper of the Service for the Church Year* (New York: The H. W. Gray Co., 1947). See also the seasonal offertories of the *Worship Supplement*, pp. 30ff.

The General Prayer

The *General Rubrics* of *The Lutheran Liturgy* (p. 421) prescribe that

> before the General Prayer at the Altar the Officiant may announce special Petitions, Intercessions, or Thanksgivings which have been requested. He may also make mention of the birth, contemplated marriage, death, etc. of members of the Congregation.

When special prayers are included in the general prayer, it is desirable that an appropriate announcement thereof be made before the general prayer. It is appropriate that in announcing the special petition, intercession or thanksgiving which has been requested, the celebrant name the full name ("William Smith," "Mary Anderson," "Jane, the wife of Harold Peters," etc.) of the persons concerned. In the prayer itself, however, he will be careful to mention only the Christian names ("William," "Mary," "Jane," etc.) of those prayed for, that is, the names that were given to them in holy baptism, by which they are known in the Book of Life.

In selecting the intercessions to be used in connection with the general prayers, the celebrant should be careful to choose prayers that are addressed to the Father. If he does not, the structure of the general prayer is violated by the interpolation of a prayer addressed to the Son or to the Holy Spirit. When a special intercession is read in the general prayer, the termination of that intercession is not read. That is, the termination, "through Jesus Christ our Lord," or another termination, is not read. It is not necessary to read the termination of any special intercession since the termination of the general prayer itself is sufficient.

The rubrics prescribe that "one of the General Prayers appointed for the Services shall always be used" (*The Lutheran Liturgy*, p. 421). There is no rubrical place for the seasonal general prayers in the service. These prayers may be used in conjunction with sermons preached apart from the service, at special devotions, and in similar circumstances. The "General Prayers appointed for the Services" are those contained in *The Lutheran Liturgy* on pp. 251–277 and in *The Lutheran Hymnal* on pp. 13–14, 23–24, 110–112.[35] It should be noted that the rubrics provide that "the Litany may

---

33   Cf. Ralph Gehrke, *Planning the Service* (Saint Louis: Concordia Publishing House, 1961) for a discussion of the hymn of the week together with practical suggestions for its use.

34   The original function of the offertory chant was to cover the offertory procession.

35   See the forms of the intercessions, *Worship Supplement*, pp. 33ff.

be used instead of the General Prayer, except when there is a Communion," that is, the litany cannot replace the general prayer at a celebration of the sacrament of the altar.

Although the way in which the amen at the end of the general prayer is printed indicates that the celebrant will say the amen, it is appropriate for the congregation to join with the celebrant in the amen.[36]

It is better not to follow the rubric which permits the singing of a hymn after the general prayer. The continuity of the service from the offertory through to the completion of the communion is stressed by proceeding at once to the salutation of the preface. (*The Order of Holy Communion*, 1959, p. 12, makes no provision for a hymn at this point.)

The Preface

In some editions of *The Lutheran Hymnal* and *The Lutheran Liturgy* the preface ends with the words, "through Jesus Christ our Lord," because of an editorial mistake. The words should be struck at this point in those copies of these books in which they appear, and inserted at the beginning of the prefaces for Advent, the Ascension, and Whitsunday.

Although the rubric does not so specify, the preface of Christmas should be used through January 5, the preface of the Epiphany through January 13, the preface of Easter through the Wednesday after Rogate Sunday, the preface for the Ascension through the Saturday after Exaudi, the preface for Whitsunday on Pentecost and throughout the week following, the preface of the holy Trinity on Trinity Sunday through the first Sunday after Trinity, the preface of apostles and evangelists on all days of apostles and evangelists except the day of Saint John the apostle and evangelist, when the preface of Christmas is said. (The preface of Christmas is said daily through January 5, including Saint Stephen's Day and Holy Innocents' Day.) The preface of the holy Trinity may be used on any Sunday for which no other preface is appointed, according to the rubrics of *The Lutheran Liturgy*, that is, on the Sundays of the post-Epiphany season, the Sundays of Pre-Lent, and the Sundays of the season after Trinity.

In general, it is wise to consult the Lutheran Church Year Calendar. On the reverse side of the calendar sheet for each month the correct use of the proper prefaces is carefully noted.

The Sanctus

When the sanctus is spoken, the text of the sanctus given in *The Lutheran Liturgy*, p. 23, should be followed. That is, the word, "Hosanna," and the phrase, "Blessed is He," should not be said three times when the sanctus is spoken. The repetition of "Hosanna" and "Blessed is He" is an accommodation to the musical setting of the sanctus in *The Lutheran Hymnal*.

Although there is no rubrical authority for the inclusion of a eucharistic prayer in the rite of *The Order of the Holy Communion*, the celebrant may—in view of the great antiquity and meaningfulness of the eucharistic prayer—feel justified in praying a eucharistic prayer immediately after

---

36   It is probably desirable to make provision for the congregation's participation in the General Prayer. For example, after each paragraph the people might say "Hear us, O Lord," or some similar response. This would tend to lessen the tedium of the people listening to the lengthy, uninterrupted prayer by the celebrant.

The rubrics do not prescribe the posture of the congregation during the general prayer. It is desirable that the congregation stand or kneel for the general prayer, although as far as the rubric goes, the congregation may remain seated for it.

the sanctus. The *Worship Supplement* of our synod now includes a eucharistic prayer in all of the rites for the celebration of holy communion. The celebrant may, then, wish to pray one of the eucharistic prayers given in the *Worship Supplement*, pp. 45–47. If the celebrant does this, after the eucharistic prayer or the prayer of thanksgiving (as it is called in the *Worship Supplement*), he proceeds with the Our Father, followed by the pax and agnus dei.

The Lord's Prayer

The Music for the Liturgy, which is as authoritative as any of the other liturgical books of our rite, prescribes that the Our Father be introduced with the words, "Let us pray."

The Words of Institution

The Pax Domini

The Order of Holy Communion, 1959, p. 21, authorizes the ancient response, "and with thy spirit," instead of "amen" after the pax domini.

The Agnus Dei[37]

The Distribution

When the celebrant, in accordance with good Lutheran precedent, administers the holy communion to himself, he may, by way of private preparation, say the following prayers in a low voice:

O Lord Jesus Christ, who saidst unto thine apostles, "Peace I leave with you, my peace I give unto you;" regard not my sins, but the faith of thy church, and grant unto her that peace and unity which is according unto thy will, who livest and reignest God, world without end. Amen.

O Lord Jesus Christ, Son of the living God, who according to the will of the Father, and by the cooperation of the Holy Ghost, hast by thy death given life to the world; deliver me by this thy most holy body and blood from all mine iniquities and from every evil, and make me ever to cleave unto thy commandments, and suffer me never to be separated from thee, who with the Father and the Holy Ghost livest and reignest one God, world without end. Amen.

Let the partaking of thy body, O Lord Jesus Christ, which I, though unworthy, do presume to receive, according to thy loving kindness be profitable to me for the receiving of forgiveness of sins, life and salvation, who with the Father and the Holy Ghost livest and reignest one God, world without end. Amen.

---

[37] The significant words of the agnus dei should be a part of the worship of the entire congregation, people and ushers. There should, obviously, be no bustling about with kneeling cushions or rail gates. When necessary, these arrangements can be completed after the agnus dei.

I will receive the bread of heaven and call upon the name of the Lord.
Lord, I am not worthy that thou shouldest come under my roof; but speak the word only, and my soul shall be healed.

The body of our Lord Jesus Christ, which was given for me, preserve my body and soul unto everlasting life.

What reward shall I give unto the Lord for all his benefits toward me? I will take the cup of salvation and call upon the name of the Lord. I will call upon the Lord who is worthy to be praised; so shall I be saved from mine enemies.

The blood of our Lord Jesus Christ, which was shed for me, preserve my body and soul unto everlasting life.

The rubrics do not prescribe that the words of distribution be spoken to each communicant, or, for that matter, to each rail of communicants. The requirement of the rubric is adequately met if the minister who administers our Lord's body says the words pertaining to the consecrated bread in a loud voice at the beginning of the distribution and if the minister who distributes our Lord's blood does the same with the words pertaining to the chalice. Thereafter, following ancient precedent, the clergyman distributing the hosts says to each communicant "the body of Christ" (or "the body of Christ, given for thee"), and the clergyman who administers the chalice says, "the blood of Christ," (or "the blood of Christ, shed for thy sins").

The authorized formula of distribution should, however, always be said at the beginning of the distribution, as a clear confession of the faith of the church concerning the sacrament of the altar.

"If the consecrated bread and wine be spent before all have communed, the celebrant shall consecrate more, saying aloud so much of the Words of Institution as pertains to the elements to be consecrated" (*The Lutheran Liturgy*, p. 421). In this rubric, "aloud" does not require a greater volume of voice than is necessary for those who are in the chancel to hear what the celebrant is saying. **Under no circumstances should a clergyman administer hosts or wine that have not been consecrated.**

The Nunc Dimittis
According to ancient tradition, gloria patri was omitted from the fifth Sunday in Lent through holy Saturday, wherever it occurred in the eucharistic liturgy.

The Thanksgiving

The Salutation and Benedicamus
These are very old parts of the eucharistic liturgy and should not be omitted.

The Benediction
Neither this nor any other blessing should be introduced with, "and now."

Chapter Five:
The Celebration of the Holy Eucharist

I. Preparations for the Celebration of the Holy Eucharist

The missal stand or cushion for the service book is placed at the epistle corner of the altar.[38] The front edge of the missal stand or cushion is parallel to the front edge of the altar.[39]

A linen cloth is placed on the credence. The following items are then placed on the credence: a cruet or flagon of wine, a cruet of water (if the celebrant will add a small quantity of water to the chalice and wash his hands at the offertory), the bread box or ciborium, and a lavabo bowl and towel (if the celebrant will wash his hands at the offertory.)[40]

The altar candles are lighted.
The chalice and paten are prepared in the sacristy.

First a purificator is placed over the mouth of the chalice.

Then the paten is placed on top of the purificator. Then a large host may be placed on top of the paten.

Then the pall is placed on top of the paten.

Conduct of the Services   35

Then the chalice veil is placed over the chalice and paten, and adjusted to form a trapezoid when viewed from the front.

Then the burse, containing the corporal and additional purificators is placed on top of the vested chalice.

The celebrant marks the service book. If the service book does not contain the liturgical lessons, the lectionary will be placed toward the back of the altar behind the cushion or stand which holds the service book.

The vested chalice and burse may be placed on the altar before the service begins, if this is the custom of the parish. See the instructions on p. 36 for placing the vested chalice and burse on the altar. If the celebrant places the vested chalice and burse on the altar before the service begins, he may also open the service book at the introit before the service begins.

---

38 Although the older practice is to place the missal stand or cushion at the epistle corner of the altar, it is also possible—where some simplification of the ceremonial is desired—to place the missal stand or cushion at the left of the midst of the altar on an angle to the front edge of the mensa.

39 If the celebrant will not be assisted by a server, the service book must be placed on its stand or cushion before the service begins. Traditionally, the service book is placed on the stand or cushion with its front cover facing down so that the open edge of the book faces the crucifix. This old ceremony recalls the teaching of Rev. 5:1–5.

40 If there is no server, these items may be placed toward the back of the altar at the epistle corner. If, however, the credence is quite close to the altar, these items may be placed on the credence even if there is no server.

II. The Celebration of the Holy Eucharist: Celebrant and Server

During the opening hymn—or, if the opening hymn is omitted, at the hour appointed for the celebration of the eucharist—the celebrant goes to the foot of the altar.

The celebrant may be preceded by a server. The server carries the service book in both hands before his chest. When he has arrived at the foot of the altar, he steps to his right and, when the celebrant arrives at the foot of the altar, the server reverences the altar with the celebrant. The server then goes up to the epistle corner of the altar and places the service book on its stand or cushion with the front cover facing down so that the open edge of the service book faces the crucifix. Having placed the service book on its stand, the server returns to the foot of the altar and stands at the celebrant's left on the floor of the chancel. Note that the server always stands on the side of the altar *opposite* the location of the service book.

The celebrant carries the vested chalice and burse, with the knop of the chalice in his left hand, and his right hand on top of the burse. When he has arrived at the foot of the altar, he reverences the altar, goes up to the midst of the altar, and places the chalice on the altar to the left of the midst of the altar. The celebrant then takes the corporal from the burse, places the corporal still folded in the midst of the altar, and lays the burse at the rear of the altar left of center or leans it against the gradine or reredos left of center. He then unfolds the corporal with a minimum of motion.[41] Then he places the vested chalice in the midst of the corporal and adjusts the chalice veil. With his hands joined before him, the celebrant half-turns with his right shoulder toward the congregation and goes to the epistle corner. He opens the service book at the introit. The celebrant then turns with his left shoulder toward the congregation, returns to the midst of the altar, faces the crucifix, turns by his right shoulder to the congregation, goes down the steps to the floor of the chancel, and turns by his left shoulder to the altar.

The Confession of Sins

Facing the altar, the celebrant says, "In the name of the Father and of the Son and of the Holy Ghost." (As he says these words he may make the sign of the cross on himself.) With his hands joined, the celebrant turns by his right to the congregation, faces them, and says, "Beloved in the Lord! Let us draw near... to grant us forgiveness."[42] The celebrant then turns by his left to the altar. (The celebrant and congregation may kneel.) With his hands joined the celebrant says, "Our help is in the name of the Lord."[43] With his hands joined, he continues, "I said, I will confess my transgressions unto the Lord." The celebrant and congregation say the confession of sins.

---

41 The corporal should always be folded into nine divisions in this way: front, back, right, left.
42 "When turning at the altar, the Officiant shall ordinarily turn by his right side to face the Congregation and by his left side to face the altar." *The Lutheran Liturgy*, p. 417.
43 As the celebrant says these words he may make the sign of the cross on himself.

Then the celebrant stands, turns by his right to face the congregation and, with hands joined, says: "Upon this your confession... the grace of God unto all of you." Then he places his left hand flat against his body just below his chest, raises his right hand, fingers together and palm toward the congregation, to the level of his shoulder and continues: "And in the stead and by the command of my Lord Jesus Christ I forgive you all your sins in the name of the Father..." At the words, "and of the Son," the celebrant makes the sign of the cross over the congregation. As the congregation says "amen," the celebrant rejoins his hands before his chest and turns by his left shoulder to the altar.

The Introit

After pronouncing the absolution, the celebrant goes up to the midst of the altar, bows his head, (half-turns with his right shoulder toward the congregation, goes to the epistle corner of the altar) and faces the altar.[44]

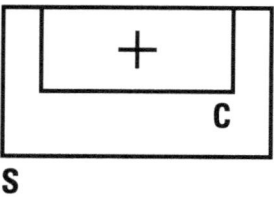

If the service is choral, the choir and/or congregation sing-(s) the introit while the celebrant goes to the altar. If the service is not choral, the celebrant first goes to the altar and, when he arrives at the service book, reads the introit.

In either case, the celebrant may bow slightly to the crucifix at the words, "Glory be to the Father and to the Son and to the Holy Ghost." Since the introit is actually the beginning of the service proper, the celebrant may make the sign of the cross on himself as he reads the first words of the introit.

The Kyrie

When the introit is completed, the celebrant (half-turns with his left shoulder toward the congregation, goes back to the midst of the altar, and) faces the altar throughout the kyrie, keeping his hands joined.

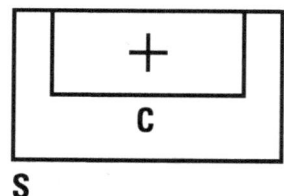

The Gloria in Excelsis

The celebrant remains at the midst of the altar, facing it, with his hands joined.

At the words, "Glory be to God on high," the celebrant may open his hands and immediately rejoin them, bowing his head slightly as he does. He may also incline his head at the words, "we worship Thee," "Jesus," "receive our prayer." At the words, "art most high in the glory of God the Father," he may sign himself with the cross.

---

44 Although the older practice is to read the introit, collect, lesson, epistle, and gradual at the epistle corner of the altar, and the gospel at the gospel corner of the altar, it is also possible—where simplification of the ceremonial is desired—to read these parts of the service at the midst of the altar. The lesson, epistle, gradual, and gospel may also be read at the lectern.

The Salutation

His hands still joined, the celebrant turns by his right to the congregation and says, "The Lord be with you."

As he says, "The Lord be with you," he may separate his hands to the width of his body and rejoin them. He may acknowledge the congregation's response by inclining his head slightly toward the congregation ***after*** "and with thy spirit." He may again separate and rejoin his hands as he says, "Let us pray."

The Collect for the Day

Having said, "Let us pray," the celebrant (half-turns with his right shoulder toward the congregation, goes to the epistle corner of the altar and) faces the altar. (As the celebrant prays the collect he may separate his hands to the width of his body; he rejoins his hands before him as he begins the termination of the collect.)

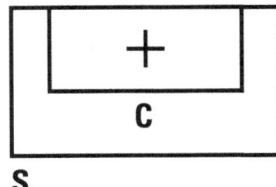

The Old Testament Lesson

The celebrant (still standing at the epistle corner of the altar) takes the service book or lectionary and turns by his right to face the congregation. He reads the lesson.

The Old Testament lesson may also be read by the server. In that case, after the congregation has responded to the collect by saying "amen," the server goes to the credence table, takes the lectionary, proceeds to a point in the chancel in front of the epistle corner of the altar, turns by his left, faces the congregation, and reads the lesson.

The Epistle

The celebrant (still standing at the epistle corner of the altar) reads the epistle. Having read the epistle, the celebrant turns by his left to the altar and places the lectionary on the altar. If the Old Testament lesson and epistle were read from the service book, the celebrant replaces the service book on its cushion or stand.

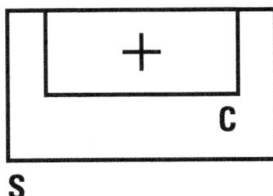

The epistle may also be read by the server. (See above under the Old Testament lesson.) Having read the epistle, the server turns by his right, faces the altar and takes the lectionary back to the credence.

The Gradual[45]

The celebrant (still standing at the epistle corner) reads the gradual from the service book. (It is customary for him to place his hands at the edges of the service book while he does so.)

Having read the gradual, the celebrant carries the service book, together with its cushion or stand (and the lectionary) to the gospel corner of the altar.[46] He places the service book and its cushion or stand at an angle to the front edge of the altar. The celebrant may then return to the midst of the altar, place his joined hands on the mensa, and, bowing moderately, say the traditional prayers, "Cleanse my heart, etc." (See p. 27) Having said these prayers, he returns to the gospel corner of the altar.

When the gradual is sung by the choir and/or congregation, it is not necessary that the celebrant read it as well. Rather, having read the epistle, the celebrant faces the altar (and proceeds with the ceremonies described above.)

The Holy Gospel

The celebrant takes the book containing the gospel in his hands and, if he is standing at the gospel corner of the altar, turns by his left to face the congregation.[47] If he is standing at the midst of the altar, he turns by his right to face the congregation.

When the celebrant announces the gospel, he may with his right thumb trace the sign of the cross on the first word of the text of the gospel for the day and then with his right thumb make the sign of the cross on his forehead, lips and heart.[48]

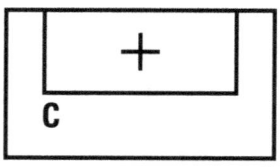

After he has read the gospel, he may raise the book to his lips, kiss the beginning of the gospel he has read and say in a low tone of voice "By the gospel words today may our sins be done away."[49]

Having concluded the gospel, the celebrant turns by his right, replaces the service book on its cushion or stand, or replaces the lectionary on the altar, moves the cushion or stand with both hands to within about a foot of the center of the altar, turns by his right, goes with joined hands to the midst of the altar, and faces the altar.

---

45 If the celebrant feels justified in splitting the gradual—see p. 33 n. 9.—and so reads the gradual proper after the Old Testament lesson, and the alleluia verse or tract after the epistle, the celebrant, having read the Old Testament lesson, turns by his left and, facing the altar, reads the gradual proper. Having read the gradual proper, he turns by his right to face the congregation, and reads the epistle. Having read the epistle, he turns by his left and, facing the altar, reads the alleluia verse or tract. If the server reads the Old Testament lesson and the epistle, he faces the altar while the gradual proper and the alleluia verse or tract are said or sung. 46   The celebrant himself carrying the service book to the gospel corner of the altar is a last vestige and reminder of the gospel procession. Cf. Joseph Jungmann, *The Mass of the Roman Rite* (Missarum Sollemnia), translated by Francis A. Brunner (New York: Benziger Brothers, 1951), I, 447, n. 30. It is also possible for the server to transfer the service book to the gospel corner of the altar.

47 This variation in the usual rubric recognizes "the ghost of the deacon," who traditionally read the gospel, still lingering about the altar.

48 Members of the congregation may likewise make the sign of the cross on themselves in this manner, praying silently, "May thy gospel be in my mind, on my lips, and in my heart. Amen."

The Nicene Creed

The celebrant says the creed, facing the altar, with his hands joined.

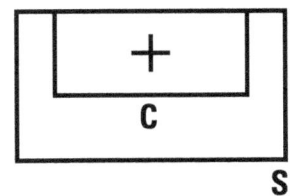

The celebrant may begin the creed by saying, "I believe in one God." Then the congregation continues, "The Father almighty, etc." As the celebrant says, "I believe in one God," he may, as at the beginning of the gloria in excelsis, open his hands and immediately rejoin them, bowing his head as he does. He may, as always, bow his head at the holy name of Jesus. He may bow from the waist at the words, "and was incarnate" and remain bowed through the words, "was crucified also for us." He stands erect again before the words, "under Pontius Pilate" are said.[50] In some parts of the church of the Augsburg Confession the celebrant placed the extremities of his fingers on either side of the corporal and knelt on his right knee from the words And was incarnate" through the words "and was made man."[51] The celebrant may bow his head at the words, "worshiped and glorified."[52] At the words, "and the life of the world to come," the celebrant may sign himself with the cross.[53]

The creed ended, the celebrant, with his hands joined, turns by his right shoulder, goes down the altar steps to the floor of the chancel, and (preceded by the server) goes to his chair.

---

49 This ancient custom survived after the Reformation in many parts of the church of the Augsburg Confession. It is a mark of reverence for the written word of God. In our own generation it is highly desirable that we do everything that we can in the course of our worship to encourage reverence for the written word of God.

50 The bow at this point is in reverence for the mystery of the incarnation. It is customary to stand erect before the words "under Pontius Pilate" are said. The explanation given for this was that the soldiers of the Roman procurator knelt and bowed before our Lord in mockery during his passion.

51 Luther said of the ceremonies connected with the words "and was incarnate..." of the creed:

The Word...condescends to assume my flesh and blood, my body and soul. He does not become an angel or another magnificent creature; He becomes man. This is a token of God's mercy to wretched human beings; the human mind cannot grasp or understand, let alone express it. However, we Christians can at least learn to prize and esteem these words; they were acknowledged and preserved even in the papacy ... They were sung daily in every Mass in a slow tempo and were set to a special melody different from that of the other words. And when the congregation came to the words "from the Virgin Mary, and was made man," everyone genuflected and removed his hat. It would still be proper and appropriate to kneel at the words "and was made man," to sing them with long notes as formerly, to listen with happy hearts to the message that the Divine Majesty abased Himself and became like us poor bags of worms, and to thank God for the ineffable mercy and compassion reflected in the incarnation of the Deity...

The following tale is told about a coarse and brutal lout. While the words "And was made man" were being sung in Church, he remained standing, neither genuflecting nor removing his hat. He showed no reverence, but just stood there like a clod. All the others dropped to their knees when the Nicene Creed was prayed and chanted devoutly. Then the devil stepped up to him and hit him so hard it made his head spin. He cursed him gruesomely and said: "May hell consume you, you boorish ass! If God had become an angel like me and the congregation sang 'God was made an angel,' I would bend not only my knees but my whole body to the ground! Yes I would crawl ten hells down into the ground. And you vile human creature, you stand there like a stick or a stone. You hear that God did not become an angel but a man like you, and you just stand there like a stick of wood."

Martin Luther, "Sermons on the Gospel of St. John, Chapters 1-4," *Luther's Works* (St. Louis: Concordia Publishing House, 1957) XXII, 102 and 105. Cf. Martin Luther, "Auslegung des ersten und zweiten Kapitels Johannes in Predigten 1537 and 1538," *D. Martin Luthers Werke. Kritische Gesammtausgabe* (Weimar: Hermann Böhlaus Nachfolger, 1912) XLVI, 627 and 792.

52 This is a confession of the deity of the Holy Spirit.

53 It is said that the sign of the cross is made at this point since it is only through the death of Christ and his subsequent resurrection that we have the hope of the resurrection. A bodily gesture at this point signifies that our bodies share in the full redemption accomplished for us by Christ.

The Hymn

The celebrant, seated at his chair, joins the congregation in singing the hymn.

The Sermon

If the celebrant is also the preacher, he may find it convenient to remove the maniple and chasuble before going into the pulpit, although it is not necessary for him to do so. If he does, he will resume the chasuble and maniple after the votum. The changing of vestments is best done in the sacristy, out of sight of the assembled congregation.

The Lutheran Liturgy, p. 412, authorizes "the preacher (to) raise his hand in blessing and make the sign of the holy cross when saying the Votum at the close of the Sermon." It is better not to avail oneself of this privilege.

The Offertory

When the sermon is ended, the celebrant (having resumed the chasuble and maniple) goes to the midst of the altar. **When he arrives at the altar**—and not before—he and the congregation sing or say the offertory.[54]

When the offertory has been said, the celebrant may wash his hands.[55] With his hands joined, the celebrant turns with his right shoulder toward the congregation and goes to the epistle corner of the altar. As he goes he begins to say the psalm Lavabo (psalm 26) in a low voice. When he has arrived at the epistle corner, the celebrant holds the extremities of his thumbs and forefingers over the bowl held by the server; the server pours water over them. When the celebrant has washed his fingers, he takes the lavabo towel from the server's left arm and, facing the altar, wipes his fingers dry. He then replaces the towel on the server's arm, turns once more to the altar, and completes the psalm. At the words, "Glory be to the Father and to the Son and to the Holy Ghost," he bows toward the crucifix and stands erect again at the words, "As it was in the beginning, etc." The celebrant then turns with his left shoulder toward the congregation and returns to the midst of the altar.[56]

---

54 There should be a definite break between the sermon and the offertory. The sermon concludes the liturgy of the word; the offertory begins the liturgy of the sacrament.

55 The lavabo is a ceremony that goes back at least to the fourth century since it is described in the catechetical lectures of Saint Cyril of Jerusalem. Its significance is obvious: purity of heart and mind and body as we approach the holy mysteries of Christ's body and blood. It also has an obvious utilitarian value: it is decent to wash one's hands before handling the food of the sacred meal, just as it is customary to wash one's hands before going to the table for an ordinary meal. Originally, the hands were washed before preparing the elements. By the end of the middle ages, however, it had become customary in some places for the celebrant to wash his hands *after* preparing the elements. The reason for this change is not wholly clear. However, it is interesting to note that it had at the same time become customary to cense the bread and wine after they had been placed upon the altar. There could be an obvious utilitarian value in washing one's hands after handling the censer. Apart from this consideration, the older position for the washing of the celebrant's hands seems to make better sense. Cf. Jungmann, II, 76ff.

56 If the celebrant has no server, the lavabo may still be performed in the following way: The lavabo bowl is filled with water and placed on the credence before the service. At the customary time the celebrant simply dips his thumbs and forefingers into the bowl. Then he dries them on the towel.

The celebrant then takes hold of the back part of the chalice veil and removes it with both hands. He folds it on the altar to the right of the corporal, then places it close to the rear of the altar near the corporal.

With his right hand the celebrant takes the chalice by the knop and moves it off the corporal toward the epistle side. With his right hand he removes the pall from the chalice and places it on the right side of the outspread corporal.

Then he takes the paten and goes to the epistle corner of the altar. (***Note***: If the celebrant is not assisted by a server, and the bread-box and cruets have been placed on the credence, the celebrant will, instead of merely going to the epistle corner of the altar, go to the credence. If the celebrant is not assisted by a server, and the bread-box and cruets have been placed toward the back of the altar on the epistle side, the celebrant will merely go to the epistle corner of the altar as directed below.) Holding the paten in his left hand, the celebrant takes as many hosts as he thinks will be sufficient from the bread-box (held by the server) and places them on the paten. (If he uses a large host to communicate himself, he will place the large host on top of the small hosts.)

After the celebrant has placed the necessary number of hosts on the paten he turns with his left shoulder toward the congregation and returns to the midst of the altar where he places the paten on the forepart of the corporal.

If the number of communicants is so large that the hosts required cannot safely be placed on the paten, the celebrant, having placed the paten on the corporal, will return to the epistle corner and procure the ciborium (from the server). He will take the ciborium to the midst of the altar and place it toward the back of the corporal.

The celebrant removes the purificator from the chalice, takes the chalice by the knop in his left hand, and goes to the epistle corner of the altar. The celebrant takes the wine cruet (from the server) with his right hand, pours the requisite amount of wine into the chalice (and returns the wine cruet to the server. The celebrant may then take the water cruet from the server, pour a very small quantity of water into the chalice, and return the cruet to the server.)

Then the celebrant carries the chalice in both hands, the foot in his left hand, the knop in his right hand, to the center of the altar, where he places the chalice on the corporal behind the paten. Placing his left hand on the foot of the chalice, with his right hand he covers the chalice with the pall.

If the number of communicants is so large that the wine cannot safely be contained in the chalice, the celebrant, having covered the chalice with the pall, returns to the epistle corner and procures an additional cruet or flagon of wine (from the server). The celebrant takes it to the center of the altar and places it toward the back of the corporal.[57]

---

57 The offerings of the people may be brought to the celebrant at this point in the service. The server takes the large receiving bason, goes to the ushers, receives the alms basons from them, and brings the alms basons to the celebrant. The celebrant receives them from the server and places them toward the epistle corner of the altar. The server may remove the alms basons from the altar to the credence following the general prayer. An alternate procedure is this: if the offerings of the people are received at the door of the church—see pp. 12ff—the offerings may be brought forward during or immediately after the singing of the offertory chant. After placing the offerings on the altar, the celebrant proceeds with (the lavabo and) the preparation of the bread and wine for the communion.

Diagram showing the position of the sacred vessels and linens on the altar

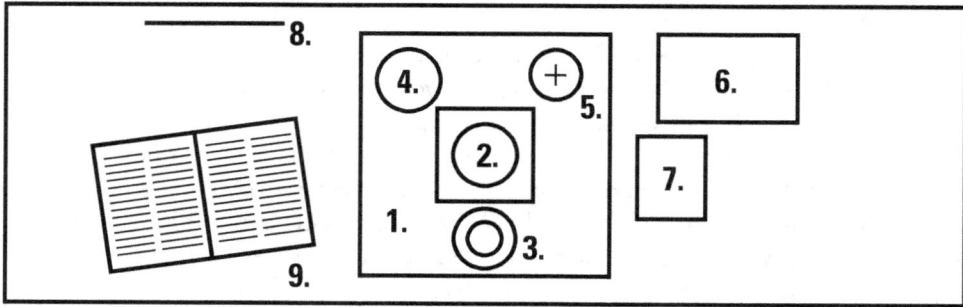

1–outspread corporal
2–chalice covered with the pall
3–paten
4–ciborium (if needed)
5–cruet or flagon (if needed)
6–folded chalice veil
7–purificators
8–burse (leaning against the reredos or gradine)
9–service book

The General Prayer

If there are special intercessions, the celebrant, before beginning the general prayer, will turn by his right to the people, announce the intercessions, and then turn back to the altar by his left.

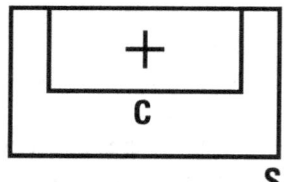

Still standing at the midst of the altar, the celebrant offers the general prayer.

> The celebrant may extend his hands the width of his body during the general prayer, rejoining them at the words, "through Jesus Christ, etc."
>
> At the words, "Receive, O God, our bodies and souls ... that we may live unto thee" (*The Lutheran Hymnal*, p. 24) he may extend his hands over the bread and wine, palms down, fingers together, the thumbs of both hands touching each other. The same procedure may be followed at the words, "Accept, we beseech thee, our bodies and souls ... which is our reasonable service," (*The Lutheran Hymnal*, p. 13) when the general prayer which contains these words is prayed at a celebration of the eucharist.[58]

---

58 Extending hands over the bread and wine—a ceremony tantamount to the laying on of hands—is a gesture of identification. The individual extending his hands over or laying his hands on some object identifies himself with that object. At this point in the liturgy, the celebrant, representing the people, identifies himself and the people with the offerings of bread and wine, since the offerings of bread and wine are the tokens of our lives and our work given to Christ for his purpose. This ceremony has its roots in Old Testament times (Ex. 29:10).

The Preface

The general prayer ended, the celebrant turns by his right to the people and says, "The Lord be with you."

As he says this he may separate his hands the width of his body and rejoin them. He may acknowledge the congregation's response by inclining his head slightly toward the congregation **after** "and with thy spirit." As he says, "Lift up your hearts," he may raise and extend his hands the width of his body, his palms facing each other. After the response of the congregation, "We lift them up unto the Lord," he rejoins his hands before his chest and says, "Let us give thanks unto the Lord, our God."

After the congregation responds, "It is meet and right so to do," the celebrant turns by his left to the altar and (with hands extended as at the collect) says the preface.

The Sanctus

The celebrant, still facing the altar, joins the congregation in the sanctus.

At the words, "Holy, holy, holy," the celebrant may join his hands—which he had extended during the preface—and resting the tips of his fingers on the edge of the mensa, he may bow moderately from the waist until the first "Hosanna in the highest" has been completed. Thereafter he resumes his erect position.[59]

At the words, "Blessed is He," the celebrant may sign himself with the holy cross.

The Lord's Prayer[60]

Still facing the altar, the celebrant prays the Our Father.

If the celebrant says, "Let us pray," before the Our Father—as authorized in *The Music for the Liturgy*—he may separate and join his hands again. Then, with hands extended as at the collect, he says or chants the Our Father through the petition, "But deliver us from evil." During the congregational response, "For Thine is the kingdom, etc." he joins his hands.

The Words of Institution[61]

If a ciborium or pyx is used, the celebrant uncovers it before he proceeds with the words of institution. At the words, "took bread," he takes a host from the paten—the large host, if one is being used—raises it slightly, and replaces it on the paten. Then he touches the ciborium or other vessels in which hosts to be consecrated are contained, thus indicating that he is including them in the consecration.

---

59 The bow during the sanctus expresses the awe of the worshipers as they join in the hymn of the seraphim around the throne of grace.
60 If the celebrant prays the eucharistic prayer, "the prayer of thanksgiving," immediately after the sanctus—see p. 30—he may extend his hands at the collect for the day while praying the eucharistic prayer. He follows the directions on p. 44ff. for the words of institution. He rejoins his hands before him for the termination of the eucharistic prayer.
61 Cf. Formula of Concord, Solid Declaration, VII, 75–82 on the doctrine of consecration. Note the words of the Formula which speak of the words of institution as said "over the bread and chalice."

At the words, "when He had given thanks," the celebrant makes the sign of the cross over the hosts on the paten and over the other vessels containing hosts to be consecrated.[62] At the words, "He brake it," the celebrant may break the large host or one of the other hosts on the paten. At the words, "Take, eat," the celebrant takes the large host between the thumb and forefinger of both hands (leans forward and rests his elbows on the altar, preferably outside the corporal), and says with particular distinctness, attention, and reverence, "This is My body, which is given for you. This do in remembrance of Me," over the host which he holds and over all the others which are to be consecrated.[63] Then he replaces the host on the paten.[64]

If a ciborium or bread-box is in use, the celebrant covers it after he has said the words, "This do in remembrance of Me."

Then the celebrant uncovers the chalice. To obviate the danger of spilling he holds the foot of the chalice with his left hand while he removes the pall with his right hand. He places the pall on the chalice veil. If a cruet or flagon is used, the celebrant removes the stopper or opens the lid. At the words, "He took the cup," the celebrant takes the chalice by the knop with his right hand, his left hand supporting the foot of the chalice, raises the chalice three or four inches above the corporal and then replaces it. Then he touches each vessel containing wine to be consecrated to indicate that he is including it in the consecration.

---

62 The custom has become general in Lutheran churches for the celebrant to make the sign of the cross over the hosts at the words, "This is my body." In view of the connection between "giving thanks" and "blessing," both of which reproduce the Latin *benedicere*, it would be more appropriate to make the sign of the cross over the bread at the words, "when he had given thanks."

63 After the words, "This do in remembrance of me," it had become customary during the middle ages for the celebrant to elevate the large host. This custom persisted in some places in the church of the Augsburg Confession after the Reformation. The celebrant bowed profoundly from the waist or genuflected. Then, keeping his eyes fixed on the host, he reverently elevated it as far as he conveniently could so that it could be seen by the people. He then lowered it slowly and with his right hand placed it on the corporal (or paten). Thereupon he again bowed profoundly from the waist or genuflected. On the whole subject of the elevation of the host, cf. Carl F. Wisloff, *The Gift of Communion: Luther's Controversy with Rome on Eucharistic Sacrifice*, translated by Joseph M. Shaw (Minneapolis: Augsburg Publishing House, 1964), pp. 156-165. See also Edward Frederick Peters, *The Origin and Meaning of the Axiom: "Nothing Has the Character of a Sacrament Outside of the Use" in Sixteenth Century and Seventeenth-Century Lutheran Theology*, Unpublished Doctor's Thesis, Concordia Seminary, St. Louis, 1968, pp. 61ff, 149ff, 271ff, 372ff, 464ff. The elevation was abolished neither in Luther's Formula Missae of 1523 nor in his Deutsche Messe of 1526. Cf. Martin Luther, "An Order of Mass and Communion for the Church at Wittenberg, 1523," *Luther's Works* (Philadelphia: Fortress Press, 1965) 53, 28; Martin Luther, "The German Mass and Order of Service, 1526," *Luther's Works* (Philadelphia: Fortress Press, 1965) 53, 82. See Martin Luther, "Formula Missae et Communionis 1523," *D. Martin Luthers Werke. Kritische Gesammtausgabe* (Weimar: Hermann Böhlau, 1891) XII, 212, and Martin Luther, "Deutsche Messe und Ordnung Gottesdiensts 1526," *D. Martin Luthers Werke. Kritische Gesammtausgabe* (Weimar: Hermann Böhlaus Nachfolger, 1897) XIX, 99.

It was anciently customary to ring the bell in the church tower a total of seven strokes, the first at the beginning of the consecration, three strokes at the consecration of the hosts and three more at the consecration of the chalice. Later, with the multiplication of masses, hand bells were substituted. It seems that the widespread custom in the Lutheran church of ringing the church bell during the recitation of the Our Father is a survival of this ancient custom, transferred to another element in the service after the custom of celebrating the holy communion every Sunday and major holy day unhappily became less common.

64 The celebrant was careful from this point on to keep his thumbs and forefingers joined, except when it was necessary to separate them, lest a fragment of one of the hosts adhering to his thumb or finger fall to the ground. With the same reverent concern he would later lightly rub his thumbs and forefingers together over the chalice to remove any fragments of the hosts which may be adhering to them. See p. 18–19. The use of the houseling-cloth (from the middle-English word "housel"-host) developed from the same concern. See pp. 11–12.

He makes the sign of the cross over the chalice and over the other vessels containing wine to be consecrated at the words, "and when He had given thanks." At the words, "Drink ye all of it," the celebrant takes the chalice with his right hand, the thumb and forefinger together above the knop and the other fingers below, and supporting the foot with his left hand, the thumb and forefinger above and the other fingers below, he (inclines slightly, resting his elbows on the edge of the altar, lifts the chalice a little above the corporal and, holding it in such a way that it is perfectly upright, says with particular distinctness, attention, and reverence the words, "This cup is the New Testament in My blood which is shed for you for the remission of sins." He then places the chalice on the corporal, saying, "This do, as oft as ye drink it, in remembrance of Me."[65]

After the celebrant has said the words, "This do, as oft as ye drink it, in remembrance of Me," he covers the chalice with the pall. If a cruet or flagon is used, he replaces the stopper or closes the lid at this point.

The Pax Domini

When the consecration is completed, the celebrant places his left hand on the corporal and turns by his right to the congregation as far as he conveniently can. (As he says, "The peace of the Lord be with you always!" he may make the sign of the cross over the congregation three times or once, depending on local custom.) After the congregation has responded, the celebrant again faces the altar.

The Agnus Dei

The celebrant remains facing the altar.

During the singing of the agnus dei by the congregation, the celebrant may say the words of this prayer in a low voice. Traditionally, he strikes himself on the chest with the tips of the last three fingers of his right hand at the final word of the three petitions, his left hand resting meanwhile on the corporal.

The celebrant reverently administers the holy communion to himself.

By way of private preparation, he may say the prayers on p. 31 with his hands joined. The celebrant says, "I will receive the bread of heaven and call upon the name of the Lord. Lord, I am not worthy that thou shouldest come under my roof, but speak the word only, and my soul shall be healed." Anciently, this prayer, "Domine, non sum dignus," was said three times. The celebrant struck his chest each time with the extremities of the last three fingers of his right hand, his left hand resting on the corporal. Taking the parts of the host, one on top of the other,

---

65   It was once customary to elevate the chalice at this point in the same way in which the host had been elevated. See n.** 23 above.

in his right hand, and holding the paten in his left hand under the host as he conveys it to his lips, he says in a low voice, "The body of our Lord Jesus Christ, which was given for me, preserve my body and soul unto everlasting life. Amen." Then bending forward moderately, he reverently places the host upon his tongue. He replaces the paten on the corporal and rubs his thumbs and forefingers over it to remove any fragments of consecrated bread. His head erect, he joins both hands before his face, and remains for a brief time in meditation on the holy eucharist. Then he places the ends of the last three fingers of his left hand on the foot of the chalice and removes the pall with his right. He places both hands on the corporal, bows reverently from the waist and says, "What reward shall I give unto the Lord for all his benefits toward me? I will take the cup of salvation and call upon the name of the Lord. I will call upon the Lord who is worthy to be praised; so shall I be saved from mine enemies." Then, still standing, the celebrant reverently raises the chalice as high as his chest and says, "The blood of our Lord Jesus Christ, which was shed for me, preserve my body and soul unto everlasting life. Amen." He then places the chalice to his lips and reverently receives the precious blood. He then replaces the chalice on the corporal. Placing his left hand on the base of the chalice, with his right hand he covers the chalice with the pall. After this he meditates for a short time on the gift that he has received.

The *General Rubrics* of *The Lutheran Liturgy* provide that "if there be another minister to assist in the Distribution, he may approach the altar during the singing of the Agnus Dei."

The Distribution
If the celebrant is assisted by a server, the server kneels on the footpace toward the epistle corner of the altar. The celebrant administers the sacrament to the server. The server may remain kneeling in this place or he may kneel or stand at some convenient place in the chancel. He does not sit during the distribution of holy communion.

The celebrant administers the sacrament to the congregation. If another minister assists in the distribution, the assisting minister administers the chalice.

Note the directions on p. 31 concerning the formula of distribution. We are required by the rubric to speak the entire formula of distribution at least once.

"When all have received the holy sacrament, the celebrant shall cover what remains of the bread and wine with the veil" (*The Lutheran Liturgy*, p. 421). The celebrant places the purificator over the mouth of the chalice. He places the paten on top of the purificator. He places the pall on top of the paten. If a breadbox or ciborium and cruet or flagon rest on the corporal, he removes them from the corporal at this point. He places the chalice and paten to the right of the corporal. Then he folds the corporal: front, back, right, left. He places the corporal in the burse. He replaces the chalice and burse on top of the veiled chalice and paten and places the ciborium or breadbox and flagon or cruet behind the veiled chalice and paten.

The Nunc Dimittis[66]

The celebrant stands before the midst of the altar, facing the altar with his hands joined. (He may bow as he says the words, "Glory be to the Father and to the Son and to the Holy Ghost.")

The Thanksgiving

The celebrant stands before the midst of the altar facing the altar.

The celebrant may extend his hands when praying the collect of thanksgiving, but he does not extend his hands when saying the versicle preceding it. The celebrant joins his hands before him at the termination of the collect.

At the doxology of the collect of thanksgiving ("through Jesus Christ, etc.") the celebrant closes the book (in such a way that the open edge is toward the crucifix in the midst of the altar [See n. 2, p. 36]).

The Salutation and Benedicamus

The celebrant, standing in the midst before the altar, turns by his right to the congregation and says, "The Lord be with you," to which the congregation responds, "And with thy spirit." (The ceremonial is the same as that described in connection with the salutation before the collect for the day.) Then, with his hands joined, the celebrant says, "Bless we the Lord."

The Benediction

The celebrant places his left hand flat against his chest, raises his right hand, fingers together and palm toward the congregation, not higher than his head, and pronounces the prescribed blessing. At the words, "and give thee peace," he makes the sign of the cross over the congregation. He rejoins his hands before him and faces by his left toward the altar while the congregation responds "Amen." Thereafter all engage in silent prayer.

The server goes up to the altar, takes the closed service book, returns to the floor of the chancel and steps to the right of center. The celebrant takes hold of the front of the chalice veil with both hands and folds it back over the burse resting on top of the veiled chalice. Then he grasps the chalice by the knop with his left hand and places his right hand on top of the burse.

The celebrant turns by his right and (carrying the veiled chalice and paten with the burse on top of them) goes down to the floor of the chancel, turns by his left, faces the altar, then turns by his right and (preceded by the server) returns to the sacristy.

---

66 In the Lutheran church, the parts of the service beginning with the nunc dimittis are part of the "ordinary," not of the "propers." It is, therefore, not necessary, as it formerly was in the rite of the Roman Catholic church, to have the service book returned to the epistle corner of the altar.

III. The Celebration of the Holy Eucharist: Celebrant, Deacon, Subdeacon, and Acolytes

Before the service begins, the service book is placed on its cushion or stand, open at the introit. The veiled chalice and paten with the burse on top of them are placed on the credence. The lectionary, the cruet or flagon of wine, the cruet of water, the ciborium or breadbox, the lavabo bowl and towel are placed on the credence.

The Introit[67]

The procession goes to the altar in this order: thurifer, server carrying the processional cross, flanked by two taperers, subdeacon carrying the book of the gospels, deacon, and celebrant. When he has arrived at the foot of the altar, the thurifer takes the censer to the sacristy and returns to his place in the chancel. The server and taperers take the processional cross and candles to the appointed places, and then go to their places in the chancel. The subdeacon steps to the left, the deacon steps to the right. When the celebrant arrives between them, all three go up to the altar. The subdeacon places the gospel book on the altar toward the gospel corner. Then the celebrant, deacon and subdeacon reverence the altar. They then go to the positions shown in the diagram. The celebrant, deacon and subdeacon reverence toward the altar crucifix at the words, "Glory be to the Father and to the Son and to the Holy Ghost."

The Kyrie

The deacon and subdeacon line up behind the celebrant. Toward the end of the kyrie, the celebrant, deacon, and subdeacon go to the midst of the altar.

The Gloria in Excelsis

While the celebrant intones, "Glory be to God on high," the deacon and subdeacon stand in line behind him, as shown in the diagram.

Order of Procession
Thurifer
Taperer; Server; Taperer
Subdeacon
Deacon
Celebrant

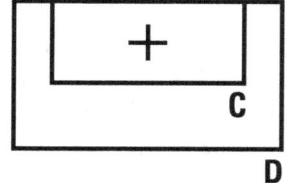

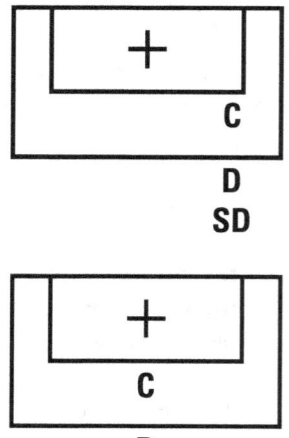

---

[67] These directions assume that the confession of sins will have been conducted prior to the beginning of the eucharistic liturgy. If the celebrant wishes to include the confession of sins in the service proper, the ministers and servers go in procession to the chancel. When the celebrant, deacon, and subdeacon arrive at the foot of the altar the confession of sins is held. After the absolution has been pronounced, the choir and/or congregation sing(s) the introit and the celebrant, deacon, and subdeacon go to the altar.

When the congregation takes up the chant, "And on earth peace, etc.," the deacon goes to the celebrant's right; the subdeacon, to the celebrant's left. Both bow slightly to the crucifix on arriving. At the end of the gloria in excelsis, the deacon and subdeacon again line up behind the celebrant as at the intonation of the gloria.

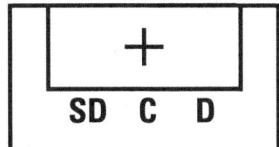

The Salutation

The deacon and subdeacon remain standing in line behind the celebrant. After the celebrant has chanted, "Let us pray," the celebrant, deacon, and subdeacon go back to the epistle corner of the altar and stand in line.

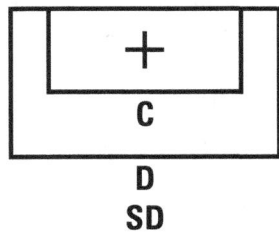

The Collect for the Day

The celebrant, deacon, and subdeacon stand in line at the epistle corner. At the words, "through Jesus Christ, thy Son, our Lord," the three bow toward the altar crucifix.

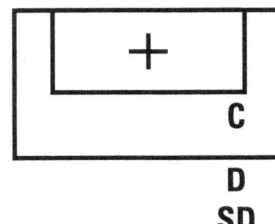

The Old Testament Lesson

When the collect has been sung, the deacon goes to the side of the celebrant and stands facing north. The server hands the book containing the Old Testament lesson and the epistle to the subdeacon who goes to a place on chancel level in line with the epistle corner of the altar to sing the lesson.

(The server himself may sing the lesson. In that case, the subdeacon remains standing behind the celebrant and the server goes to sing the lesson. When the server has sung the lesson, he hands the lectionary to the subdeacon who then goes to sing the epistle. The server returns to his customary place.)

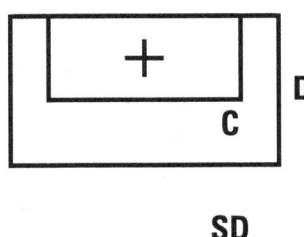

The Epistle

The subdeacon, standing in line with the epistle corner of the altar, sings the epistle. When he has sung the epistle, he returns the lectionary to the server who places it on the credence.

The Gradual

After the subdeacon has returned the lectionary to the server, the subdeacon removes the service book to the gospel corner of the altar and goes to stand at the foot of the altar steps.

The celebrant moves toward the midst of the altar. The thurifer may bring the censer and incense boat to the celebrant; the celebrant puts some incense into the censer. The thurifer then goes to the floor of the chancel and stands a short space behind the subdeacon.

The deacon kneels before the midst of the altar and quietly at the altar offers the prayer, "Cleanse my heart... through Jesus Christ, our Lord. Amen." Still kneeling, the deacon asks the celebrant's blessing (see p. 27). The celebrant blesses the deacon and hands the gospel book to him.

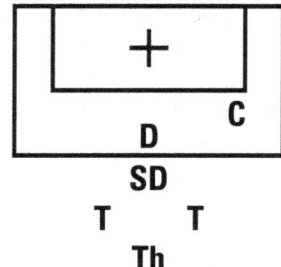

Meanwhile, the taperers procure their candles and come to stand at the foot of the altar behind the subdeacon.

When the deacon has received the gospel book from the celebrant, the deacon stands and turns to the people. At this, the thurifer, taperers and subdeacon turn, and the gospel procession goes to the place where the gospel will be sung.

The Holy Gospel

The celebrant stands at the altar, toward the epistle corner, facing the place where the gospel is sung.

When he arrives at the place where the gospel will be sung, the deacon hands the gospel book to the subdeacon.

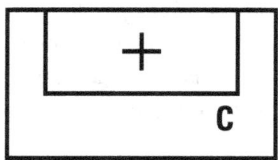

After the deacon has announced the gospel, he may take the censer from the thurifer and cense the gospel book. He swings the censer once to the center, once to the left, once to the right, and returns the censer to the thurifer. The thurifer swings the censer while the deacon sings the gospel.

When the gospel has been completed, the deacon may kiss the gospel book; or, the deacon may step aside, and the subdeacon, carrying the gospel book, may go directly to the celebrant and present the gospel to him to be kissed. (The subdeacon would then take the gospel book to the credence and, when the deacon has returned to the altar, stand behind him.)

The gospel procession returns to the altar. The thurifer and taperers deposit the censer and candles in the usual places and take their customary places in the chancel.

The deacon stands behind the celebrant; the subdeacon hands the gospel book to the server who places it on the credence; and the subdeacon then stands behind the deacon.

The Nicene Creed

The celebrant, deacon, and subdeacon stand in line at the midst of the altar while the celebrant intones the creed, "I believe in one God."

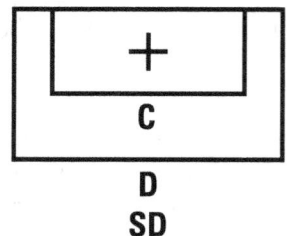

As the people respond, "the Father almighty, etc.," the deacon goes to the celebrant's right; the subdeacon, to the celebrant's left.

Both bow slightly toward the crucifix when they arrive beside the celebrant.

At the end of the creed, the deacon and subdeacon again line up behind the celebrant.

Then the celebrant, deacon, and subdeacon go to their chairs.

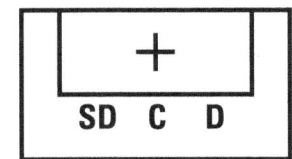

The Hymn

The Sermon

(For convenience the celebrant may, if he preaches, remove the chasuble and maniple before preaching. If the deacon preaches, he may remove his dalmatic and maniple before preaching. After the sermon, the celebrant resumes the chasuble and maniple; if the deacon preached, the deacon resumes his dalmatic and maniple.

The Offertory

When the sermon has ended, the subdeacon, deacon and celebrant return to the foot of the altar in that order. The subdeacon steps to the left, the deacon steps to the right, and, when the celebrant arrives between them, all three reverence the altar together.

The celebrant goes up to the altar, the deacon stands behind him, the subdeacon stands behind the deacon. Then the offertory is sung.

The deacon and subdeacon then go to the credence.

The subdeacon may take the lavabo bowl, towel, and water cruet and go to the epistle corner of the altar, where he is met by the celebrant. The subdeacon pours water over the celebrant's thumb and forefingers, the celebrant dries his hands on the towel, the subdeacon replaces the cruet, bowl and towel on the credence.

Meanwhile, the deacon takes the burse from the credence, goes to the midst of the altar, removes the corporal from the burse, lays the corporal still folded on the midst of the altar, places the burse toward the back of the altar or against the reredos or gradine toward the gospel corner of the altar, and unfolds the corporal.

The subdeacon brings the veiled chalice and paten, sets it down to the right of the corporal and returns to the credence.

The deacon unveils the chalice, folds the veil and places it at the right of the corporal toward the back of the altar.

The subdeacon brings the bread-box to the deacon.[68] The deacon, having removed the pall from the chalice, places enough hosts on the paten for the communion, and hands the paten to the celebrant who places the paten on the front part of the corporal.

---

[68] The server may hand the bread-box, ciborium, cruets, and flagon to the subdeacon.

(If there will be many communions, the subdeacon hands the ciborium to the deacon, who hands it to the celebrant. He in turn places the ciborium on the back part of the corporal.)

The subdeacon brings the cruets of wine and water to the deacon. The deacon removes the purificator from the chalice, places the purificator to the right of the corporal, takes the wine cruet, and pours wine into the chalice. (The subdeacon then adds a small quantity of water.) The deacon hands the chalice to the celebrant who places the chalice on the corporal behind the paten. Then the deacon, placing his left hand on the foot of the chalice, with his right hand covers the chalice with the pall. (If there will be many communions, the subdeacon hands the cruet or flagon to the deacon who then hands it to the celebrant. He in turn places it toward the back part of the corporal.)

The deacon and subdeacon line up behind the celebrant.

The General Prayer
The deacon and subdeacon stand behind the celebrant.

The Preface
The deacon and subdeacon remain standing behind the celebrant.

At the words, "evermore praising Thee and saying," the deacon goes to the celebrant's right; the subdeacon, to the celebrant's left.

The Sanctus
The celebrant, deacon, and subdeacon bow from the waist while the words, "Holy, holy, holy Lord God of Sabaoth; Heaven and earth are full of Thy glory; Hosanna in the highest," are sung.

The Lord's Prayer[69]
The deacon and subdeacon return to stand behind the celebrant.

The Words of Institution
The subdeacon kneels. The deacon goes to the celebrant's right. During the words of institution, the deacon assists the celebrant by uncovering and covering the chalice with the pall. During the words of consecration, "This is My body which is given for you. This do in remembrance of Me... this cup is the new testament in My blood, which is shed for you for the remission of sins. This do, as oft as ye drink it, in remembrance of Me," the deacon and subdeacon bow profoundly.

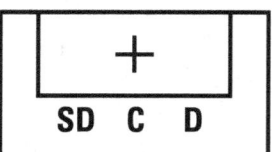

---

[69] If the celebrant prays a eucharistic prayer immediately after the sanctus, the deacon and subdeacon assume the positions indicated for the words of institution. At the end of the eucharistic prayer they assume the positions indicated for the Our Father.

The Pax Domini

The celebrant, deacon, and subdeacon remain in position.

The Agnus Dei

The deacon goes to the celebrant's right; the subdeacon, to the celebrant's left.

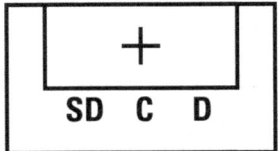

The Distribution

The deacon and subdeacon bow while the celebrant receives the sacrament.

The deacon and subdeacon then kneel on either side of the altar step to receive the sacrament.

The celebrant administers the host and cup to the deacon. The celebrant then administers the body of our Lord to all who are in the chancel, kneeling in their places: the subdeacon, server, thurifer, and taperers. The deacon follows the celebrant and administers the chalice. After the subdeacon has received the sacrament, he may kneel or stand to the north of the altar or in some other convenient place. The thurifer, server and taperers kneel or stand in some convenient place. They do not sit.

The celebrant administers the host to the congregation; the deacon follows and confirms with the chalice.

When all have received the sacrament, the deacon places a purificator over the mouth of the chalice, places the paten on top of it, places the pall on top of the paten, and removes the chalice from the corporal to the right of the corporal. He covers the chalice with the veil, folds the corporal, places the corporal in the burse, and places the burse on top of the chalice. The deacon may then either place the veiled chalice with the burse on top of it in the midst of the altar, or hand them to the subdeacon to be replaced on the credence.

(If a ciborium and flagon or cruet are on the corporal, the deacon would, of course, remove them from the corporal before folding it. The deacon may hand the ciborium and flagon or cruet to the subdeacon to be placed on the credence, or, if the veiled chalice and burse are left on the altar, the deacon may place the ciborium and flagon or cruet behind the veiled chalice and burse.)

The Nunc Dimittis, Thanksgiving

Salutation, and Benedicamus

The celebrant, deacon, and subdeacon stand in line at the midst of the altar.

The deacon sings the benedicamus.

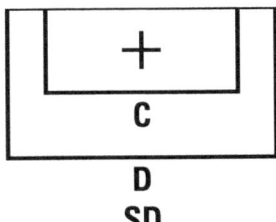

The Benediction

During the benediction, the deacon may kneel slightly to the right of the midst; the subdeacon, slightly to the left of the midst.

After the benediction, the celebrant turns back to the altar. The deacon and subdeacon stand, if they have knelt during the benediction. They return to the floor of the chancel, the deacon standing to the right of the midst; the subdeacon, to the left. They face the altar. The server gets the processional cross; the taperers get their candles and come to stand at the foot of the altar. The thurifer gets his censer and comes to stand at the foot of the altar behind the server and taperers.

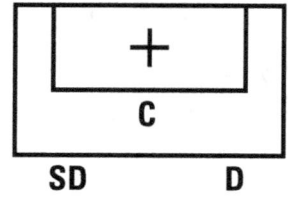

The celebrant turns back to the people. He comes down the steps to stand between the deacon and subdeacon. The celebrant turns back to the altar. Then the celebrant, deacon, and subdeacon together reverence the altar and turn to the people. The thurifer then turns to the people and leads the procession back to the sacristy in this order: thurifer, server carrying the processional cross flanked by the taperers, sub-deacon, deacon, celebrant.

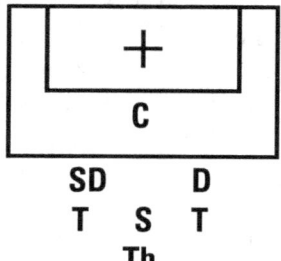

NOTE: If some simplification of the foregoing directions is desired, it is possible to dispense with the "liturgical positioning" of the deacon and subdeacon at the altar. This means that throughout the service—except at the ceremonies of the gospel, the offertory, and the communion—the deacon would stand on chancel level in line with the epistle corner of the altar. The subdeacon would stand on chancel level in line with the gospel corner of the altar. Both would face the altar. It is also possible to dispense with the use of the processional cross, lights, and incense. In that case, only the server would assist the celebrant, deacon and subdeacon.

CHAPTER SIX
THE CELEBRATION OF THE HOLY EUCHARIST FACING THE PEOPLE

I. Introduction

In his *German Mass* of 1526 Martin Luther wrote: "In the true mass, however, of real Christians, the altar should not remain where it is, and the priest should always face the people as Christ undoubtedly did at the Last Supper."[70] The practice to which Luther here alludes was common in Christian antiquity.[71] The celebration of the Eucharist facing the people should not, however, be regarded as a kind of liturgical "orthodoxy." The celebration in the so-called eastward position—the celebrant turning his back to the people so that he faces the (liturgical) east—also has a venerable history. It is still the most common practice among Lutherans, has not ceased to be the usage of the Eastern Orthodox communion, and probably is still the use of the majority of Anglican congregations.[72]

The celebration of the Eucharist facing the people serves to emphasize that the altar is a table and that the Holy Eucharist is a ***meal***.[73] The family of God gathers around the Lord's ***table*** for the family meal. This way of celebrating the Eucharist provides for a kind of involvement of the people with the action of the presiding minister which is not possible when the Holy Eucharist is celebrated by a minister with his back to the people.

The following directions distinguish sharply between the service of the Word and the service of the sacrament. The first part of the great service centers in the holy Word, the second centers in the holy food. The Lord of the church comes through the Word and through the bread and wine of the holy meal. A ***book*** is the focus of the service of the Word; ***bread and wine on a table*** are the focus of the service of the sacrament. To emphasize this distinction ***no part of the service prior to the eucharistic meal itself is conducted at the altar***. There is no need for the altar, that is, the table, before the meal is to be prepared and eaten. A table is necessary neither for the prayers and hymns nor for the reading of the lessons in the service of the Word: for this a book is sufficient. Also to emphasize the table

---

70 Martin Luther, "Deutsche Messe," in *D. Martin Luthers Werke. Kritische Gesammtausgabe* (Weimar: Hermann Böhlaus Nachfolger, 1897), XIX, 80. (Hereafter this edition of Luther's works will be referred to as WA.) Martin Luther, "German Mass and Order of Service," in *Luther's Works*, 53 (Philadelphia: Fortress Press, 1965), 25. (Hereafter this edition of Luther's works will be referred to as LW.)
71 Joseph A. Jungmann, *The Mass of the Roman Rite: Its Origins and Development (Missarum Sollemnia)*, trans. Francis A. Brunner (New York: Benziger Brothers, 1951), I, 274ff. Basil Minchin, *The Celebration of the Holy Eucharist Facing the People* (n.p., n.d.7, pp. 3-12, 19–27).
72 "To pray to the East is a Christian custom that has its roots in apostolic worship since the primitive church celebrated the Eucharist in expectation of the Lord's return. (I Cor. xi. 26) It was believed that the ***parousia*** would be heralded by the sign of the cross in the Eastern sky, as mentioned in Matt. xxiv. 30. Hence to turn to the East was an acknowledgment that the Eucharist was being celebrated in expectation of the second Advent." Cyril E. Pocknee, *The Parson's Handbook*, 13th edition (London: Oxford University Press, 1966), p. 21. See Jungmann, I, 70f.

character of the altar and the meal character of the Eucharist, the corporal (the linen cloth on which the vessels for the bread and wine are placed) is not spread on the altar nor are the sacred vessels themselves placed on the altar until the eucharistic meal itself is about to begin, that is, at the offertory.

Celebrating the Eucharist facing the people reflects an approach to the liturgy, common to the pre-medieval period, which emphasizes the involvement of the whole church in the eucharistic action. In the pre-medieval period the bishop, seated behind the altar and facing the people, preached and offered the great eucharistic prayer, but the remaining portions of the liturgy were almost wholly conducted by others. The celebration of the Eucharist was understood as the action of the whole church of God in a given place, an action in which each member functioned "in his vocation and ministry." This idea was given form by assigning various parts of the liturgy to various persons or groups of persons. Even during the Middle Ages—and for many years after the Reformation in some parts of the Lutheran Church—the normal Sunday and festival service of at least the large city churches was the "high mass," a Eucharist celebrated by a priest assisted by deacon and subdeacon, servers, choir and congregation. But with the passage of time many Christians have come to look on this full type of service involving many participants as extraordinary, and to regard a service conducted by a solitary clergyman as normal. This development is probably regrettable, since it has unduly clericalized worship and has given the impression that the Eucharist is a rite to be read by the minister rather than an action in which the whole church participates. A return to the ancient ideal would give concrete expression to the thought that the Eucharist is the action of the body of Christ, an action in which the several members of the body of Christ have various functions to carry out.[74] For this reason these ceremonial directions encourage the participation of as many people as possible: reading the lessons, bringing the gifts of bread and wine to the altar, and so on.

In terms of the rationale of this type of eucharistic celebration, the use of the term "celebrant" for the minister who presides at the celebration is misleading. For the whole church celebrates the Eucharist; the minister only presides at the Eucharist according to his vocation. But while the term "celebrant" is misleading, the term has been retained in the following directions for the sake of convenience. More accurately one should speak of "the minister who presides at the celebration of the sacrament," or of "the president of the eucharistic assembly." But while these phrases are more accurate, they are also quite awkward.

The following directions provide for two kinds of eucharistic service: first, a simple way of celebrating the Holy Eucharist facing the people; second, a way of celebration involving greater use of traditional ceremonial features.

Except in cases where the prescriptive "shall" rubrics of our synod's authorized service books are cited, the following directions should be regarded merely as suggestions rather than normative prescriptions. These directions suggest *a way*—of celebrating the Eucharist facing the people, a way which reflects the long history of how this has been done among the people of God, which is sensitive to ecumenical consensus, and which may prove to be an orderly and helpful way of doing the liturgy at the present time.

---

73 In Christian tradition the altar is also the symbol of Christ in the church and, therefore, of the presence of God with His people. The altar is by definition a place of sacrifice and therefore stands in the church as the symbol of the one perfect sacrifice of Christ on the cross, of which the Eucharist is the memorial.

74 On this whole matter see Jungmann, I, 22ff., 67ff., 195ff. See also Basil Minchin, *Every Man in His Ministry* (London: Darton, Longmans and Todd, 1960), pp. 188ff.

Celebrating facing the people is much more demanding on the officiating clergy than celebrating in the "eastward" position. The officiants are continually in full view of the people. This makes it absolutely necessary to avoid all nervous habits. The officiants must be conscious of facial expression. They should not stare at the congregation, since the members of the congregation would in this way be made most uncomfortable. The minister should look at the people when addressing them, for example, during the salutation. To grin or grimace or wink the eyes or roll them around is intolerable. (This does not, however, imply that the celebrant should look grim or unhappy.) When one person is carrying out his function, for example, reading a lesson, the other persons in the chancel should not stare or look around, but rather look at the person who is carrying out the assigned function. When the celebrant is offering prayers he may, if he is sure of the text of the prayer, lift his eyes "to heaven." When reading a lesson, one should keep his eyes on the book as a sign that he is reading the words of another. Gestures should be bold and deliberate, without being either mechanical or theatrical. For example, when the celebrant lifts the chalice from the altar at the words, "He took the cup," he should do this deliberately and lift the chalice high enough above the mensa of the altar so that the people can clearly see what is being done.

In general, the less "liturgically minded" pastor may find it necessary to employ more ceremonial actions than he has been accustomed to use when celebrating in the "eastward" position. The more "liturgically minded" pastor may find that some ceremonial observances possible in the "eastward" position tend to be distracting when done in full view of the people.[75]

II. The Arrangement of the Altar and Chancel

The altar is the one absolutely essential piece of furniture in the church building. If there is to be a meal, there must necessarily be a table on which to prepare it. The altar should indicate by its size and dignity and position its role as the table for the eucharistic meal and the symbol of the presence of the exalted Christ among His people.

The altar is placed away from the wall of the chancel. If at all possible, the altar should be placed at some distance from the wall so that the chairs for the officiating clergy can be placed behind it.[76] The chairs should be placed as far as possible from the altar so that the clergy when viewed by the congregation do not, when at the chairs, appear to be already at the altar.

The chair of the celebrant should indicate his function of presiding over the worship of the community. Yet the chair should not have the appearance of a throne. It may, however, be placed a step higher than the altar step so that more than the celebrant's head can be seen when the celebrant is seated. If eucharistic vestments are worn, the chair should have a low back so that when the celebrant is seated the chasuble may hang down behind it.

---

75 For example, the celebrant probably should not kneel behind the altar as it may appear ludicrous to see only the celebrant's head protruding above the altar.
76 On the history of the position of the altar see the helpful summary in Basil Minchin, *The Celebration of the Holy Eucharist Facing the People*, pp. 3–12. See also Cyril E. Pocknee, The Christian Altar (London: A. R. Mowbray and Co., 1963), pp. 88ff. See also Joseph A. Braun, *Der Christliche Altar in seiner geschichtlichen Entwicklung* (München: Alte Mesiter Guenther Koch and Co., 1924), 1, 421ff.

If architectural limitations make it impossible to place the chair of the presiding minister behind the altar, it may be placed (together with other chairs for officiating clergy) against the side wall of the chancel. Chairs for lay servers may be placed at convenient locations in the chancel.

The altar should be vested in a frontal of the color of the day or season; it may also be vested in a frontlet.[77] In many places today there is a tendency to dispense with the frontal, but this is contrary to the bulk of tradition. People normally clothe their tables at mealtime. Vesting the altar in a frontal is a mark of reverence for the Lord whom the altar represents and serves to make the altar the focus of attention. The use of the frontal in the proper liturgical color also prevents the monotony of the altar appearing the same throughout the year. There may, of course, be circumstances in which one may feel free—or be compelled—to omit the frontal. This might happen when the altar is itself an extraordinary work of art or where its shape unfortunately makes impossible its vesting in the customary way. A free-standing altar should, if possible, be vested both front and back, or one may use a throw-over type of frontal, hanging down on all sides.

The altar must be vested in a fair linen cloth.[78] At the narrow ends of the altar the fair linen cloth should reach the floor.

It is customary to place a crucifix somewhere in the church in full view of the people. The crucifix must not be placed on the altar used for celebration facing the people since the crucifix would then obscure the action of the minister. For the same reason a processional crucifix should not be placed in front of the altar. A processional crucifix may be placed behind the celebrant's chair (if the celebrant's chair is behind the altar) or a large crucifix may be hung over the altar, or on the east wall of the chancel, or at the entrance to the chancel.

A candle may be placed on the altar step at either end of the altar, thus leaving the altar free of everything not really essential to the holy meal. (These candles may be brought to the altar in procession at the beginning of the service. See below, Part V.) If this is not possible, a candle may be placed on the mensa at each end of the altar.[79]

A missal stand or book rest is by no means necessary. The service book may rest directly on the altar. If a missal stand is used, it must be low and inconspicuous, lest it detract by its size and proportion from the vessels of bread and wine. Some may wish to follow the old custom of using a cushion for a book rest.[80] If a missal stand or cushion is used, it is brought to the altar only when the service book which rests on it is needed at the altar; that is, it is brought to the altar at the offertory.

There should be a credence table somewhere in the chancel, and another credence table near the entrance of the church building. Each should be decently covered with a linen cloth. The credence table in the chancel should probably be placed in such a way that it is at the celebrant's right when the celebrant faces the people.

---

77 The frontlet—the short cloth hanging down from the mensa a few inches—may be dispensed with. Historically it served only as a convenience to conceal the means by which the frontal was suspended.
78 *The Lutheran Liturgy* (St. Louis: Concordia Publishing House, n.d.), p. 426.
79 See Jungmann, I, 67ff., and D. R. Dendy, *The Use of Lights in Christian Worship*, Alcuin Club Collections (London: SPCK, 1959), XL. Dom Gregory Dix, *The Shape of the Liturgy* (London: Dacre Press, 1945), pp. 416ff.
80 Pocknee, *The Parson's Handbook*, p. 28.

The lectern for reading the lessons may be placed at any convenient place in the chancel or at the place where the nave and chancel meet. In ancient times two ambos, elevated reading desks, were in use in some places. This is still possible. In that case one could be reserved for reading the Holy Gospel and the other for reading all other lessons. (The usual arrangement of pulpit and lectern is, perhaps, analogous to the two ambos.) The point of using an ambo to read the lessons was to provide a place where the lessons could be read so as to be easily heard, and to provide a place to rest the rather unwieldly texts of the Scriptures.[81]

Diagrams indicating how the chancel might be arranged when the Holy Eucharist is celebrated facing the people:

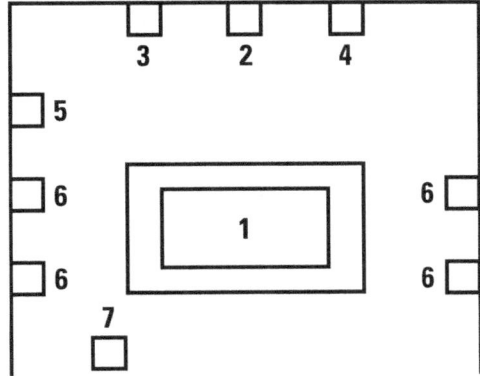

A. When it is feasible to place the celebrant's chair behind the altar.

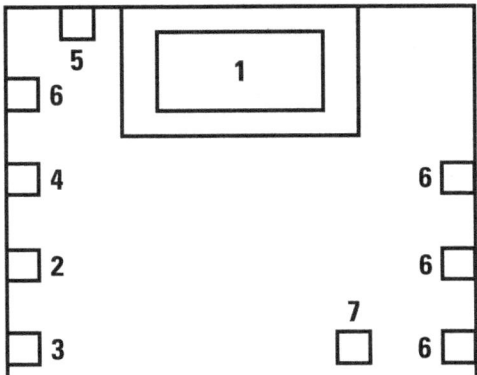

b. When the celebrant's chair must be placed elsewhere.

1 - Altar
2 - Celebrant's chair
3 - Deacon's chair
4 - Subdeacon's chair
5 - Credence
6 - Server's chair
7 - Possible position for lectern

---

81 See Jungmann, I, 411–19.

III. Preparations for the Celebration of the Holy Eucharist Facing the People

The chalice and paten are prepared in the customary way. First, a purificator is placed over the mouth of the chalice. Then the paten is placed on top of the purificator. Then the pall is placed on top of the paten. Then the chalice veil is placed over the chalice and paten, and adjusted to form a trapezoid when viewed from the front. Then the burse, containing the corporal and additional purificators, is placed on top of the veiled chalice. The veiled chalice and paten, with the burse resting on top of them, are placed on the credence in the chancel.[82]

The bread box or ciborium and the cruet or flagon are placed on the credence near the entrance of the church.[83]

The lectionary is placed on the lectern. If there is no lectern, the lectionary is placed on the credence.

The service book is placed on the credence, or if the celebrant has no server to assist him, it is placed on the celebrant's chair.

IV. A Simple Way of Celebrating the Holy Eucharist Facing the People

The Confession of Sins

During the opening hymn—in silence if the opening hymn is omitted—the celebrant goes to the entrance of the chancel or to the foot of the altar steps. There he leads the congregation in the confession of sins.[84]

The Introit

While the introit is sung, the celebrant goes to his chair. (If no one is available to sing the introit, the celebrant, having pronounced the absolution, goes to his chair and, when he arrives at the chair, reads the introit.)

The Kyrie, Gloria in Excelsis, Salutation and Collect for the Day

The celebrant remains standing at his chair.

---

82 There is some sentiment at present against the use of hosts or wafers for Holy Communion. Some feel that the hosts are so unlike the bread ordinarily eaten that people have difficulty in realizing that they are bread. If, however, a loaf of bread is used, a larger paten becomes a necessity. For this purpose a good silver alms-bason, perfectly plain, or any decent silver vessel may be used. When such a paten is used for the bread, it is obviously impossible to veil the chalice and paten in the usual way. In this case the unveiled chalice—perhaps covered with a pall or folded corporal—and the large paten will simply be placed on the credence. They may be covered with some large veil, but this is not necessary. If the loaf of bread is brought forward by representatives of the people at the offertory, an additional vessel—to hold the bread while it rests on the credence near the entrance of the church and while it is carried to the altar—may be necessary. For this purpose a bread basket may serve.

Instead of a loaf of bread, whole-wheat wafers may be used. These are usually somewhat larger and thicker than the wafers now in use and have a consistency more like the bread eaten at table today.

83 The bread and wine are then brought to the altar at the offertory by representatives of the people.

84 If the confession of sins is separated from the order of the Holy Communion, the minister will come into the church in advance of the hour appointed for the celebration of the Eucharist. He will conduct the confession of sins in the usual way and then return to the sacristy. At the hour appointed for the celebration of Holy Communion the introit is sung by the choir. While the introit is sung, the minister enters the church and goes to his chair. (If no one is available to sing the introit, the minister enters the church in silence, goes to his chair, and, when he arrives at his chair, reads the introit).

The Old Testament Lesson and the Epistle

After the celebrant has prayed the collect for the day he sits. A layman may come forward to the lectern and read the Old Testament lesson. He may then return to his place and another layman may come forward and read the Epistle. (If no competent person is available to read the lessons, the celebrant, having prayed the collect, goes to the lectern and reads them.)

The Gradual

While the gradual is sung, the celebrant goes to the lectern or goes into the midst of the congregation to read the Holy Gospel.[85] (If no one is available to sing the gradual, the celebrant, standing at his chair—or, if he has read the Epistle, standing at the lectern—leads the congregation in reading the gradual. Then he may remain at the lectern or go into the midst of the congregation to read the Holy Gospel.)

The Holy Gospel

The celebrant reads the Holy Gospel at the lectern or in the midst of the congregation. After the celebrant has read the Gospel, he returns to his chair.

The Nicene Creed

Standing at his chair, the celebrant leads the people in the creed.

The Hymn

The celebrant remains at his chair. If his chair is behind the altar, he may preach from his chair. If he preaches from the pulpit, he may go into the pulpit after the hymn has been sung.[86]

The Sermon

After the celebrant has pronounced the votum ("The peace of God which passeth..."), he procures the service book, goes to the altar, and places the service book at his left on the altar.[87]

The Offertory

The celebrant, standing behind and at the midst of the altar, sings or reads the offertory with the people.[88]

---

85 At the present time there is considerable feeling that the Gospel should be read in the midst of the people as a symbol of bringing the Gospel of Christ to all men.

86 Note that if "The Holy Eucharist I" (*Worship Supplement*, pp. 19ff.) is the rite being used for the service, the sermon immediately follows the Holy Gospel. After the sermon the celebrant, standing at his chair, leads the people in the creed. Then the hymn is sung and the liturgy continues with the offertory action.

87 This is the first time the celebrant goes to the altar.

88 If "The Holy Eucharist I" is used, the offertory chant is not sung at this point. Rather, it is sung **while** the bread, wine, and money are presented and placed on the altar. The offerings of the people are first gathered. Then, while the bread, wine, and money are brought forward by the representatives of the people and placed on the altar by the celebrant, the offertory chant is sung. If the liturgy is spoken, the congregation may read the offertory sentences while these things are done, or the celebrant and people may read the offertory sentences after these actions have been completed.

Conduct of the Services

The celebrant goes to the credence. He takes the veiled chalice with the burse resting on top of it and carries them to the altar. He places the veiled chalice and burse at his right on the altar. He takes the corporal from the burse, places the folded corporal in the midst of the altar, and lays the burse on the altar behind the service book. Then he unfolds the corporal. Then the celebrant takes hold of the back part of the chalice veil with both hands and removes it from the chalice. He folds it on the altar to the right of the corporal, then places it close to the back of the altar near the corporal. The celebrant removes the pall from the chalice and places the pall on the right side of the outspread corporal.

Then the celebrant places the paten slightly to the left of the center of the corporal. He removes the purificator from the chalice and places the purificator on the altar to the right of the corporal. He places the chalice slightly to the right of the center of the corporal.[89]

Meanwhile, the offerings of the people are gathered. Representatives of the congregation then bring forward the offerings and the vessels of bread and wine which had been placed on the credence near the entrance to the church building before the service began.

The celebrant meets the representatives of the people at the rail.

Note: In the directions immediately following, it is assumed that for the sake of convenience the celebrant does not go behind the altar but remains on the side of the altar nearest the congregation when he places the offerings and the vessels of bread and wine on the altar.

The celebrant receives the alms basons, takes them to the altar, and places them toward the end of the altar.

The celebrant returns to the rail, receives the ciborium or bread box, takes the ciborium or bread box to the altar, and places it to the right of the paten. He uncovers the ciborium or bread box, places a large host or several hosts on the paten, covers the ciborium or bread box, and returns to the rail.

He receives the flagon or cruet of wine. He takes the flagon or cruet to the altar, pours wine into the chalice, places the flagon or cruet to the left of the chalice, and covers the chalice with the pall. Then the celebrant returns to his place behind the altar.[90]

---

89 The arrangement of the vessels described here is somewhat different from the arrangement in use in most parts of the Western church since the close of the middle ages, that is, the paten in front of the chalice. Apparently, the more primitive practice was to place the chalice to the right and the paten to the left on the altar. (This is still the custom of the churches of the Byzantine rite.) "The practice of placing the chalice to the right, the host to the left, continued into the later Middle Ages." (Jungmann, II, 53) In the celebration of the Eucharist facing the people the older practice is desirable. The paten can more readily be seen by the people if it is placed beside rather than—from the congregation's perspective—behind the chalice.

90 The representatives of the people may remain at the altar rail, returning to their places after they have received the sacrament.

Diagram showing the position of the sacred vessels and linens on the altar:

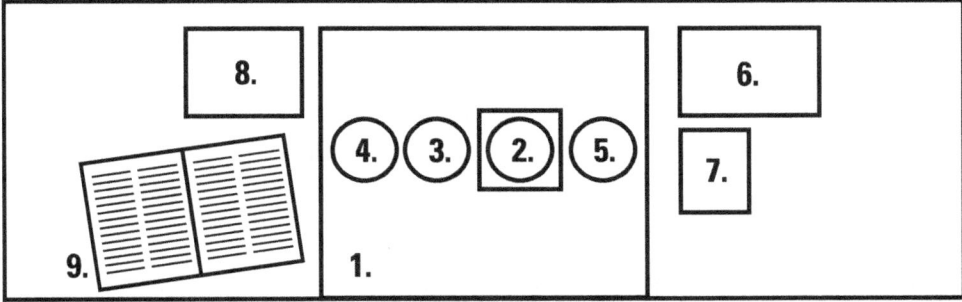

1 - Outstretched corporal
2 - Chalice covered with pall
3 - Paten
4 - Ciborium or bread box
5 - Cruet or flagon
6 - Folded chalice veil
7 - Purificators
8 - Burse
9 - Service book

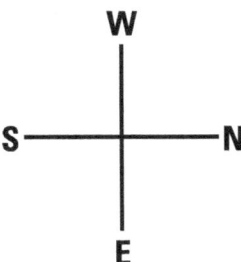

The General Prayer
   Standing behind the altar, the celebrant prays the general prayer.

The Preface, Sanctus, and the Lord's Prayer
   The celebrant continues to face the people throughout these parts of the service.

The Words of Institution
   The celebrant removes the cover from the ciborium or bread box. With hands joined he begins the words of institution. At the words "took bread" he takes the paten in both hands and lifts it as high as his chest. He then replaces the paten on the altar. At the words "when He had given thanks" the celebrant places his left hand on the altar to the left of the corporal and with his right hand makes the sign of the cross over the paten and over any other vessel in which there is bread to be consecrated. At the words "He brake it" the celebrant may take a large host in both hands, break it into two pieces, and replace the pieces on the paten. While he says the words of consecration, "Take, eat; this is My body which is given for you," the celebrant holds the paten in both hands before his chest. He

pronounces the words of consecration with particular distinctness, attention, and reverence. After the words "in remembrance of Me" he replaces the paten on the corporal and covers the ciborium or bread box.

He then uncovers the flagon or cruet of wine. Placing his left hand on the base of the chalice, with his right hand the celebrant removes the pall from the chalice. At the words "He took the cup" the celebrant takes the chalice by the knop in his right hand and, placing his left hand under the foot of the chalice, lifts the chalice as high as his chest, and then replaces it on the corporal. At the words "when He had given thanks" the celebrant places his left hand on the altar to the left of the corporal and with his right hand makes the sign of the cross over the chalice and over any other vessel in which there is wine to be consecrated. While he says the words of consecration, "Drink ye all of it; this cup is the new testament in My blood, which is shed for you for the remission of sins," the celebrant again lifts the chalice from the altar and holds it before his chest. He pronounces the words of consecration with particular distinctness, attention, and reverence. After the words "in remembrance of Me" he places the chalice on the corporal. Placing his left hand on the foot of the chalice—to avoid the possibility of accidentally causing the chalice to be overturned—with his right hand he covers the chalice with the pall. Then he covers the flagon or cruet.

The Pax Domini and Agnus Dei

The celebrant continues to face the people across the altar throughout these portions of the service. After the celebrant has sung or said the pax domini, the greeting of peace may be exchanged among the people.

The Distribution

The celebrant reverently receives the Holy Sacrament. Then he administers the Holy Communion to the people. (If the representatives of the people have remained at the altar rail since bringing forward the bread, wine, and money at the offertory, they return to their places after they have received the Holy Communion.)

If another minister assists in the distribution, the **celebrant** administers the consecrated bread and the assisting minister administers the chalice.

When all have received the sacrament, the celebrant places the chalice in the midst of the outspread corporal. He then places the purificator over the mouth of the chalice. He places the paten on top of the purificator. He places the pall on top of the paten. He covers the chalice and paten with the veil. The flagon or cruet and the ciborium or bread box are placed in their usual positions. (See the diagram of the position of the sacred vessels on the altar.)[91]

---

91 The sacred vessels may be returned to the credence at this point. The celebrant takes the flagon or cruet and the ciborium or bread box to the credence. Then he removes the veiled chalice from the corporal, folds the corporal, places the corporal in the burse, and places the burse on top of the veiled chalice. Then he removes the veiled chalice and paten with the burse resting on top of them to the credence. He then returns to his place behind and at the midst of the altar.

The Nunc Dimittis, Thanksgiving, Salutation, Benedicamus, and Benediction
   The celebrant stands behind the altar, facing the people. After pronouncing the benediction, the celebrant may pause for silent prayer. Then he goes around to the front of the altar, reverences the altar, and returns to the sacristy.

V. The Celebration of the Holy Eucharist Facing the People: Celebrant, Deacon, Subdeacon, and Acolytes[92]

KEY TO DIAGRAMS IN PART V
C—Celebrant   S—Server
D—Deacon   T—Taperer
SD—Subdeacon   L—Layman
R—Representatives of the people who bring forward the gifts of bread, wine, and money.

   While the opening hymn is sung—in silence, if the opening hymn is omitted—the ministers and acolytes go in procession to the entrance of the chancel. The server carrying the processional cross, flanked by two taperers, leads the procession.[93] The subdeacon, carrying the gospel book, follows them. The deacon follows the subdeacon. The celebrant follows the deacon. The servers with cross and lights stop at the entrance of the chancel. The subdeacon steps to the left, the deacon steps to the right, and the celebrant stands between them.

The Confession of Sins
   The celebrant leads the people in the confession of sins. (The servers with cross and lights do not kneel.)

The Introit[94]
   While the introit is sung, the servers with cross and lights lead the procession into the chancel. The subdeacon follows them; the deacon follows the subdeacon; the celebrant follows the deacon. When the servers arrive at the foot of the altar steps, they pause, take their ornaments to the appointed place, and then take their places in the chancel.[95] The subdeacon places the gospel book on the altar and goes to his chair.[96] The deacon reverences the altar and goes to his chair. The celebrant reverences the altar and goes to his chair. The celebrant stands before the chair in the midst; the deacon stands at his right; the subdeacon stands at his left.[97]

T S T	T S T	T S T
SD	SD	SD C D
D	D	
C	C	
Procession	Procession into Chancel	At the Entrance to the Chancel

The Kyrie and Gloria in Excelsis
   Everyone remains standing in his place.

The Salutation and the Collect for the Day

While the people sing the response to the salutation, the server brings the service book from the credence. He stands before the celebrant, slightly to the celebrant's left, holding the service book open at the collect. After the collect for the day has been sung, the server returns the service book to the credence.

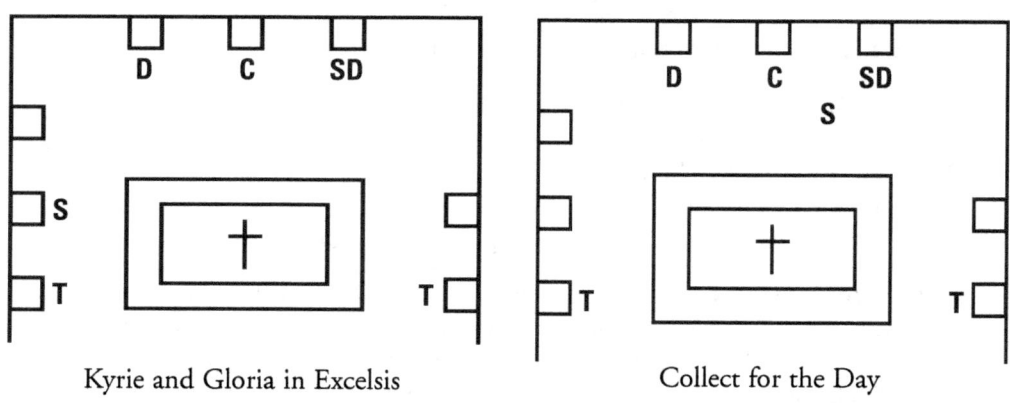

Kyrie and Gloria in Excelsis   Collect for the Day

---

92 The ceremonial here described follows the broad outline of eucharistic ceremonial generally followed in the Western church since about the seventh/eighth century. Certain medieval developments retained in some places at the Reformation are included. But these directions are obviously a contemporary adaptation and reflect the actual practice of some of our parish churches.

93 If incense is used, the thurifer precedes the servers with cross and lights. According to historical evidence, lights and incense were carried before the celebrant as a mark of honor for Christ, whom the celebrant represents. The Apology of the Augsburg Confession says: "Ministers do not represent their own persons but the person of Christ, because of the church's call, as Christ testifies (Luke 10:16), 'He who hears you, hears me.' When they offer the Word of God or the sacraments they do so in Christ's place and stead" (Apology of the Augsburg Confession VII, 28). Some historical evidence suggests that the lights and incense were more closely related to the gospel book which was carried in procession: the gospel book which represented Christ (Jungmann, I, 446). We might wish at the present time to relate the lights (and incense) to the processional cross, which is also a symbol of Christ. On the use of incense in general, see Horace D. Hummel, "On the Use of Incense," Una Sancta, 24 (Resurrection 1967), 76-80.

94 If the confession of sins is omitted or held at some hour prior to the celebration of the Eucharist, the eucharistic liturgy begins with the introit. The servers and ministers enter the church and go in procession to the altar while the introit is sung.

95 As noted above (see Part II), the candles carried by the servers may be the candles placed on the floor at either end of the altar. They are carried into the church by the servers and placed at either end of the altar at this point.

96 The gospel book was placed on the altar before the beginning of the Eucharist according to *Ordo Romanus Primus*, ca. seventh-eighth century. (Cf. "Ordo Romanus Primus," *Patrologiae Latinae*, ed. J. P. Migne [Paris: Garnier Brothers, 1895] LXXVIII, 940. Hereafter Migne's edition will be referred to as MPL.) The usage is, however, probably much older. "The Lord's Board was too holy (too 'awful' is another view) to bear anything but the Mystic Oblation itself, and such objects, the cup, the paten, the linen cloth, as were necessary for the offering of the sacrifice. If indeed the Book of the Gospels lay on the Altar from the beginning of Mass until the Gospel was read, it is to be remembered that the Gospel Book was regarded as representing our Lord Himself, just as the Altar came to be conceived of as the throne of the Great King" (Edmund Bishop, *Liturgica Historica: papers on the liturgy and religious life of the Western Church* [Oxford: Clarendon Press, 1945]), p. 412. In the rite of the Eastern Church to this very day the gospel book rests on the altar (Archdale A. King *The Rites of Eastern Christendom* [Rome: Catholic Book Agency, 1947], II, 113). "In the Middle Ages it was the rule (to a great extent) to place the Gospel Book on the altar at the beginning of Mass .... When in the present day high Mass the deacon lays the Gospel Book on the altar after the Epistle, it is doubtless a reminiscence of the ancient symbolic ritual. The older, fuller ceremony was probably omitted from the Missal of Pius V (Rit. serv. vi. 5) because the Gospel is contained in the Missal and the latter is on the altar from the start" (Jungmann, I, 444). The rite of the Roman Church now directs that the gospel book, which has been carried in procession, is to be placed on the altar at the beginning of mass.

97 The deacon, as the "first assistant" to the celebrant, occupies the "place of honor" at the celebrant's right.

98 The reading of the Epistle was originally the work of a lector. In the seventh/eighth century the reading of the Epistle became at Rome the work of the subdeacon ("Ordo Romanus Primus," MPL, LXXVIII, 942). As early as the time of Saint Justin Martyr (ca. A.D. 150) we hear that someone other than the presiding minister read the liturgical lessons (Jungmann I, 23). For a discussion of who read the liturgical lessons, see Jungmann, I, 410ff.

The Old Testament Lesson and the Epistle

Everyone sits. A layman may come forward from the congregation to read the Old Testament lesson, or the Old Testament lesson may be read by the server or the subdeacon. At the conclusion of the Old Testament lesson, the layman or server returns to his place and the subdeacon comes to the lectern to read the Epistle.[98] If the subdeacon has read the lesson, he simply remains at the lectern to read the Epistle.

After the subdeacon has read the Epistle, he goes to the foot of the altar steps.

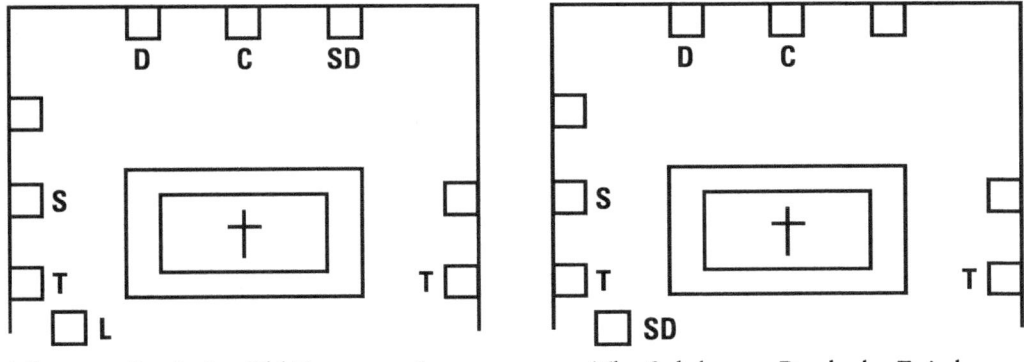

A Layman Reads the Old Testament Lesson   The Subdeacon Reads the Epistle

The Gradual[99]

If incense is used in connection with the reading of the Holy Gospel, the thurifer brings the censer and incense boat to the celebrant, and the celebrant puts some incense into the censer. Then the deacon asks for and receives the celebrant's blessing.[100] Then the deacon

---

99   Incense may be used in connection with the reading of the Holy Gospel. Lights (and incense) are used at the Gospel as a mark of honor for the written Word of God. Martin Luther in his "Formula Missae et Communionis" of 1523 wrote: "Sixth, the Gospel lesson follows, for which we neither prohibit nor prescribe candles or incense. Let these things be free" (Martin Luther, "An Order of Mass and Communion," LW 53, 25. "Formula Missae et Communionis," WA XII, 211). Saint Jerome, writing from Bethlehem in A.D. 378, says: "Throughout all the churches of the East when the Gospel is to be read lights are kindled ... not to dispel the darkness but to exhibit a token of joy... and that under the symbol of corporeal light that light may be set forth of which we read in the psalter, 'Thy word is a lamp unto my feet and a light unto my path!'" (Jerome, "Contra Vigilantium," MPL, XXIII, 346)

If incense is used in connection with the reading of the Holy Gospel, the thurifer brings the censer and incense boat to the celebrant, and the celebrant puts some incense into the censer. Then the deacon asks for and receives the celebrant's blessing. (See below, footnote 31.) Then the deacon goes around to the front of the altar. Meanwhile, the thurifer goes to stand on chancel level a short distance behind the taperers, who stand on chancel level behind the subdeacon. The deacon takes the gospel book from the altar and turns to the people. When the deacon turns to the people, the thurifer, taperers, and subdeacon turn to the people, and the thurifer leads the procession to the place where the Gospel will be sung. After the deacon has announced the Gospel, he takes the censer from the thurifer and censes the gospel book. He swings the censer once to the center, then to the left, then to the right, and returns the censer to the thurifer. While the deacon sings the Gospel, the thurifer swings the censer. After the Gospel has been sung, the procession returns to the altar in the same order in which it came to the place where the Gospel was sung. The thurifer and taperers take the censer and lights to the usual places and return to their places in the chancel.

100 The deacon turns to the celebrant and says in a low voice: "Give me your blessing." The celebrant answers in a low voice: "The Lord be in your heart and on your lips that you may worthily and competently proclaim His Holy Gospel in the name of the Father and of the ✠ Son and of the Holy Spirit." At the words "and of the Son" the celebrant makes the sign of the cross over the deacon.

goes around to the front of the altar. Meanwhile, the thurifer goes to stand on chancel level a short distance behind the taperers, who stand on chancel level behind the subdeacon. The deacon takes the gospel book from the altar and turns to the people. When the deacon turns to the people, the thurifer, taperers, and subdeacon turn to the people, and the thurifer leads the procession to the place where the Gospel will be sung. After the deacon has announced the Gospel, he takes the censer from the thurifer and censes the gospel book. He swings the censer once to the center, then to the left, then to the right, and returns the censer to the thurifer. While the deacon sings the Gospel, the thurifer swings the censer. After the Gospel has been sung, the procession returns to the altar in the same order in which it came to the place where the Gospel was sung. The thurifer and taperers take the censer and lights to the usual places and return to their places in the chancel.

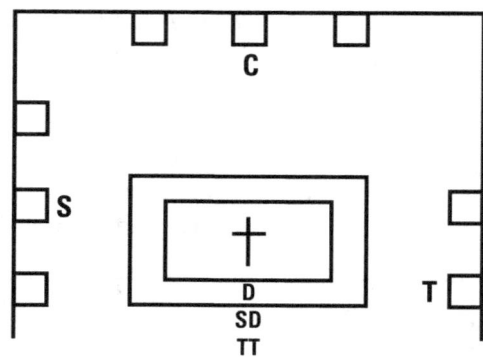

The Gospel Procession Forms at the Altar

Everyone stands. The deacon may ask for and receive the celebrant's blessing. Then the deacon goes around to the front of the altar. The taperers get their lights and stand on chancel level behind the subdeacon. The deacon takes the gospel book from the altar and turns to the people. When the deacon turns, the subdeacon and taperers turn to the people and lead the deacon to the place where the Gospel will be read.

When they arrive at that place, the deacon, subdeacon and taperers take the positions indicated in the diagram.[101] The deacon hands the book to the subdeacon, who holds the book for the deacon to read.[102] The celebrant and server remain at their places and face in the direction of the place where the Holy Gospel is read.

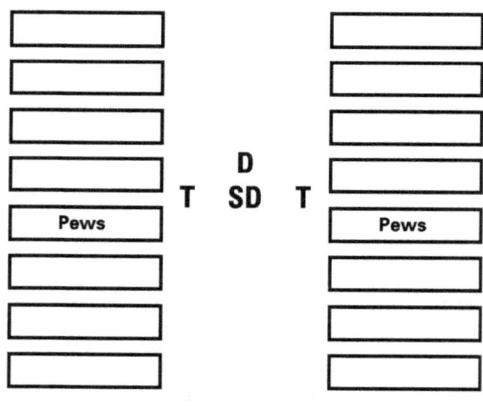

Holy Gospel

The Holy Gospel

After the Gospel has been sung, the procession returns to the altar in the same order in which it came to the place where the Gospel was sung. The subdeacon carries the gospel book and places it on the credence or lectern before resuming his place at the celebrant's left. The taperers take their lights to the usual places and resume their positions. The deacon resumes his place at the celebrant's right.

---

101 When the taperers flank the subdeacon during the reading of the Gospel, they face each other.
102 The *Apostolic Constitutions* (fourth century) and Saint Jerome (ca. 342—420) already mention the reading of the Gospel by the deacon (Jungmann, I, 443).

The Nicene Creed
Everyone remains standing in his place.

The Hymn
At the end of the hymn the celebrant may go into the pulpit. If the celebrant's chair is behind the altar, he may preach from his chair.

The Sermon[103]

The Offertory
The offertory chant is sung.[104]

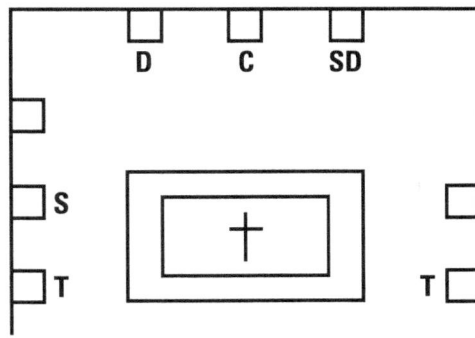

The Creed

The server brings the service book (on its cushion or stand) to the altar and places it to the left of the midst of the altar at an angle convenient for reading.[105]

The deacon brings the veiled chalice with the burse on top of it and places the veiled chalice and burse to his right at the midst of the altar. The deacon removes the corporal from the burse, lays the folded corporal in the midst of the altar, lays the burse behind the service book, and unfolds the corporal. Then he unveils the chalice, folds the veil, and places the veil to the right of the corporal toward the back of the altar. The deacon removes the pall from the chalice and places the pall on the right side of the outspread corporal. He moves the chalice slightly to the right of the midst of the corporal, places the paten to the left of the midst of the corporal, removes the purificator from the chalice, and places the purificator on the altar to the right of the corporal. (See the diagram above of the position of the sacred vessels on the altar.)[106]

Meanwhile, the offerings of the people are gathered. When they have been gathered, representatives of the congregation bring forward the offerings and the vessels of bread and wine, which before the service began had been placed on a credence near the entrance to the church building. The celebrant, deacon, and subdeacon come to the altar and stand behind it. (See diagram.)

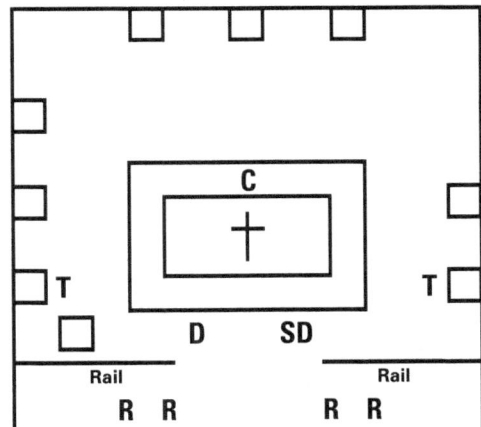

The Deacon and Subdeacon receive the bread, wine and money from the representatives of the people

---

103 See Footnote 17.
104 See Footnote 18.
105 While the deacon and server are preparing the altar, the subdeacon may assist the celebrant in washing his hands. The subdeacon takes a lavabo bowl, towel, and water cruet to the celebrant. The subdeacon pours water over the celebrant's thumbs and forefingers, the celebrant dries his hands on the towel, and the subdeacon replaces the cruet, bowl, and towel on the credence. The "lavabo," or washing of the celebrant's hands, goes back at least to the fourth century since it is described in the catechetical lectures of Saint Cyril of Jerusalem. Its significance is obvious: purity of heart and mind and body as we approach the holy mysteries of Christ's body and blood. It also has an obvious utilitarian value: it is decent to wash one's hands before handling the food of the sacred meal, just as it is customary to wash one's hands before going to the table for an ordinary meal. See Jungmann, II, 76ff.

When the representatives of the people arrive at the altar rail, the subdeacon and deacon go to meet them. The subdeacon receives the offerings and places them toward the end of the altar; he returns to the rail, receives the ciborium or bread box, and places it to the south of the paten on the corporal. The celebrant places some hosts on the paten. Meanwhile, the deacon receives the flagon or cruet and places it to the north of the chalice on the corporal. The celebrant fills the chalice with wine and covers it with the pall.

The deacon and subdeacon then resume their usual positions with the celebrant behind the altar.

The representatives of the people may remain at the rail until after they have received the Holy Communion. The servers may move closer to the altar. (See diagram.)

The General Prayer and the Preface

The celebrant remains standing in the midst behind the altar, facing the people, with the deacon at his right and the subdeacon at his left.

The Sanctus

Everyone may bow moderately from the waist as the words "Holy, holy, holy, Lord God of Sabaoth; Heaven and earth are full of Thy glory. Hosanna in the highest" are sung.

The Lord's Prayer

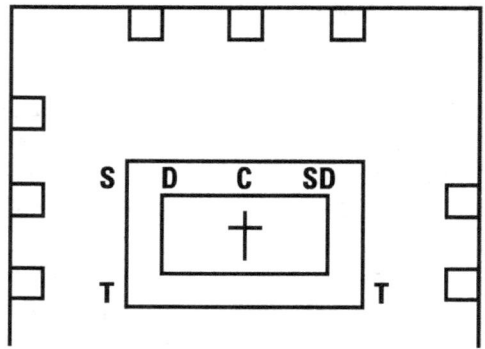

Positions during the Service of the Sacrament: General Prayer through Benediction

The Words of Institution

When the celebrant begins the words of institution, the subdeacon may uncover the ciborium or bread box. As the celebrant pronounces the words of consecration "This is My body which is given for you. This do in remembrance of Me," everyone may bow.[107] After these words have been said, the subdeacon may cover the bread box or ciborium. When the celebrant begins the second half of the words of institution, the deacon, placing his left hand on the foot of the chalice, removes the pall from the chalice with his right hand and places the pall on the altar. The deacon may also remove the stopper from the cruet or open the flagon. As the celebrant pronounces the words, "This cup is the new testament in My blood, which is shed for you for the remission of sins. This do, as oft as ye drink it, in remembrance of Me," everyone may again bow. After these words have been said, the deacon, again steadying the foot of the chalice with his left hand, covers the chalice with the pall. He then replaces the stopper in the cruet or closes the flagon.

---

106 From ancient times the deacon has spread the corporal, thus preparing the Lord's table for the eucharistic meal. It has also been his office to assist in the preparation of the food for the meal. See Jungmann I, 71; II, 52f.

107 Luther writes: "This is not the word and ordinance of a prince or emperor, but of the divine Majesty at whose feet every knee should bow and confess that it is as he says and should accept it with all reverence, fear, and humility." Large Catechism, Fifth Part: The Sacrament of the Altar, 11.

The Pax Domini[108]

The Agnus Dei

The Distribution
During the celebrant's communion, the deacon and subdeacon should reverently bow their heads. Having received the sacrament himself, the celebrant administers the consecrated bread and cup to the deacon. The celebrant then administers the host to the subdeacon and to all who are in the chancel; the deacon follows and administers the chalice to the subdeacon and to all who are in the chancel. After the subdeacon has received the sacrament, he goes to a convenient place within the chancel and there stands or kneels during the communion of the people. After the taperers and server have received the sacrament, they stand or kneel in some convenient place. The representatives of the people return to their places in the congregation. The celebrant administers our Lord's body to the congregation; the deacon administers our Lord's blood.

When the celebrant has administered the host to the congregation, he may place the paten or ciborium on the altar, go to his chair, and stand there in silent meditation.

When all have received the sacrament, the deacon hands the ciborium or bread box and the flagon or cruet to the subdeacon to be placed on the credence. Then the deacon places the purificator over the mouth of the chalice, places the paten on top of it, places the pall on top of the paten, and removes the chalice and paten from the corporal. He folds the corporal and places the corporal in the burse. He covers the chalice with the veil, places the burse on top of it, and hands the veiled chalice with the burse on top of it to the subdeacon who places them on the credence.

The Nunc Dimittis, Thanksgiving, Salutation
The celebrant, deacon, and subdeacon resume their usual places behind the altar.

The Benedicamus
The deacon sings the benedicamus.[109]

---

108 After the celebrant has sung the pax domini, the greeting of peace may be exchanged. The celebrant greets the deacon and subdeacon, who then greet the others in the chancel. The greeting is exchanged throughout the congregation.
109 The singing of the benedicamus has been the duty of the deacon from ancient times. See Jungmann, II, 433ff.

The Benediction

After the benediction, the server takes the processional cross and stands on chancel level flanked by the servers holding lights.

Followed by the deacon and the celebrant, the subdeacon comes around to the foot of the altar steps. The subdeacon steps to the left, the deacon steps to the right, and the celebrant stands between them. The three ministers reverence the altar. Then the servers with cross and lights lead the procession back to the Sacristy in the same order in which it first came to the altar.[110]

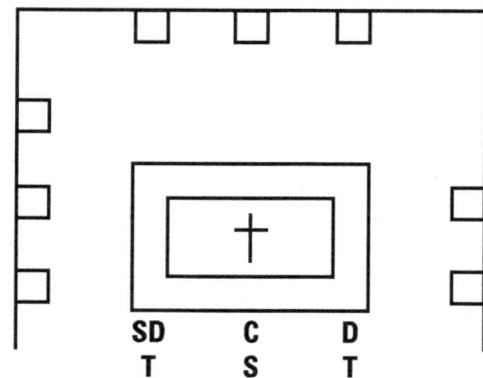

After the Benediction the Procession forms at the foot of the Altar

---

110 If incense is used, the thurifer precedes the servers with cross and lights.

Chapter Seven: Matins and Vespers

I. The Rite of the Order of Matins

"A Hymn of Invocation of the Holy Ghost or another Hymn may be sung." The omission of this hymn is preferable. It is difficult to ascertain the sense of the opening versicle, "O Lord, open thou my lips," when the opening versicle follows the singing of a hymn.

The Versicles and Gloria Patri

"The Congregation shall rise. Then shall be said or chanted the Versicles here following. During the Penitential Seasons the Hallelujah shall be omitted. All shall stand to the end of the Venite."

Hallelujah is omitted beginning at matins on Septuagesima Sunday. It is sung again at the first vespers of Easter, i.e. at vespers on Holy Saturday.

Hallelujah is **not** omitted during Advent.

Anciently, gloria patri was omitted at matins on Maundy Thursday, Good Friday, and Holy Saturday. (This omission recalls the time in the church's history when gloria patri had not yet been added to the church's worship. The solemnity of these three days resisted what was felt to be an innovation.)

The Invitatory and the Venite

"Then shall follow the Invitatory with the Venite or on Feast Days the special Invitatory."

"The Invitatory varies with the season and is always used with Psalm 95 at Matins. It is divided into two parts, separated by a colon. The first part, or the whole of the Invitatory, may be sung or said by the Minister or sung by a single voice or by the choir before the Psalm; and after the Psalm and Gloria Patri the whole Invitatory shall be sung." (*The Lutheran Hymnal*, p. 95)

"The Invitatory always precedes the Venite, Psalm 95. It varies with the Season. See *The Lutheran Liturgy* pages 216–224. Other appropriate Invitatories may be used. After the Venite and the Gloria Patri the whole Invitatory shall be repeated." (*The Lutheran Liturgy*, p. 422)

The invitatory is in reality an antiphon. An antiphon should always be repeated after the psalm. The rubrics clearly indicate that the invitatory should be repeated after the venite.

The minister or a cantor or the choir may sing or say the first half of the invitatory and the choir and/or congregation may sing or say the second half. When the invitatory is repeated after the venite, it should be sung or said in its entirety by all.

The seasonal invitatory is used throughout the season, except on minor festivals occurring within the season. For example, on Saint Stephen's Day the common invitatory is said, although Saint Stephen's Day is celebrated during Christmastide. Although the rubrics do not so specify, the invitatory for the Trinity season should be used only on

Trinity Sunday and during its octave.

The correct use of the invitatory is indicated on the *Lutheran Church Year Calendar, The Lutheran Liturgy* Edition, published annually by the Ashby Co., Erie, Pennsylvania.

The Hymn

"Then shall be sung The Hymn."

This is the one required hymn at matins, the so-called "office hymn."

It is preferable to use a hymn which concludes with a doxological stanza. If a hymn without a doxological stanza is sung, a doxology of the same meter and rhyme pattern may be added. See *The Lutheran Hymnal*, p. 838, for a list of doxological stanzas according to meter.

Traditional Matins office hymns included in *The Lutheran Hymnal* and in the *Worship Supplement* are:

General–*The Lutheran Hymnal* 550, *Worship Supplement* 788
Advent–*The Lutheran Hymnal* 60, 63, 68; *Worship Supplement* 704
Christmas through January 13 (except on Saint Stephen's Day, Saint John's Day, and Holy
    Innocents' Day)–*The Lutheran Hymnal* 98, 104; *Worship Supplement* 709, 721
Holy Innocents' Day–*The Lutheran Hymnal* 273
Circumcision of Christ–*The Lutheran Hymnal* 104, 115, 361
Transfiguration–*Worship Supplement* 723
Judica Sunday through Wednesday of Holy Week–*Worship Supplement* 728
Eastertide–*Worship Supplement* 737
Ascensiontide–*The Lutheran Hymnal* 212
Pentecost–*The Lutheran Hymnal* 236
Trinity Sunday and its octave–*The Lutheran Hymnal* 240, 564

The proper use of the office hymn is noted on the Lutheran Church Year Calendar.

The Psalmody

"One or more Psalms shall be said or chanted. At the end of each Psalm or at the end of the Psalmody the Gloria Patri shall be said or chanted. The Congregation may be seated during the Psalmody and rise at the last Gloria Patri. Instead of one of the Psalms, the Athanasian Creed (page 45) may be used on Trinity Sunday. An Antiphon may be used with each Psalm." (*The Lutheran Liturgy*, p. 28.)

"When an Antiphon is used with the Psalm, it shall be chanted before the Psalm and repeated after the Gloria Patri."

At least three psalms should be said. The core of the divine office is the praying of the psalter. To curtail the recitation of the psalter by reducing the number of psalms to one is to suggest misunderstanding of the essential nature of the office.

After the Reformation it became customary in the church of the Augsburg Confession to pray psalms 1–109 at matins, reserving psalms 110–150 for vespers. The longer psalms may be divided into sections and each section regarded as a separate psalm.

The Lutheran Hymnal, p. 166, provides a scheme for praying the entire psalter every month.

The rubric on p. 4 of *The Lutheran Hymnal*—"On Trinity Sunday, at Matins, the Athanasian Creed may be used instead of the Psalmody"—is regrettable. It implies that one may dispense with the psalter at matins on Trinity Sunday. This would be a liturgically indefensible procedure, since the core of the office is the praying of the psalter. The more carefully formulated rubric on p. 28 of *The Lutheran Liturgy* should be followed. Following this rubric, one would say or chant at least two psalms perhaps psalms 8 and 67 (Cf. *The Lutheran Hymnal*, p. 160) and the Athanasian Creed with the antiphon, "Glory be to Thee, coequal Trinity" (*The Lutheran Hymnal*, p. 99) and gloria patri.

The psalms are prayed responsively by whole verses. The caesura colon in the middle of each verse indicates a pause in the recitation. This should be strictly observed. If this principle is followed, the corporate recitation of the psalter will be greatly facilitated: the people will never be in doubt as to where the pause is to be made. In gloria patri, a pause is similarly made before the words, "and to the Holy Ghost," and before the words, "world without end."

It is preferable, where possible, to pray the psalter in the following way: The antiphon up to the colon is intoned by a cantor; the entire choir and/or congregation sing the remainder of the antiphon. The cantor then intones the first verse of the psalm up to the colon; his side of the choir and/or congregation then completes the first verse of the psalm. (It is preferable to begin the recitation of the psalter with the gospel side of the choir and congregation.) The opposite side of the choir and/ or congregation sings the second verse; the third verse is again sung by the cantor's side of the choir and/or congregation, and so on to the end. The gloria patri is rendered as if it were two verses of a psalm. Then the choir and/or congregation repeat the antiphon.

In practice, it will be difficult, if not impossible, for the congregation to join in singing the antiphon, though the congregation may well sing the psalms if the music is placed before them and the simpler psalm tones are used.

When matins is said, the same scheme may be followed.

Less desirable is the custom of the minister reading the antiphon, the psalm then being prayed responsively by whole verses between the minister and congregation, and the antiphon being repeated by the minister and congregation after the psalm.

N. B. If the opening words of the psalm are identical to the antiphon, the opening words of the psalm are not repeated. For example, if the antiphon of psalm 31 should be, "In Thee, O Lord, do I put my trust; let me never be ashamed," the cantor or minister says or chants: "In Thee, O Lord, do I put my trust; let me never be ashamed." His side of the choir and/or congregation immediately continues with the words, "deliver me in Thy righteousness." Then the opposite side of the choir and/or congregation continues with the second verse of the psalm, and so on.

The Lection

"One Lesson shall, more may, be read. On Sundays or Festivals one Lesson shall be read from the Epistles and one from the Gospels. A Lesson from the Old Testament may precede the Lesson from the Epistles. See *The Lutheran Liturgy* page 438. Lessons shall not be chosen from the Psalter. The Epistle and the Gospel for the Day shall not be used as Lessons at Matins. In announcing the Lesson, the Officiant shall say: The First (or Second or Third) Lesson is written in the _____ chapter of _____ beginning at the _____ verse. The Lesson ended, he shall say: Here endeth the First (or Second or Third) Lesson.[111] After that, facing the altar, he may say or chant: But Thou, O Lord, have mercy upon us." (*The Lutheran Liturgy*, p. 422)

The rubrics require the reading of at least two lessons at Matins on Sundays and festivals. One lesson is to be taken "from the Epistles" and one "from the Gospels." This does not mean that the epistle and gospel for the day are to be read: that is clearly forbidden by the rubric. (It is assumed that in addition to matins there will be a celebration of the holy eucharist on Sundays and festivals. The epistle and gospel for the day are read at the eucharist.) The terms "Epistles" and "Gospels" in the rubric refer to the books of the New Testament which have those titles. A lesson from the Old Testament may be read before the lesson "from the Epistles."

The "Second Series" of the table of lessons, *The Lutheran Hymnal*, p. 159, may well be followed in choosing lessons for matins. (The "First Series" of this table is the lectionary for the holy communion. It is not to be used at matins and vespers.)

The table of lessons is incomplete. It provides no lessons for matins and vespers on the minor festivals and several other occasions. Since our rite does not make adequate provisions, the minister will himself choose appropriate lessons "from the Epistles" and "from the Gospels." In choosing lessons the minister may find helpful the lectionary for matins and vespers in the *Service Book and Hymnal*, pp. 280f.

On non-festival weekdays throughout the year, the table of lessons for morning and evening throughout the year may be followed. (*The Lutheran Hymnal*, pp. 161–164)

When the office is sung, the lessons too should be sung. The words, "Here endeth the Lesson," may be omitted when the lesson is sung.

The Responsory

"After the Lesson or Lessons a Responsory may be said or chanted." (*The Lutheran Liturgy*, p. 28)

"The Responsory varies with the Season and may be sung by the Choir after the last Lesson. See *The Lutheran Liturgy* pages 216 to 227. Other appropriate Responsories may also be used." (*The Lutheran Liturgy*, p. 422)

"The Responsory varies with the Season and may be sung after the last Lesson at Vespers and Matins. At the end of the Responsory is sung Glory be to the Father and to the Son and to the Holy Ghost (but not "As it was in the beginning," etc.), followed by the repetition of the last sentence of the Responsory." (*The Lutheran Hymnal*, p. 95)

When the responsory is said, the minister reads all but the last sentence—in some cases, e.g. Christmas (*The Lutheran Hymnal*, p. 96), the last phrase—of the opening

---

111   The word "lection" is never used in announcing or concluding a lesson.

section of the responsory. The people read this last sentence or phrase. Then the minister reads the verse; the people repeat the last sentence or phrase; the minister reads the first half of gloria patri, and the people again repeat the last sentence or phrase.

When the responsory is sung, a cantor sings the parts said by the minister and the choir sings the response.

While the rubric does not so specify, the responsory for the Trinity season, *The Lutheran Hymnal*, p. 99, should be used only on Trinity Sunday and during its octave.

It would be appropriate to use the responsory for Christmas on the festivals of the Presentation of our Lord, the Annunciation of the blessed virgin Mary and the Visitation of the blessed virgin Mary. (The rubrics of the *Worship Supplement*, p. 99, prescribe the use of the Christmas responsory for the Presentation of our Lord and for the Visitation of the blessed virgin Mary.)

Note that "other appropriate Responsories may also be used." The *Worship Supplement* provides proper Responsories for the Annunciation of the blessed virgin Mary and for apostles' and evangelists' days. (*Worship Supplement*, p. 99)

The Canticle

"Matin Canticles

"The Te Deum. Proper at Matins on all Sundays except in Advent and from Septuagesima to Good Friday; also proper on Feasts and Festivals and during their Seasons.

"The Benedictus. Proper on all Sundays in Advent and from Septuagesima to Good Friday; also proper for daily use.

"The Benedicite. Proper on Feasts and Festivals and during Eastertide, when the Te Deum is not used. See *The Lutheran Liturgy* page 282.

"The Dignus Est Agnus. Proper during Eastertide and Ascensiontide. May also be used during the Trinity Season. See *The Lutheran Liturgy* page 289.

"The Beatitudes. Proper during Trinity Season, but may be used any other time except Sundays. See *The Lutheran Liturgy* page 288.

"Any of the other Canticles, except the Magnificat and the Nunc Dimittis, may be used at Matins on any Day except a Sunday or a Feast or a Festival. See *The Lutheran Liturgy* page 282. Confitebor Tibi is traditionally associated with Monday, Ego dixi with Tuesday, Exultavit cor meum with Wednesday, Cantemus Domino with Thursday, Domine audivi with Friday, and Audite coeli with Saturday.

"An Antiphon may be sung with any of the Canticles except the Te Deum. It should be sung before the Canticle and repeated after the Canticle by the entire Choir. See *The Lutheran Liturgy* pages 216–227." (*The Lutheran Liturgy*, p. 423)

Note that the proper canticle for matins on Sundays and festivals is te deum laudamus. The proper matins canticle on Sundays during Advent and on Sundays from Septuagesima through Palmarum is benedictus. But on ***festivals*** occurring during Advent, Pre-Lent, and Lent, te deum laudamus is said at matins: i.e. on Saint Andrew's Day, Saint Thomas' Day, the Conversion of Saint Paul, the Presentation of our Lord, Saint Matthias'

Day, and the Annunciation of the blessed virgin Mary. It is also appropriate to say te deum laudamus at matins throughout the octaves of the greater festivals: i.e. Christmas, Epiphany, Easter, Pentecost, Trinity Sunday, Reformation Day.

Note that the canticle may be sung or said responsively in the same way that the psalmody is sung or said (cf. above, pp. 77–78).

Gloria patri is said after every canticle except the te deum.

Note that an antiphon may be used with any canticle except the te deum.

The Prayers

"Then shall be said the Prayers here following or the Suffrages (*TLH* p. 113), the Litany (*TLH* p. 110), or other Prayers. All shall say or chant The Kyrie ... Then all shall say or chant The Lord's Prayer ... Then shall be said or chanted the Salutation, the Collect for the Day or other Collects and the Collect for Grace. Each Collect may be preceded by a Versicle. After each Collect the Congregation shall say or chant: Amen." (*The Lutheran Hymnal*, p. 31)

"Instead of the Prayers appointed, the Suffrages, the Litany, or other prayers may be used. The Bidding Prayer may be used in the same manner on any Wednesday or Friday in Lent and on Good Friday." (*The Lutheran Liturgy*, p. 423)

"The Collect for the Sunday is ordinarily said at Matins throughout the week. The Collect for Grace shall be the last Collect used at Matins. A Versicle may be used before any Collect after the first." (*The Lutheran Liturgy*, p. 423)

At no point in the praying of the divine office is there, perhaps, more confusion among us than at this point. The confusion stems in part from a printing error in an early printing of *The Lutheran Hymnal* in which the titles, "The Kyrie," "The Lord's Prayer," etc., were printed in gothic type identical to the title, "The Prayers." Some have been misled by this printing error into thinking that "The Prayers" is yet another item in the service rather than the title of all that follows through to the benedicamus. The printing error has been corrected in subsequent printings of *The Lutheran Hymnal*, but the misunderstanding persists.

What is implied by the rubric is clear. After the canticle, the minister and congregation are ***immediately*** to continue with the kyrie and the Our Father, or the litany, or the morning suffrages, or the suffrages, or the bidding prayer. (In other words, the minister is not to insert prayers between the canticle and the kyrie.) After the kyrie and the Our Father—or the litany, or the morning suffrages, or the suffrages, or the bidding prayer—have been prayed, the service continues with the salutation, the collect for the day, other collects, and the collect for grace.[112]

When the litany is used at matins, the litany concludes with the Our Father. When the suffrages are used at matins, they conclude with the words, "Hear my prayer, O Lord, etc." on p. 114 of *The Lutheran Hymnal*. When the morning suffrages are used, they conclude with the words, "Hear my prayer, O Lord, etc." When the bidding prayer is used, it concludes with the Our Father. In every case, the minister then proceeds to the salutation.

---

[112] When a layman conducts the service, the salutation is omitted. "V. Hear my prayer, O Lord: R. And let my cry come unto Thee" is traditionally said in its place.

The following chart may serve to clarify these directions.
1. ***The Prayers*** [The Kyrie; The Lord's Prayer; The Salutation; The Collect for the Day; Other Collects; The Collect for Grace*] ***The Benedicamus**, **The Benediction***.
2. ***The Prayers*** [The Suffrages (through "Hear my prayer, O Lord," p. 114); The Salutation; The Collect for the Day; Other Collects; The Collect for Grace*] ***The Benedicamus**, **The Benediction***.
3. ***The Prayers*** [The Morning Suffrages** (through "Hear my prayer, O Lord"); The Salutation; The Collect for the Day; Other Collects; The Collect for Grace*] ***The Benedicamus**, **The Benediction***.
4. ***The Prayers*** [The Litany (though the Our Father); The Salutation; The Collect for the Day; Other Collects; The Collect for Grace*] ***The Benedicamus**, **The Benediction***.
5. ***The Prayers*** [The Bidding Prayer (through the Our Father); The Salutation; The Collect for the Day; Other Collects; The Collect for Grace*] ***The Benedicamus**, **The Benediction***.

*At vespers, the collect for peace is prayed here.
**At vespers, the evening suffrages.

On Sundays, festivals, and days within the octaves of Christmas, Epiphany, Easter, Pentecost, Trinity Sunday, and Reformation Day, the kyrie and the Our Father are said, followed by the salutation and the proper collects.

On other days of the year, the suffrages, the morning suffrages, or the litany—in each case followed by the salutation and proper collects—may be said. According to tradition, these prayers are not used on Sundays, festivals, and days within the octaves of greater festivals. Wednesday and Friday were the traditional days for praying the litany both before and after the Reformation.

The use of the bidding prayer should probably be restricted to the "Morning Service without Communion" (*The Lutheran Hymnal*, pp. 5ff) or the holy communion on Good Friday. The bidding prayer is an ancient form of the prayer of the church which concluded the service of the word at the celebration of holy communion. The bidding prayer, therefore, has its origin in the eucharistic liturgy—not in the office. The rubrics, however, permit the use of the bidding prayer at matins on Wednesdays and Fridays in Lent and at matins on Good Friday.

Psalm 130 may be included in the praying of the suffrages at matins. Psalm 51 may be included in the praying of the suffrages at vespers. (See *The Lutheran Hymnal*, p. 113) If this is done, psalm 130 would not be prayed in the psalmody at matins; psalm 51 would not be prayed in the psalmody at vespers. After psalm 130 or psalm 51 has been prayed, the suffrages continue with the versicle, "Turn us again, O God of hosts," *The Lutheran Hymnal*, p. 114.

There is a typographical error in the response to the versicle, "Give peace in our days, O Lord," *The Lutheran Hymnal*, p. 114. The text of the response should read: "Because there is none other that fighteth for us except Thee, O God."

When the Our Father is said at the office, the minister traditionally says, "Our Father," and the people continue, "who art in heaven, etc." When the Apostles' Creed is said at the office, the minister traditionally says, "I believe in God," and the people continue, "the

Father almighty, etc." If this custom is consistently followed, the people will be certain at what point they are to join in the praying of the Our Father and the creed, and a ragged beginning of these prayers will be avoided.

The first collect at matins is always the collect for the day; the last collect is the collect for grace. On the proper use of the collect for the day see above pp. 20-21. (The collect for the day which is prayed at the holy eucharist is also prayed at matins.)

Note that a versicle may be used before any collect after the first. When matins is sung, these versicles may be sung by a cantor. See *The Lutheran Hymnal*, pp. 95ff., for appropriate versicles.

The first and last collects at matins take the full termination, "who liveth and reigneth, etc." Other collects take the short termination.

The Benedicamus and the Benediction

When matins is sung, benedicamus may be sung by a cantor. "Matins and Vespers end with the Benedicamus if the Minister is not conducting the Service. If the Minister is the Officiant, he shall pronounce the Benediction and the Benedicamus may be omitted" (*The Lutheran Hymnal*, p. 4). By "the Minister" the rubric means an ordained clergyman. Even if an ordained clergyman is officiating, benedicamus should not be omitted.

II. The Rite of the Order of Vespers

"A Hymn of Invocation of the Holy Ghost or another Hymn may be sung." The omission of this hymn is preferable. It is difficult to ascertain the sense of the opening versicle, "O Lord, Open Thou my lips," when the opening versicles follow the singing of a hymn.

The Versicles and Gloria Patri, cf. p. 76

The Psalmody, cf. pp. 77–78

The Lection, cf. pp. 79

The Responsory, cf. pp. 79–80

The Hymn

"Then shall be sung The Hymn.

This is the one required hymn at vespers, the so-called "office hymn." It is preferable to use a hymn which concludes with a doxological stanza. If a hymn without a doxological stanza is sung, a doxology of the same meter and rhyme may be added. See *The Lutheran Hymnal*, p. 838, for a list of doxological stanzas according to meter.

Traditional vespers office hymns included in *The Lutheran Hymnal* and in the *Worship*

Supplement are:

General–*The Lutheran Hymnal* 564, 790 (especially when Vespers is said late in the evening)
Advent–*Worship Supplement* 703
Christmas–*The Lutheran Hymnal* 95, 98; *Worship Supplement* 701, 721
Holy Innocents' Day–*The Lutheran Hymnal* 273
Circumcision of Christ–*The Lutheran Hymnal* 95, 98, 117, 350; *Worship Supplement* 701, 721
Transfiguration–*Worship Supplement* 723
Epiphany–*The Lutheran Hymnal* 131
Invocavit through the Friday after Laetare–*The Lutheran Hymnal* 559
Judica Sunday through Wednesday of Holy Week–*The Lutheran Hymnal* 168; *Worship Supplement* 729, 730
Easter–*Worship Supplement* 733, 737
Ascension–*The Lutheran Hymnal* 212
Trinity–*The Lutheran Hymnal* 564

The Versicle

"Then, all standing, may be said or chanted this Versicle. On Feast Days a special Versicle may be used." (*The Lutheran Liturgy*, p. 34)

A special versicle may be used throughout the festival half of the church year and on all festivals. See *The Lutheran Hymnal*, pp. 95ff.

The Canticle[113]

"An Antiphon may be said or chanted with the Canticle." (*The Lutheran Liturgy*, p. 34)

"The Magnificat or the Nunc Dimittis may be used on Sundays. Other Canticles may be used on other days. See *General Rubrics*." (*The Lutheran Liturgy*, p. 34)

"Vesper Canticles. The Magnificat: The proper Canticle at Vespers at all times. The Nunc Dimittis: A proper substitute for the Magnificat only when Vespers are said or sung as a late Office. The Dignus Est Agnus: Proper during Eastertide and Ascensiontide. May also be used during the Trinity Season. See page 289." (*The Lutheran Liturgy*, p. 42)

Antiphons for the seasons of the church year are found on pp. 95ff. of *The Lutheran Hymnal*.[114]

The canticle at vespers may be sung or said in the same way that the psalmody is sung or said. See pp. 77-78.

---

[113] Versicle 11, *The Lutheran Hymnal*, p. 101, was traditionally used from the first vespers of Invocavit Sunday through vespers on the Friday after Laetare Sunday. On Days of apostles and evangelists, versicle 9, *TLH*, p. 101, is appropriate. On the day of the Presentation of our Lord, the Annunciation of the blessed virgin Mary, and the Visitation of the blessed virgin Mary, versicle 3 of Christmas, *TLH*, p. 96, may be used. On the day of Saint Michael and All Angels, versicle 11 *TLH*, p. 101, may be used. On All Saints' Day, versicle 1 (or 2) of the commemoration of the dead, *TLH*, p. 100, may be used.

[114] On days of apostles and evangelists and on All Saints' Day, one of the antiphons of the commemoration of the dead, *TLH*, p. 100, may be used. On the day of the Presentation of our Lord, the Annunciation of the blessed virgin Mary, and the Visitation of the blessed virgin Mary, one of the Christmas antiphons, *The Lutheran Hymnal*, p. 95, may be used.

The Prayers, cf. pp. 81–83

"The Collect for the Sunday is ordinarily said at Vespers throughout the week until Friday; but on Saturday the Collect for the following Sunday is said. The Collect proper for any Festival may be used at Vespers of the day before. The Collect for Peace shall be the last Collect in the Order of Vespers. A Versicle may be used before any Collect after the first."

For the proper use of the collects see pp. 20–21.

Note that the rubrics say that the collect for a Sunday or festival is said at vespers **the day before**. This service is regarded as the "first vespers" of the Sunday or festival, and the antiphons, versicles, lessons and hymn should be those appropriate to the Sunday or festival. The collect of the ***preceding*** Sunday is not said.

When a day of greater rank occurs before a day of lesser rank, the second vespers of the day of greater rank is said, and the first vespers of the day of lesser rank is merely commemorated by praying the collect for the day of lesser rank after the collect for the day of greater rank. For example, on October 31 vespers is of Reformation Day; the collect for All Saints' Day is prayed after the collect for Reformation Day.

When a day of lesser rank occurs before a day of greater rank, the first vespers of the day of greater rank is said and the second vespers of the day of lesser rank is merely commemorated by praying the collect for the day of lesser rank after the collect for the day of greater rank. For example, if the Nativity of Saint John the Baptist, June 24, falls on the Monday after the second Sunday after Trinity, vespers on Sunday, June 23, is of the nativity of Saint John the Baptist, and the collect for the second Sunday after Trinity is said after the collect for the nativity of Saint John the Baptist.

Certain days in the church year traditionally do not have first vespers. These days are Ash Wednesday, Monday of holy week, Tuesday of holy week, Wednesday of holy week, Maundy Thursday, Good Friday, Holy Saturday, Easter Monday, Easter Tuesday, Monday of Whitsun Week, Tuesday of Whitsun Week. On the eves of these days, the collect for the following day is not said at vespers, nor are the antiphons, versicle, lessons and hymn those of the following day. For example, on Wednesday of holy week, the collect for Wednesday of holy week is prayed; the collect for Maundy Thursday is not prayed after the collect for Wednesday of holy week.

Saint Stephen's Day, Saint John's Day, Holy Innocents, Day, and All Saints, Day in theory have first vespers. In practice, however, the first vespers of these days is merely "commemorated." That is, the antiphons, versicle, lesson, hymn and collect are those of the foregoing day. The collect for the following day is added by way of "commemoration" after the collect for the day. For example, at vespers on December 25, the office is of Christmas Day; the collect for Saint Stephen's Day is prayed after the collect for Christmas Day. At vespers on October 31, the office is of Reformation Day; the collect for All Saints' Day is said after the collect for Reformation Day.

The traditional rules for the use of propers during octaves also apply to vespers. It must be remembered that the liturgical day begins at vespers the day before. For example, at vespers on the eve of the first Sunday after the Epiphany, the office is of the first Sunday after the Epiphany, and the collect for the Epiphany of our Lord is said after the collect for the first Sunday after the Epiphany.

In general, it is best to consult the *Lutheran Church Year Calendar* for the correct sequence of collects at vespers.

The Benedicamus and Benediction, cf. p. 83

III. The Ceremonial of Matins and Vespers
Matins and Vespers

Matins and vespers are "choir offices." That is, matins and vespers of the Lutheran rite are in content the old pre-Reformation daily services sung in the choir—the portion of the church between the nave and the sanctuary—of monastery, cathedral and parish churches. It is desirable that we remind ourselves of the historic roots of these services by our way of conducting them. Matins and vespers, therefore, should not be read at the altar. They should be read from a chair and prayer desk within the chancel. But there is more than a historical reason for refraining from reading the offices at the altar. The altar is essentially the table for the eucharistic meal. If the minister refrains from using the altar for other purposes, its real purpose will be more clear in the minds of the people.

The altar is vested in the customary way for the choir offices: with a frontal (and frontlet) of the proper color, and with a fair linen cloth. The two altar candles are lighted. The origin of the custom of lighting the two altar candles only for the holy eucharist is difficult to discover; this custom is without historic precedent in the church of the Augsburg Confession.

The minister and any persons assisting in the conduct of matins and vespers wear the cassock and surplice. The stole is not worn for matins and vespers.

If the choir is seated in the chancel, it enters the chancel by the shortest route during the organ prelude or, during Advent and Lent—when the organ is traditionally used only to support the singing—in silence. At the end of the service the choir leaves the chancel by the shortest route during the postlude or, during Advent and Lent, in silence. There should be no sung "processional" and "recessional" at matins and vespers, nor is there any need for the choir to walk the entire length of the center aisle of the church if it is possible for it to enter the chancel from a door in or near the chancel. There is no need to carry a processional cross and lights before the choir and/or clergy at matins and vespers.

The offering received on occasion at matins and vespers should not be brought to the altar. If it is brought to the altar, there is too close an approximation to the offertory action of the eucharist. In general, the tendency to approximate the ceremonies of the eucharist in the praying of matins and vespers should be resisted.

The Ceremonial of Matins

At the hour appointed for the service, the minister enters the chancel, reverences the altar, and goes to the prayer desk. He may kneel and offer silent prayer. (When the choir is seated in the chancel, the minister may follow the choir as it enters the church and takes its place in the chancel. If there are lectors, they walk immediately before the minister.)

If an opening hymn is sung, it is begun *after* the minister (and choir) are in their places. During the versicles and gloria patri, the invitatory and the venite, the minister stands before his chair and faces the opposite wall of the chancel. Whenever the minister stands at his chair during the offices he faces directly toward the opposite wall. He does not turn toward the altar.[115]

The minister sits in his chair for the hymn, rising for the last stanza if it is a doxology.

The minister stands or sits at his chair during the psalmody. If he sits for the psalmody, he rises during the last half verse of the last psalm for the last gloria patri. (*The Lutheran Liturgy*, p. 28)

After the psalmody has been said, the minister goes to the lectern to read the lection. If there is no lectern, he may read the lection from the pulpit or standing at his chair, facing the people. He need not face the altar for the versicle and response, "But Thou, O Lord, have mercy upon us." The *General Rubrics* state: "When the Officiant stands before the altar, he faces The altar for all sacrificial acts and the Congregation for all sacramental acts" (*The Lutheran Liturgy*, p. 417). Since he is not standing "before the altar," the rubric does not apply.

It is desirable that someone other than the officiating minister read the lection. If this is done, the minister sits at his chair, and the person assigned to read the lesson goes to the lectern or pulpit or to some convenient place within the chancel and reads the lesson. After he has read the lesson, the reader returns to his place.

The minister stands or sits at his chair during the responsory.

The minister stands before his chair during the canticle.[116]

It is an old custom for the minister and all present to bow for the words of the te deum: "Holy, holy, holy, Lord God of Sabaoth; Heaven and earth are full of the majesty of Thy glory," and at the words, "We therefore pray Thee, help Thy servants, whom Thou best redeemed with Thy precious blood." It was once customary in some places to kneel while the words, "We therefore pray Thee, etc.," were sung.

The minister stands before his chair during the prayers. Though the rubric does not so specify, the minister and congregation may kneel for the prayers, except that the minister always stands for the salutation and collects. The prayers are always said in a standing position on Sundays, festivals, during octaves of greater festivals, and during Eastertide, i.e. from Easter through the Saturday after Pentecost.

The minister stands before his chair during the benedicamus.

The minister turns toward the people to pronounce the benediction. He may make the sign of the cross as he says the benediction.

---

115 At the words, "O Lord, open Thou my lips," the minister and congregation may make the sign of the cross on their lips, using their right thumb. At the words, "Make haste, O God, to deliver me," all may sign themselves with the cross in the usual way.

116 At the opening words of the "gospel canticles"—benedictus, magnificat, nunc dimittis—all may make the sign of the cross. The "gospel canticles" are daily memorials of the incarnation. The sign of the cross is the symbol of our redemption: the Son of God became man that he might redeem us.

After the benediction all may kneel for silent prayer. The minister then rises and returns to the sacristy, reverencing the altar as he passes it. When the choir is seated in the chancel, the minister may, after silent prayer, follow the choir as it leaves the church. (The lectors walk immediately before the minister.)

The Ceremonial of Vespers

At the hour appointed for the service, the minister enters the chancel, reverences the altar, and goes to the prayer desk. He may kneel and offer silent prayer. (When the choir is seated in the chancel, the minister may follow the choir as it enters the church and takes its place in the chancel. If there are lectors, they walk immediately before the minister.)

If an opening hymn is sung, it is sung ***after*** the minister (and choir) are in their places.

During the versicles and gloria patri, the minister stands before his chair and faces the opposite wall of the chancel.[117]

The minister stands or sits at his chair during the psalmody. If he sits for the psalmody, he rises during the last half first of the last psalm for the last gloria patri. (*The Lutheran Liturgy*, p. 28)

After the psalmody has been said, the minister goes to the lectern to read the lection. If there is no lectern, he may read the lection from the pulpit or standing at his chair, facing the people. He need not face the altar for the versicle and response, "But Thou, O Lord, have mercy upon us." (See p. 88).

It is desirable that someone other than the officiating minister read the lection. If this is done, the minister sits at his chair and the person assigned to read the lesson goes to the lectern or pulpit or to some convenient place within the chancel and reads the lection. After he has read the lesson, the reader returns to his place.

The minister stands or sits at his chair during the responsory and the hymn. He rises for the last stanza of the hymn if it is a doxological stanza.

The minister stands before his chair during the versicle and response, the canticle, the prayers, and the benedicamus.[118] Though the rubric does not so specify, the minister and congregation may kneel for the prayers, except that the minister always stands for the salutation and collects. The prayers are always said standing on Sundays, festivals, during the octaves of greater festivals, and during Eastertide, i.e. Easter Day through the Saturday after Pentecost.

The minister, standing at his chair, turns toward the people to pronounce the benediction.

After the benediction all may kneel for silent prayer. The minister then rises and returns to the sacristy, reverencing the altar as he passes it. When the choir is seated in the chancel the minister may, after silent prayer, follow the choir as it leaves the church. (The lectors walk immediately before the minister.)

---

117 See footnote 1 above.**
118 See footnote 2 above.**

The Sermon and the Offering at Matins and Vespers

When Matins and Vespers of *The Lutheran Hymnal* are used, the sermon may follow the responsory. Since, however, the position of the sermon is governed by a "may" rubric, the sermon may be preached after the benedicamus or before the opening versicles. The *Worship Supplement* states that the sermon may be preached before the opening versicles or after the benedicamus. See *Worship Supplement*, p. 52.

As noted above, the offering should not be brought to the altar at the offices. The minister, therefore, is in no way involved in that part of the service.

Some Additional Ceremonies

The officiating minister may wear a cope over his surplice at matins and vespers on Sundays and festivals. On occasions of great solemnity the cantors may also wear copes over their surplices.

During the middle ages, the altar was censed during the magnificat. The custom of offering incense at evening is very ancient. We read of this custom in the Old Testament (Ex. 30:1ff). The use of incense during the canticle agrees very well with the versicle commonly sung before the magnificat: "Let my prayers be set forth before thee as incense, and the lifting up of my hands as the evening sacrifice." The magnificat is the climax of vespers, and is a daily memorial of the incarnation. Some may, therefore, wish from time to time to mark the singing of the magnificat with the offering of incense. (See Appendix C for the method of censing the altar.)

Taperers may come into the chancel and stand on chancel level in line with the corners of the altar during the magnificat. They may hold their candles before the minister while he sings the collects. (The taperers stand on either side of the minister, facing each other.)

When lights and incense are used at vespers, the thurifer and taperers may precede the choir and/or lectors and minister when they enter the chancel during the prelude. A server, walking between the taperers, may carry a cross, though there seems to be little precedent for this. The departure from the chancel at the end of the service may be made in the same way.

The above ceremonies may on occasion also be used in connection with matins. If this is done, the altar is censed during the canticle.

Chapter Eight: Processions

Introduction

"The procession is a distinct, significant act of worship: it is not an aimless walk around the church; but it has a definite objective, such as the Rood, the Lord's Table, or the Font."[119] Processions are mentioned in the sacred scriptures.[120] A procession is a symbol of the church as the ***pilgrim*** people of God. It represents the wanderings of the church militant here on earth on its way to the eternal city, the new Jerusalem. "For here have we no continuing city, but we seek one to come" (Heb. 13:14).

In the middle ages processions were frequent, and the rules for their observance were complicated.

At the present time it would seem appropriate to reserve processions for the great festivals of the year.

The Route of the Procession

A procession always begins before the altar, makes a circuit of the nave, and returns to the altar.[121] The customary route of the procession is as follows: from the altar down the south aisle of the church and up the center aisle to the altar. If a longer route is desired, the following route may be followed: from the altar, down the center aisle, up the north aisle, across the front of the church, down the south aisle, and up the center aisle to the altar.

At least one "station" should be made in every procession at the end of the procession before the altar. A versicle, response, and collect are sung. A station may also be made at the entrance to the chancel, especially if the rood (the crucifix, often accompanied by figures of Saint Mary and Saint John) hangs over the entrance to the chancel. At Christmas and Epiphany it is appropriate to make a station at the creche. On Epiphany it is appropriate to make a station at the font, since Epiphany was anciently observed in commemoration of our Lord's baptism.[122] At Easter and Pentecost a station may be made at the font, since through baptism we share in Christ's death and resurrection and receive the gift of the Holy Spirit.

The Order of the Procession

The order of the procession before the holy eucharist is as follows: thurifer, crucifer flanked by the taperers, choir, assisting clergy, subdeacon, deacon, celebrant. Other processions follow this same basic order. On festivals, banners may be carried in procession. If banners are to be effective, they should not be placed too closely together.

---

119 Percy Dearmer, *The Parson's Handbook*, twelfth edition (London: Geoffrey Cumberlege, 1932), p. 254.
120 Joshua 6, II Samuel 6, I Chronicles 16, Matthew 21.
121 On Palm Sunday the procession begins at the place where the Palms have been blessed. The palms may be blessed at some place outside the church. Then the procession moves into the church.
122 If a station is made at the font during the Epiphany procession, the gospel of our Lord's baptism, Matthew 3:13-17, may be sung before the usual versicle, response and collect of the station.

When a number of clergymen walk in procession, e.g. at an ordination, the more recently ordained clergymen walk before those who have served longer in the sacred ministry. (This is in accord with the general principle for the order of processions: persons of greater dignity walk after those of lesser dignity.)

It is desirable—though not always possible—that the congregation participate in processions. The people should be instructed to walk in pairs, following the celebrant or officiating minister. If this is done, it will almost be a necessity to use the longer processional route described above. The people join the procession as it passes down the center aisle; they return to their pews as the procession goes up the center aisle to the altar.

A procession is really a separate service, usually held before the celebration of holy communion.

At the hour appointed for the service, the servers and clergy go from the sacristy to the altar by the shortest route. The celebrant, deacon, and subdeacon stand at the foot of the altar steps. (The celebrant wears a cope over his amice, alb, cincture and stole. If the procession is not held in connection with the holy communion, the officiating minister wears the cope over his surplice.) The crucifer and taperers stand behind the celebrant, deacon, and subdeacon. Other servers and clergy stand in some convenient place. If incense is used, the thurifer brings the censer to the celebrant and the celebrant puts some incense into the censer. Then the thurifer goes to stand behind the crucifer and taperers. The ministers turn to the people, and the deacon—if there is no deacon, the officiating minister himself—sings, "Let us go forth in peace." The choir and people sing, "In the name of Christ. Amen." (From Easter Day through the Saturday after Pentecost, "alleluia" may be added to this versicle and to the response.) The organ introduces the hymn and the people join in singing it. The thurifer—if incense is not used, the crucifer and taperers—turns and the procession moves off in the customary order. When the procession returns to the altar, the ministers again take their places before the altar as at the beginning of the procession and the station is made. Then all may return by the shortest route to the sacristy. If holy communion follows, the celebrant removes his cope and vests in the maniple and chasuble for the celebration of the eucharist. If the ministers and servers have returned to the sacristy, they then go back to the altar in the usual way.

Examples of Festival Processions[123]

On Christmas, before the midnight eucharist
1. "Let us go forth in peace, etc."
2. Hymn 710 "O, Come, All Ye Faithful"
3. Station at the creche: versicle and response 5 of Christmas, *TLH*, p. 96; collect for Christmas Day, *TLH*, p. 56
4. Hymn 98 "Of the Father's Love Begotten"
5. Station before the high altar: versicle and response 3 of Christmas, *TLH*, p. 96; collect 41, *TLH*, p. 107

---

[123] On Trinity Sunday, the Athanasian Creed may be sung in procession before the celebration of the eucharist. It is appropriate to sing antiphon 2 of the Trinity season, *TLH*, p. 99, before the creed and after the gloria patri at the end of the creed. Versicle 3 of the Trinity season, *TLH*, p. 99, and the collect for Trinity Sunday may be sung after the procession has returned to the altar.

On Easter Day
1. "Let us go forth in peace, alleluia, etc."
2. Hymn 202 "Welcome, Happy Morning!"
3. Station at the Font: versicle and response 1 of Easter, *TLH*, p. 97; collect–"Grant, O Lord, that as we are baptized, etc."–*TLH*, p. 111
4. Hymn 738 "Come, Ye Faithful, Raise the Strain"
5. Station before the high altar: versicle and response 3 of Easter, *TLH*, p. 97; collect–"Grant, we beseech Thee, almighty God, that we who celebrate, etc." *TLH*, p. 68

On Pentecost
1. "Let us go forth in peace, alleluia, etc."
2. Hymn 233 "Come, Holy Ghost, Creator Blest"
3. Station at the font: versicle and response 1 of Whitsuntide, *TLH*, p. 98; collect 51, *TLH*, p. 107
4. Hymn 224 "Come, Holy Ghost, God and Lord.'"
5. Station before the high altar: versicle and response 2 of Whitsuntide, *TLH*, p. 98; collect for Monday of Whitsun Week, *TLH*, p. 72.

The Litany in Procession

The Litany was anciently sung in procession on April 25 and on the Rogation days—the Monday, Tuesday, and Wednesday before Ascension Day. The singing of the Litany on April 25 dates from the time of Saint Gregory the Great. The processional litany on the Rogation days was introduced by Saint Mamertus, the archbishop of Vienne in Gaul (c. 470 A.D.), as an act of intercession against earthquakes and other perils.[124] Martin Luther reintroduced the litany in Saint Mary's Church, Wittenberg, in view of the peril of the Turkish invasion in 1529.[125] To sing the litany in procession is a most impressive way of marking a day of prayer and repentance. The litany may be sung in procession in time of war or in view of any disaster. At the present time the Sundays in Lent may commend themselves as an appropriate time for singing the litany in procession before the celebration of the eucharist. In rural areas especially, the litany may well be sung in procession on one of the Rogation Days or, if that is not possible, on Rogate Sunday. It would be appropriate for the entire congregation to walk to the nearest field, singing the litany as they go, imploring God's blessing on the fruits of the earth.[126]

When the litany is sung in procession, the usual route of the procession may be reversed as a way of distinguishing a procession of prayer and penitence from a festival procession. In some places the penitential procession moved from the altar, down the

---

[124] F. L. Cross, *The Oxford Dictionary of the Christian Church* (London: Oxford University Press, 1957), pp. 847 and 859.
[125] Arthur Carl Piepkorn, "Let us Pray for the Church," *Response*, VI, St. Michael and All Angels, 1964, pp. 69ff.
[126] For a helpful discussion of the Rogationtide procession, see Arthur Carl Piepkorn, "Processions In The Lutheran Church," *Sursum Corda*, I (Reformation 1939), 14f., I (Christmas 1939), 15f., II (Lent-Easter 1940), 13f., II (Pentecost 1940), 33f. These articles contain historical background and practical suggestions not only for the Rogationtide procession, but also for the other processions of the church year.

north aisle, and up the center aisle to the altar. The explanation given for this was that the penitential procession moved toward the cold north, rather than toward the warm and sunny south side of the church. If a longer route is desired, the procession leaves the altar, moves down the center aisle, up the south aisle, across the front of the church, down the north aisle, and up the center aisle to the altar.

The customary order of the procession is observed (see above). It is, perhaps, appropriate to omit the use of incense. The celebrant or officiant generally wears a violet cope. When the ministers and servers arrive at the altar, the Exsurge, Domini may be sung:

> Arise, O Lord, our God, help Thy servants and liberate us, for Thy holy Name's sake. Ps. We have heard with our ears, O God: our fathers have told us what works Thou didst in their days. Glory be to the Father ... world without end. Arise, O Lord... for Thy holy Name's sake.

Then all may kneel, and the Litany is begun. After "O God the Holy Ghost: have mercy upon us" has been sung, all rise and the procession begins. The procession should be timed so that it returns to the altar before the Our Father. The responses should be sung after each petition, rather than being sung after each group of petitions. After the Our Father, psalm 70, together with the collects for pardon ("Hear, we beseech Thee, O Lord"), for deliverance from sin ("We beseech Thee, O Lord, in Thy clemency"), for peace ("O God, from whom all holy desires"), and for divine guidance and help ("Direct us, O Lord"), may be sung. If the holy eucharist follows, the celebrant removes his cope and vests in the maniple and chasuble. (The ministers and servers may go to the sacristy for the changing of the vestments. They then go back to the altar in the usual way.) If the eucharist does not follow, the officiant may dismiss the people with a blessing and return to the sacristy.

APPENDIX C

Manner of Censing the Altar

The use of incense has become very rare in our churches since the Reformation. This is strange in view of the fact that incense is so frequently mentioned in the sacred scriptures. (Cf. Horace D. Hummel, "On the Use of Incense," *Una Sancta*, 24 Resurrection 1967, 76-80.) In his Formula Missae of 1523 Luther permitted the retention of incense at the gospel in the service of holy communion.

If on occasion the altar is censed during the canticle at matins and vespers, this may be done in the following way. The minister goes to the altar and reverences it. The thurifer brings the censer and incense boat to the minister at the midst of the altar. The minister puts some incense into the censer. The thurifer hands the censer to the minister and leaves the altar. The minister censes the altar. He swings the censer toward the altar crucifix three times. Then he walks toward the epistle corner of the altar, swinging the censer three times toward the back of the mensa as he goes. Arrived at the epistle corner, the minister lowers the censer and swings it at the side of the altar; he then swings it somewhat higher at the side of the altar. Then he returns to the midst of the altar, swinging the censer three times across the front part of the mensa as he goes.[127] He then proceeds to the gospel corner of the altar, swinging the censer three times toward the back of the mensa as he goes. Arrived at the gospel corner, the minister lowers the censer and swings it once at the side of the altar; he then swings it once somewhat higher at the side of the altar. Then the minister returns to the midst of the altar, swinging the censer three times across the front part of the mensa as he goes. He then goes as far toward the gospel corner as necessary and, beginning at the gospel corner of the altar, swings the censer six times toward the front of the altar as he walks to the epistle corner of the altar. Arrived at the epistle corner of the altar he hands the censer to the thurifer. The minister returns to the midst of the altar, reverences it, and returns to his chair in the chancel (See "Diagram of the Censing of the Altar").

If the altar stands free of the chancel wall, the altar is censed in the following way. The minister goes behind the altar to the midst of the altar and reverences it. The thurifer brings the censer and incense boat to the minister. The minister puts some incense into the censer. The thurifer hands the censer to the minister and leaves the altar. The minister censes the altar. He walks to the north corner of the altar, swinging the censer three times over the mensa as he goes. The minister then censes the north side of the altar twice. Then he walks before the front of the altar, swinging the censer six times toward the front of the altar as he goes.[128] (As he comes to the midst of the front of the altar, he may turn to the altar, and swing the censer three times toward the crucifix. Then he continues to walk toward the south corner of the front of the altar, completing the censing of the front of the altar as he goes.) He then censes the south side of the altar twice. Then he walks

---

127 Whenever the minister passes the midst of the altar, he turns and reverences the altar.
128 Whenever the minister passes the midst of the altar—front and back, he turns and reverences the altar.

toward the midst of the back of the altar, swinging the censer three times over the mensa as he goes. Then he returns to the south corner of the altar and walks to the north corner, swinging the censer six times toward the back of the altar as he goes. Arrived at the north corner of the altar, the minister hands the censer to the thurifer, returns to the midst and reverences the altar, and returns to his chair in the chancel (See "Diagram of the Censing of a Free-Standing Altar").

Diagram of the Censing of the Altar

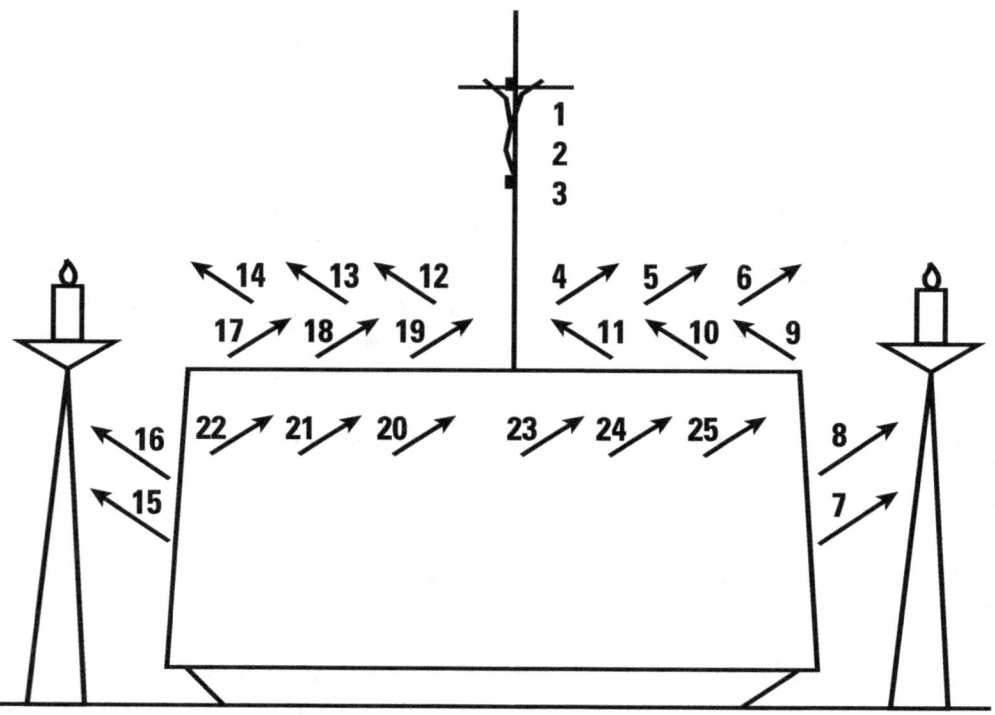

Diagram of the Censing of a Free-Standing Altar

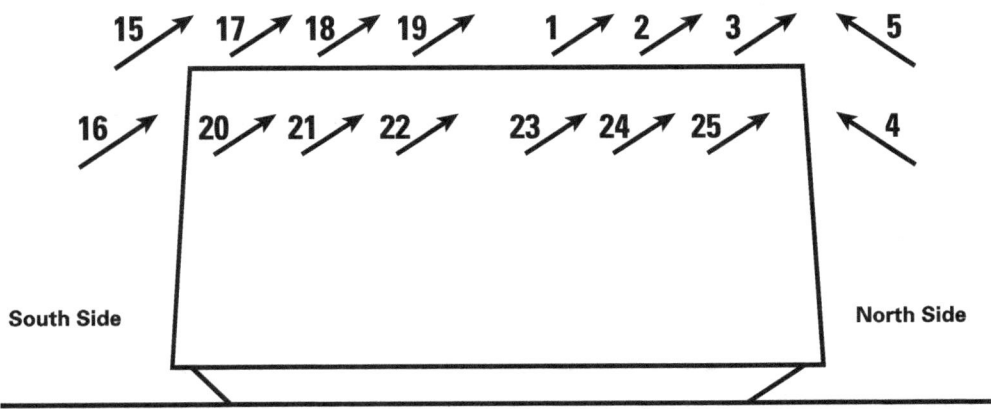

Conduct of the Services 95

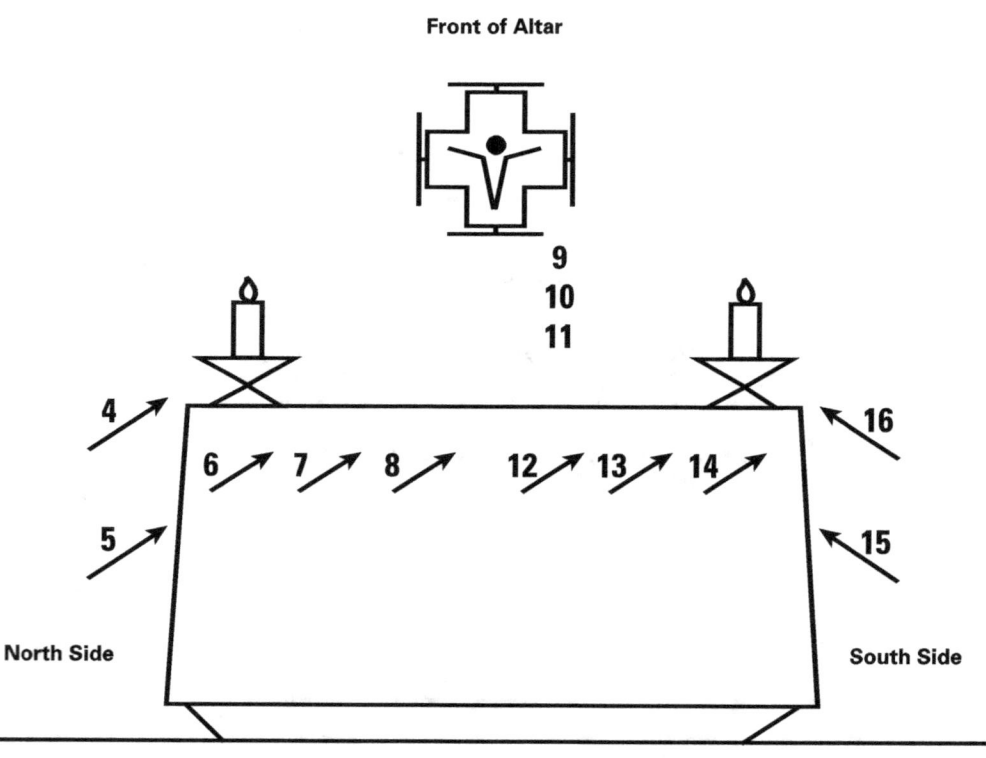

THE GENERAL RUBRICS

From The Lutheran Liturgy

GENERAL RUBRICS

These General Rubrics together with the Rubrics given in the Services are a directory to the pastor for the conduct of divine worship

✠

I. For the Order of Morning Service, the Order of the Holy Communion, the Order of Matins, the Order of Vespers

When the Officiant stands before the altar, he faces the altar for all sacrificial acts and the Congregation for all sacramental acts.

The sacrificial acts of the Morning Service and of the Order of the Holy Communion are the Trinitarian Invo-cation, the Confession, the Introit, the Hymns and Canticles, the Gradual, the Creed, the Prayers, the Offertory, the Preface, the Sanctus, and the Words of Institution; in the Order of Matins: the Hymns, the Opening Versicles, the Psalmody, the Versicle after the Lection, the Canticles, and the Prayers; in the Order of Vespers: the Hymns, the Opening Versicles, the Psalmody, the Versicle after the Lection and the Versicle after the Office Hymn, the Canticles, and the Prayers.

The sacramental acts of the Morning Service and of the Order of the Holy Communion are the Invitation to Confession, the Declaration of Grace, or the Absolution, the Salutation, the Lessons, the Sermon, the Votum, the Salutation, the Benedicamus, and the Benediction; in the Order of Matins: the Invitatory, the Lection, the Sermon, the Salutation, the Benedicamus, and the Benediction; in the Order of Vespers: the Lection, the Sermon, the Salutation, the Benedicamus, and the Benediction.

The word "shall" in the Rubrics makes that part of the Service obligatory, while the word "may" leaves it optional.

When turning at the altar, the Officiant shall ordinarily turn by his right side to face the Congregation and by his left side to face the altar.

Whenever Holy Communion is celebrated in a Church Service, the Order of the Holy Communion shall be used in its entirety.

The Propria, or Propers (as distinguished from the fixed portions of the Service, called the Ordinary), that is, the Introit, the Collect, the Epistle, the Gradual, and the Gospel for the Day, shall be used throughout the week following, except on those Days for which other appointments are made.

Christmas, Easter, Pentecost, and Trinity Sunday are designated as the Feasts of the Church Year; all other Festival Days are designated as the Festivals of the Church Year.

The Collects

The Collect for Ash Wednesday is said in every Lenten Service after the Collect for the Day.

Whenever the Collect for the Day is said, the full termination as appointed shall be used. If other Collects are said after it, as at Matins and Vespers, the full termination shall be used with the Collect for the Day and the last Collect only. The last Collect in Matins is the collect for Grace, the last in Vespers the Collect for Peace.

The short termination of the Collects used after the Collect for the Day will usually be: through Jesus Christ, Thy Son, our Lord; or: through the same Jesus Christ, Thy Son, our

The Lutheran Liturgy   1

Lord. Exceptions to this rule will be found printed in full in the texts of the Additional Collects.

When the Petition is addressed to God the Father, the full termination is: through Jesus Christ, Thy son, our Lord, who liveth and reigneth with Thee and the Holy Ghost, ever one God, world without end.

When the Petition is addressed to God the Son, the termination is: who livest and reignest with the Father and the Holy Ghost, ever one God, world without end.

When the Petition is addressed to God the Holy Ghost, the termination is: who livest and reignest with the Father and the Son, ever one God, world without end.

When mention is made of our Lord in the body of the Petition, the termination is: through the same Jesus Christ, Thy Son, our Lord, who liv-eth and reigneth with Thee and the Holy Ghost, ever one God, world without end.

When mention is made of our Lord at the end of the Petition, the termination is: who liveth and reigneth with Thee and the Holy Ghost, ever one God, world without end.

When mention is made of the Holy Ghost in the body of the Collect, the termination is: who liveth and reigneth with Thee and the same Holy Ghost, ever one God, world without end.

When the Petition is addressed to God the Holy Trinity, the termination is: who livest and reignest, ever one God, world without end.

The Music

The music of the Service is not a part of the Liturgy and may be altered as circumstances permit or require.

Liturgical chant, more so than any other type of church music, is not a musical interpretation of the text; it is only the bearer of the text and hence should be sung in a simple, straight-forward manner. To a lesser extent, the same thing is true of Hymn tunes. This is in keeping with the spirit of objective character of liturgical worship, which disdains sentimental-ization and tawdriness, musical and otherwise.

The Officiant shall chant those portions of the Service to which the Choir or the Congregation responds with chanting.

The primary function of the Choir is to lead the Congregation in the singing of the Liturgy and the Hymns, and to sing the Propers of the Liturgy when they are beyond the capacity of the Congregation.

In view of the fact that they music presented by the Choir and organist is part of the Service of Worship, it is imperative that this music be in keeping with the spirit of the liturgical character of the Service.

From time to time the Choir may sing parts of the Ordinary in more elaborate choral settings.

Announcements

Notices to the Congregation, except in connection with requests for Intercession, ought not to be read during the Services.

Holy Baptism

Unless otherwise ordered in a congregation, public Baptism may be administered after the Opening Hymn, in which case the Opening Hymn may well be a baptismal hymn.

Midweek Evening Services

The Order of Vespers may be used for midweek evening Services. In place of the Lection during Lent, a portion of the History of our Lord's Passion may be read.

II. The Order of Morning Service and the Order of the Holy Communion

The Preparatory Service

For the Invocation and the Preparatory Service the Officiant may stand at the foot of the altar steps, advancing to the altar at the Introit.

When the Service begins with the Introit, the Officiant shall proceed to the altar at once.

Since the Preparation is not a part of the Service proper, it is preferable that the Officiant and the congregation speak the entire Preparatory Service. The Congregation may kneel until the Declaration of Grace has been spoken.

The Introit

The Introit for the Day with the Gloria Patri should be sung by the Choir. If a Choir is not available, the Introit may be said or chanted by the Officiant; in this case the Gloria Patri may be said or sung by the congregation.

The Introit for the Day, including the Gloria Patri, should either be sung or spoken throughout.

The Antiphon, which announces the keynote of the Introit, shall be repeated after the Gloria Patri.

If the Confessional Service immediately precedes the Communion Service, the latter shall begin with the Introit.

The Kyrie

The Kyrie shall be said or sung by the congregation.

A ninefold, but not a fourfold or sixfold (the Officiant speaking the first line; the Officiant speaking each line) Kyrie may be substituted for the threefold Kyrie. In place of the English text, the Greek form, "Kyrie Eleison, Christe Eleison, Kyrie Elei-son," may be used in either a threefold or a ninefold form.

The Gloria in Excelsis

The Gloria in Excelsis shall be used on all Feast and Festival Days; at other times a versified form of the Gloria in Excelsis (Hymns 237, 238, in *The Lutheran Hymnal*), or another hymn of praise, may be used. The Gloria in Excelsis shall also be used at all services of Worship in which the Administration of Holy Communion takes place, except that in this case it may be omitted during the Seasons of Advent, Pre-Lent, and Lent.

The Lessons

Before the Epistle for the Day an appointed Lesson from the Old Testament (cf. pp. 438, 439) may be read, but the Epistle for the Day and the Gospel for the Day shall always be read.

When the Minister announces the Gospel for the Day, the Congregation shall rise and then chant, Glory be to Thee, O Lord.

The Gradual for the Day and the Hallelujah

The Gradual for the Day or the Sentence for the Season should be sung by the Choir. If a choir is not available, the Officiant may say the Gradual or the Sentence for the Season; or the Congregation may simply sing the Hallelujah after the Epistle has been read. Hallelujah is not sung during Pre-Lent and Lent.

Special choir music may be sung in place of, or preferably in addition to, the Gradual, between the Epistle and the Gospel. When this is done, it is important that the textual content of the choral selection harmonize with the theme of the Liturgy and Service. A hymn of Invocation to the Holy Ghost may be sung to replace the Gradual; the classical Gradual Hymn of the Lutheran Church is "We Now Implore

God the Holy Ghost" (*The Lutheran Hymnal*, Hymn 231).

THE CREED

The Nicene Creed shall be chanted or said by the Congregation on all Feasts and Festivals and whenever there is a Communion; at other times the Apostles' Creed may be used in its stead, or a versified form of these Creeds may be sung. Cf. Hymns 251, 252, 253, in *The Lutheran Hymnal*.

On Trinity Sunday, the Athanasian Creed may be used after the Gradual.

THE VOTUM

When saying the Votum at the close of the Sermon, the Preacher may raise his hand in blessing and make the sign of the cross.

THE GENERAL PRAYER

Before the General Prayer at the altar the Officiant may announce special Petitions, Intercessions, or Thanksgivings which have been requested. He may also make mention of the birth, contemplated marriage, death, etc., of members of the congregation.

One of the General Prayers appointed for the Services shall always be used. The Litany may be used instead of the General Prayer, except when there is a Communion.

THE HOLY COMMUNION

The Celebrant may make ready the Communion vessels immediately after the Offertory.

If there be another Minister to assist in the Distribution, he may approach the altar during the singing of the Agnus Dei.

THE PROPER PREFACE

The Proper Preface shall be used throughout its respective Season. The Preface of the Holy Trinity may be used on any Sunday for which no other Preface is appointed.

THE SACRED ELEMENTS

In making ready the elements for the Holy Communion, so much of the bread and the wine shall be placed in the proper vessels as in the judgment of the Celebrant will be required for the Administration.

If the consecrated bread or wine be spent before all have communed, the Celebrant shall consecrate more, saying aloud so much of the Words of Institution as pertains to the element to be consecrated.

When all have received the Holy Sacrament, the Celebrant shall cover what remains of the bread and wine with the veil.

When the Service has been completed, the Celebrant or a deacon shall remove the sacramental vessels from the altar to the sacristy and dispose of that part of the bread and wine which remains as follows: He shall carefully remove the bread from the paten and ciborium to a fit receptacle, there to be kept against the next Communion.

He shall pour what remains of the consecrated wine into the piscine or upon the ground at a proper and convenient place outside the church.

III. The Order of Matins

The Invitatory

The Invitatory always precedes the Venite, Psalm 95. It varies with the season. See pages 216-224. Other appropriate Invitatories may be used.

After the Venite and the Gloria Patri the whole Invitatory shall be repeated.

The Psalm

In the reading or chanting of the Psalter at Matins, Psalm 95 (Venite) shall not be used.

On Trinity Sunday, the Athanasian Creed may replace a Psalm.

The Antiphon

An Antiphon may be said or chanted with each Psalm.

When an Antiphon is used with the Psalm, it shall be chanted before the Psalm and repeated after the Gloria Patri.

The Lection

One Lesson shall, more may, be read. On Sundays or Festivals one Lesson shall be read from the Epistles and one from the Gospels. A Lesson from the Old Testament may precede the Lesson from the Epistles. See page 438. Lessons shall not be chosen from the Psalter.

The Epistle and the Gospel for the Day shall not be used as Lessons at Matins.

In announcing the Lesson the Officiant shall say: The First (or Second or Third) Lesson is written in the _____ chapter of _____ beginning at the _____ verse. The Lesson ended, he shall say: Here endeth the First (or Second or Third) Lesson. After that, facing the altar, he may say or chant: But Thou, O Lord, have mercy upon us.

The Responsory

The Responsory varies with the Season and may be sung by the Choir after the last Lesson. See pages 216 to 227. Other appropriate Responsories may also be used.

The Sermon

The Sermon or Address may follow the Lesson and Responsory as appointed.

Matin Canticles

The Te Deum. Proper at Matins on all Sundays except in Advent and from Septuagesima to Good Friday; also proper on Feasts and Festivals and during their Seasons.

The Benedictus. Proper on all Sundays in Advent and from Septuagesima to Good Friday; also proper for daily use.

The Benedicite. Proper on Feasts and Festivals and during Eastertide, when the Te Deum is not used. See page 282.

The Dignus Est Agnus. Proper during Eastertide and Ascensiontide. May also be used during the Trinity Season. See page 289.

The Beatitudes. Proper during Trinity Season, but may be used any other time except Sundays. See page 288.

Any of the other Canticles, except the Magnificat and the Nunc Dimittis, may be used at Matins on any Day except a Sunday or a Feast or a Festival. See page 282. Confitebor Tibi is traditionally associated with Monday, Ego dixi with Tuesday, Exultavit cor meum with Wednesday, Cantemus Domino with Thursday, Domine audivi with Friday, and Audite coeli with Saturday.

An Antiphon may be sung with any of the Canticles except the Te Deum. It should be sung before the Canticle and repeated after the Canticle by the entire Choir. See pages 216-227.

The Prayers

Instead of the Prayers appointed, the Suffrages, the Litany, or other Prayers may be used. The Bidding Prayer may be used in the same manner on any Wednesday or Friday in Lent and on Good Friday.

The Collect

The Collect for the Sunday is ordinarily said at Matins throughout the week. The Collect for Grace shall be the last Collect used at Matins. A Versicle may be used before any Collect after the first.

IV. The Order of Vespers

The Antiphon

An Antiphon may be said or chanted with each Psalm.

When an Antiphon is used with a Psalm, it shall be sung before the Psalm and repeated after the Gloria Patri by the entire Choir. The Psalm is sung to the tone of the Antiphon.

The Lection

One or more Lessons from the Old or the New Testament shall be read. See page 422.

The Epistle and the Gospel for the Day shall not be used as Lessons at Vespers.

In announcing the Lesson the Officiant shall say: The First (or Second or Third) Lesson is written in the _____ chapter of _____ beginning at the _____ verse. The Lesson ended, he shall say: Here endeth the First (or Second or Third) Lesson. After that, facing the altar, he may say or chant: But Thou, O Lord, have mercy upon us.

The Responsory

The Responsory varies with the Season and may be sung by the Choir after the last Lesson. See pages 216 to 227. Other appropriate Responsories may also be used.

The Sermon

The Sermon or Address may follow the Lesson and Responsory as appointed.

Vesper Canticles

The Magnificat. The proper Canticle at Vespers at all times.

The Nunc Dimittis. A proper substitute for the Magnificat only when Vespers are said or sung as a late Office.

The Dignus Est Agnus. Proper during Eastertide and Ascensiontide. May also be used during the Trinity Season. See page 289.

On Festivals a special Versicle, see pages 216-229, may be used before the Canticle.

An Antiphon may be sung with the Canticle. See page 216.

The Prayer

Instead of the Prayer appointed, the Suffrages or the Litany or other Prayers may be said.

The Collect

The Collect for the Sunday is ordinarily said at Vespers throughout the week until Friday; but on Saturday the Collect for the following Sunday is said. The Collect proper for any Festival may be used at Vespers of the day before. The Collect for Peace shall be the last Collect in the Order of Vespers. A Versicle may be used before any Collect after the first.

The Lutheran Liturgy

V. Miscellaneous

The Liturgical Colors

The Liturgical colors are white, red, green, violet, and black. Their significance is as follows:

White: Color of the Godhead, eternity, robe of the glorified Christ and the Angels, perfection, joy, purity.

Red: Color of fire, fervor, blood, martyrdom, love, victorious truth of Christian teaching based on the blood and righteousness of Christ.

Green: Color of abiding life, nourishment, rest; dominant color in nature.

Violet: Color of royal mourning and repentance.

Black: Absence of color, symbolical of death.

Their Proper Use

White: From and with Vespers of Eve of Nativity through the Epiphany Octave. On Maundy Thursday, when Communion is celebrated.
From and with the Vespers of Easter Eve through to the Vespers of the Eve of Whitsunday.
On the Feast of the Holy Trinity and during its Octave.
All the other Festivals of Christ, *i. e.,* Presentation, Annunciation, Visitation, and Transfiguration. On the Day of St. Michael and All Angels. On the day of the Conversion of St. Paul; the Nativity of St. John the Baptist; All Saints' Day; the Dedication of a Church and Its Anniversary; on days of general or special thanksgiving and on the festivals of saints not martyrs.

Red: From and with the Vespers on the Eve of Whitsunday through to the Vespers on the Eve of Holy Trinity.
The Festival of the Reformation and its Octave.
On commemorating the death of martyrs.

Green: From and with Matins on January 14 to Vespers of the Eve of Septuagesima. From the Second Sunday after Trinity through the Trinity Season to the Vespers on the Eve of Advent.

Violet: From and with the Vespers on the Eve of Advent to the Vespers on the Eve of the Nativity.
From and with Vespers on the Saturday before Septuagesima and throughout Pre-Lent and Lent, to Vespers on the Eve of Easter.
For the Day of Humiliation.

Black: For Good Friday *only.*

Variants: In some parts of the Lutheran Church green is used from Septuagesima through Shrove Tuesday. In that case white should be used from Matins on January 14 until, but not at, Vespers on the Saturday before Septuagesima. Violet may be used from Matins on the Monday after Rogation Sunday until, but not at, Vespers on the Wednesday before the Ascension Day, and on Holy Innocents' Day when it falls during the week.

The Solemnization of Holy Matrimony and the Order for the Burial of the Dead shall not affect the proper color for the Day or Season in use when these Services are held.

The Altar Linens

The Fair Linen, a cloth covering the altar, extending one third or two thirds or all the way to the floor at the narrow ends, shall always be upon the altar.

The Sacramental Linens

The *Corporal*, a square of very fine linen, is laid on the center of the Fair Linen cloth. Upon it the sacra-mental vessels are placed.

The *Pall*, a small square of stiff material covered or lined with linen, is used to cover the chalice. It should be removed at the Consecration.

The *Purificators*, squares of heavy linen, are used to cleanse the rim of the chalice during the Administration.

The *Veil*, made of silk or of the finest linen, is used to cover the sacra-mental vessels upon the altar or credence table. It is removed before the Preface and should be folded carefully and laid upon the altar and again placed over the sacramental vessels after the Administration at the Nunc Dimittis.

When not in use on the altar, the sacramental linens should be properly folded and kept in the *Burse*, a square envelope made of strong cardboard, covered with silk or heavy linen.

Headgear for Women

It is a laudable custom, based upon a Scriptural injunction (1 Cor. 11:3-15), for women to wear an appropriate head covering in Church, especially at the time of divine service.

On and after Easter Day, 1955, in any case of a contradiction between these General Rubrics as they are here printed and other rubrics published elsewhere in the official service books of the Evangelical Lutheran Synodical Conference of North America, these General Rubrics shall govern.

The Lutheran Liturgy

www.ingramcontent.com/pod-product-compliance
Lightning Source LLC
Chambersburg PA
CBHW081447070526
44586CB00019B/2263